DO SALESPEOPLE, MECH
BUREAUCRATS, AND BO
AROUND?

ARE YOU WORKING FOR LESS THAN THE TOP
DOLLAR?

DO YOU PAY TOO MUCH WHEN YOU BUY AND
GET TOO LITTLE WHEN YOU SELL?

ARE YOU IN THE MARKET FOR A NEW HOUSE,
A NEW CAR, OR A NEW JOB?

DO YOU PLAY A STEADY SECOND FIDDLE IN
YOUR PERSONAL RELATIONSHIPS?

The one thing you have to do is master the simple techniques and clear-cut rules that let you make the best possible deals for yourself in every area of your life without making a single enemy. It's all yours for the using in the most sensible strategy for success ever to make you the winner you deserve to be while staying the kind of decent person you want to be.

NEGOTIATION
The Art of Getting What You Want

MICHAEL SCHATZKI has, over the last five years, conducted scores of seminars on negotiating for business, organizations, and individuals, and has counseled clients on a consultation basis. A student of the field for nearly ten years, he is a negotiator by profession; as executive director of the Bergen-Passaic (NJ) Hospital and Physicians Council, a coalition of 1,800 physicians, fifteen hospitals, and two county medical societies, he negotiates with local, regional, and statewide regulatory and planning agencies.

WAYNE R. COFFEY, a former Associated Press newsman and newspaper editor, is the author of seven nonfiction books. His most recent work, HOW WE CHOOSE A CONGRESS, was published in the summer of 1980 by St. Martin's Press.

Self-Help Books from SIGNET and MENTOR

Negotiation

The Art of Getting What You Want

by
MICHAEL SCHATZKI
with Wayne R. Coffey

A SIGNET BOOK

NEW AMERICAN LIBRARY

Copyright © 1981 by Michael Schatzki

Library of Congress Catalog Card Number: 81-82817

SIGNET TRADEMARK REG. U.S. PAT. OFF. AND FOREIGN COUNTRIES
REGISTERED TRADEMARK—MARCA REGISTRADA
HECHO EN CHICAGO, U.S.A.

SIGNET, SIGNET CLASSIC, MENTOR, PLUME, MERIDIAN AND NAL
BOOKS are published by New American Library,
1633 Broadway, New York, New York 10019

First Printing, October, 1981

4   5   6   7   8   9   10   11   12

PRINTED IN THE UNITED STATES OF AMERICA

Dedications

Acknowledgments

A GREAT MANY people have made contributions to this book —it would not have been possible without them. A few warrant special mention: Judy Sjo-Gaber, for steering me in the best possible direction; Frank Coffey, for his faith in the project and his astute editorial sense; Tom Biracree, whose comments and suggestions were indispensable; Richard Curtis, my literary agent; Barbara Sher, whose unwavering support helped keep me on the right track; Norman Krisberg, whose insights were invaluable; and Daniel Lund, whose skill as a negotiator has made the difference more than once.

A special word of thanks is due my collaborator, Wayne Coffey, whose skill as a writer has transformed a set of ideas and concepts into the reality of a book, and whose patience, understanding, and warmth were ever-present to help our work along.

Finally, my deepest gratitude to my wife, Jeanne. Her perceptive critiques and her many suggestions and additions were essential in the actual writing of this book, and her love, concern, and willingness to be a true partner in this venture made it possible for me to see this project through to its completion.

M.S.

Table of Contents

PART I NEGOTIATION: THE LIFE SKILL

Introduction You Don't Have to Take No for an Answer *3*
Chapter 1 You're Already on Your Way *9*
Chapter 2 Free from Fear *12*

PART II SETTING THE STAGE

Chapter 3 An Overview of Negotiation *27*
Chapter 4 The Settlement Range: The Best Friend Your Negotiation Will Ever Have *35*
Chapter 5 Coping with Tension *54*
Chapter 6 Meeting Your Opponent: How Will He React? *59*

PART III MAPPING OUT YOUR ACTION PLAN

Chapter 7 Strategic Forces: Your Springboard to Successful Negotiating *69*
Chapter 8 Making a Better Deal Possible *86*
Chapter 9 Pulling Your Bargaining Levers *94*
Chapter 10 Tactics: Your Tools for Getting What You Want *103*
Chapter 11 Research and Planning: A Little Digging Goes a Long Way *138*

PART IV FACE TO FACE

Chapter 12 A Matter of Style *163*
Chapter 13 At the Bargaining Table: Putting It All Together *183*

PART V THE NEGOTIATOR'S WORKSHOP

Chapter 14 Twelve Common Negotiations: How to Handle Them . . . and Get What You Want *211*
Epilogue: Parting Thoughts *229*

PART I

Negotiation: The Life Skill

INTRODUCTION

You Don't Have to Take No for an Answer

Cindy Q. Citizen approaches the service desk of the auto dealership where she recently plunked down $7,000 for a new car. For weeks now the car has been stalling out in traffic, and this is the fourth time she's spent her lunch hour with the service manager. Each time, she's been told the problem has been corrected, and each time, the car behaved as if nobody had even touched it.

Cindy doesn't want to be a pain in the neck. She only wants to get her car fixed and never see the place again. The service manager consults his records.

"I'm sorry, ma'am," he says, "but we can't help you out this time. Your warranty expired three days ago."

"But it was under warranty when the problem first came up," Cindy pleads.

"Yes, but it's not now. I'm sorry. It's policy."

Cindy feels helpless. She takes no for an answer.

Harry Person puts a call in to his doctor. Harry hasn't been feeling well, and when he was in last week the doctor told him to call for a stronger prescription if his condition persisted.

Four days later, Harry gets a bill for $25 from his doctor. He's very upset about it, having paid $50 for an office visit already. He calls the office in the hope that the bill was an oversight.

"The bill is correct," the nurse says coldly. "That is the doctor's standard fee for a phone consultation."

Harry is angry. But he takes no for an answer.

Paul and Paula Public are moving out of their apart-

3

ment. They've been model tenants and don't expect any difficulty in getting back their $300 security deposit. The landlord inspects the premises and says there will be no problem.

A week later, Paul and Paula get the check they've been expecting. But it's for only $100! In a curt letter the landlord cites three damaged screens, numerous holes in the wall plaster, and "excessive wear and tear" as his reasons for keeping $200 of their deposit.

They confront the landlord with their gripe. He stands firm. They feel like they've been taken. But what can they do? They take no for an answer.

Tom Doe glances at the clock. It's 8:00 P.M., and everyone else in the office has long since departed. A loyal and industrious worker, Tom has been staying late for six weeks now, helping his boss, Al, finish a special project before the approaching deadline. Tom hasn't gotten a raise in a year, and somehow every time the subject is broached, Al manages to talk his way around it and put Tom off.

Tonight, Tom decides to inquire about it again. "You know how highly I value you," Al says warmly. "God knows I'd be lost on this project without you. But my hands are tied. There's simply nothing to spare in the budget right now. Don't you worry though. You know I'll take care of you as soon as it's humanly possible."

The pat on the head makes Tom feel good, but it does little for his increasing financial crunch. He takes no for an answer.

YOU DON'T HAVE to act like the people in the foregoing examples. You don't have to take no for an answer. You don't have to accept what is offered or back off from what you deserve. You will learn that you have recourse, that there are ways to change "No" to "Yes," that you don't have to settle for table scraps when what you deserve is a square meal. How? By learning to negotiate.

In years of studying, teaching seminars, and counseling hundreds of people on the life skill of negotiation, I've come to one inescapable conclusion: Most people don't get what they deserve out of life. I'm not talking about year-long vacations in the Caribbean or thirty-room oceanside estates—not that those wouldn't be nice. I'm talking about what's coming to you in the context of your everyday life.

This book is an outgrowth of discussions I've had with people from all walks of life. I'll be amazed if you don't see yourself in almost every page of the book—feelings you've had, situations you've been in, that are nearly identical to those of the people whose real-life experiences pack these pages. I've talked to machinists and mothers, secretaries and bosses, senior citizens and teenagers, factory workers and therapists, writers and all manner of business people. I've been on call-in radio programs and seen the switchboard light up like a Christmas tree with people calling for advice on their particular problems. Everywhere I go, the message always seems to come down to this: "I need help in negotiating. I have a hard time standing up for my own cause. Too often, I'm shamed or manipulated into acting a certain way or doing something I don't want to do. Too often, I'm thrust into the position of having to struggle to get even the short end of the stick." Well, help is here!

It's no secret why so many of us are uncomfortable negotiating for ourselves. Practically from the cradle—at home, school, church, and office—we've been conditioned to be obedient, to accept things as they are; in short, not to rock the boat. We have been brought up in a world of seemingly "fixed" prices, "inflexible" rules, and "immutable" decisions. We go into a store looking for a refund on a defective toaster. "Sorry," the salesclerk tells us, "but our policy is no refunds or exchanges." So we gulp, pick up our broken toaster, and head for home, right? Wrong! We negotiate . . . with the clerk, the clerk's boss, the boss's boss, or whoever has the clout to help us. And by the time we get to the end of this book, we're going to stand one helluva chance of walking out of that store with either a new toaster or a refund!

If we'd been brought up in a different culture, we'd have a completely different attitude toward negotiation. In many other places negotiation is a way of life, a process deeply woven into the social fabric. I was traveling in Morocco not long ago, and the people there negotiate for everything, from spices to rugs. I saw two guys bargaining like the world was at stake over the price of a chicken.

We're at the other extreme. We negotiate very infrequently. And that's because, except for diplomats, salespeople, real estate brokers, lawyers—people who make their living negotiating—the process is alien to us. Sure, we have a few ritualized negotiating situations such as buying a car or a house, for example, but for most of us that's about it.

The truth is that the negotiating opportunities in our daily lives are virtually endless. Most things really are negotiable, no matter what we've been trained to think, which is why I call negotiation a life skill. If you find yourself doubting it, ask yourself if you've ever wanted to or will ever want to

—Reach a fair settlement with an insurance company for a claim on an accident/theft/medical bill?

—Have more time to finish a big assignment at work?

—Have your landlord repair the faucet/toilet/ceiling/etc.?

—Secure a bigger budget for your department?

—Decide on a vacation both you and your spouse will be happy with?

—Spend less time on obligatory visits to your parents, in-laws, or other relatives?

—Have the dry cleaner compensate you for the skirt or jacket he ruined?

—Get a higher salary for a new job?

—Get a bigger raise than was offered?

—Get Mom and Dad to give you the car for the big date on Saturday night?

—Get the people you live with to shoulder more household responsibilities?

—Buy a house for less than the asking price, with washer and dryer thrown in to boot?

—Get your child into that special program that's always full?

—Have a repairman finish a job by the date—and for the price—he said he would?

—Convince your church/club/organization to have this year's picnic/outing/retreat where you want it instead of at the awful place they had it last year?

I could go on and on. Doubtless you can think of numerous other examples from your own life. Can we avoid negotiating in these situations? Absolutely. One student of mine was so negotiation-shy that when he went shopping for a used car, he refused to answer any advertisement that said "Make an offer." Why? Because he was afraid of making an offer the seller might find ridiculous. We can rationalize until the cows come home. We can squeeze by for another six months without the raise. The skirt the dry cleaner wrecked was about to be thrown away. And who cares about that dumb special program? The child probably would be under too much pressure in it anyhow.

In this book, we're going to learn to stop rationalizing. We're going to stop avoiding negotiation. We're going to dispel its negative image, strip away our fears and misconceptions, and come to see negotiation for what it truly is—an opportunity: a reasoned, orderly, comprehensible process that we can employ, easily and effectively, to get more of what we want out of life.

We've discussed what this book is about. Now let's discuss what it isn't about. It's not about manipulating, intimidating, or taking advantage of people. It's not about taking the money (or whatever it is you're negotiating for), running, and leaving the other poor soul to the buzzards. It is not a manual for the unscrupulous; I have only included a section on dirty tricks so that if you do encounter people who have checked their scruples at the door, you'll be able to recognize them for what they are and negotiate very warily with them, if at all.

Nor is this book about changing your basic personality. Most people view negotiation as a forbidding jungle that's fit only for the iron-willed, table-pounding breed of animal. But the fact is you don't have to be an ogre or a cutthroat or a fist-flailing fanatic to be a good negotiator. You don't have to be a hot-head or a fast talker. You can be nice, and you can be yourself! All you need is the willingness to stand up for yourself and knowledge about what you're doing.

Learning to negotiate, in many ways, is like learning to play tennis. The more we learn about the various strokes (strategies and tactics), the more we develop an overall sense of the game, of where we are on the court, and of what works and why, the better we'll be able to drive the ball (our needs) exactly where we want. And by the same token, the more we know about our opponent and his strokes, the better we'll be able to predict what's coming and fashion a winner of a return.

As in any game, learning how to negotiate takes practice. We can't step onto the court and start right in with overhead smashes. We've got to build our skills gradually and master the fundamentals first. Then, as we go on, we will learn to command more and more of the game's intricacies.

Negotiation is like tennis in another respect—it's fun! Sure, some negotiations are very serious and important, but even then the challenges, the strategies and tactics, the give and take of the negotiating process, are unquestionably fun.

Everything you need to know to negotiate effectively is between these covers. Here's hoping you get everything you deserve.

MICHAEL SCHATZKI
Basking Ridge, New Jersey

CHAPTER 1

You're Already
on Your Way

WE ARE ALL negotiators. I happen to make my living by negotiating, but even if I dug ditches all day long, I would still be a negotiator. Maybe I would have to negotiate with my boss for a longer lunch break or for a new shovel to make my digging easier. And I would certainly have to negotiate with my wife if I wanted to come home and watch Monday Night Football when her favorite movie was on another channel. The point is that we all negotiate all the time. There's no way around it, unless you're a hermit.

You already know something about negotiation, probably a lot more than you think you know. You may not have an effective, systematic approach to the subject—it's my job to furnish you with that—but you nonetheless have an intuitive sense of how to go about the process, just by virtue of being human. What is negotiation after all? It is merely an exchange between people for the purpose of fulfilling their needs. It doesn't matter if your need happens to be consummating a multimillion dollar merger or keeping your next-door neighbor's dogs away from your garden; if you have any needs at all and have to involve someone else to have them met, then you have to negotiate.

Let me give you a couple of examples to illustrate what I mean when I say you've got an intuitive sense of negotiating. A man I know was starting up a business in New York City, and he had to go to the appropriate city agency to get things properly licensed and registered. After making several phone inquiries he was told that, being a Manhattan resident, he should go to a city agency in lower Manhattan. He got on a subway and went downtown, but when he arrived a clerk told him that because he had a Queens post office box, he would have to go to the Queens office of the agency to get things

9

squared away. He got back on the subway, took a long ride out to the Queens office, and waited an hour on line. When it was finally his turn, a stone-faced clerk told him, "You were given wrong information. You have to go back to Manhattan and get a special application from one of the supervisors there."

Having squandered the better part of his day and nearing the end of his rope, the man made an impassioned plea to the clerk to deviate slightly from the sacred norm and help him solve his problem. The plea fell on deaf ears. So what did the man do? He stormed away from the line, climbed up on the nearest table, and began screaming wretched things about the New York City bureaucracy and what he would do to the place if he didn't get assistance in a hurry. A supervisor quickly emerged from behind the scenes, calmed the man down, and ironed out the problem in a matter of minutes.

Was our exasperated table-climber negotiating? Absolutely. Was he aware of it? Probably not. More likely he was simply thinking, "I'm going to expire from frustration if these jerks keep giving me the runaround, and I'm going to do something about it." Let's strip this negotiation down to its basics. What happened? The man had a need—licensing his business—that he wanted the agency to fulfill. When it became apparent the agency could not or would not meet that need, what did he do? He devised a tactic—albeit an unorthodox one—that created a need on behalf of the supervisor—a need for something not to happen, for not having the office trashed by some deranged businessman-to-be. So the supervisor sat down and helped the guy with his problem.

Even young children know how to negotiate. Indeed, they are among the best negotiators because they have a keen sense of how to exploit their relative helplessness to best advantage. Not long ago, while shopping in a mall, I witnessed a negotiation that has been played out a million times if it has been played out once. A mother and her young daughter were walking along when the helium balloon the little girl was carrying slipped out of her grasp and drifted cruelly up to the roof. The girl immediately began to cry, to which the mother replied, "I told you to be careful! Now stop crying, because I'm not going to buy you another one."

Since such encounters are of immense interest to a student of negotiation, I decided to follow mother and daughter down the mall to see how things turned out. The girl cried—no, make that wailed—relentlessly, doing a splendid job of advertising her unmet need. Mom scolded her repeatedly, to no avail. Inside of ten minutes the negotiation had been resolved, and relative tranquility was returned to the mall. When I last saw them, they were on line at a five-and-ten store . . . at the balloon stand. Persistence, as we'll see later, is a vital trait for any good negotiator.

Like the table-climber and the young child, you *do* have an idea of how to negotiate. Your system may not be terribly refined; it may not be a system at all. More likely, it's a piecemeal approach you've settled into without much thought. Being a professional negotiator, I *have* to give the negotiation process a lot of thought, and everything in this book is a product of that careful analysis. It's not my intention to set forth a mechanical formula that can be applied to each and every negotiation in your life. As much as I'd like to give you one, no such formula exists.

What you will get from this book is a highly effective negotiating system designed to help you achieve your goals in any kind of negotiation. It is a system that is predicated on what you already know intuitively. It is not a system that should be memorized. Being a push-button negotiator won't get you anywhere at all. Rather it is a system that encourages you to think and feel like a negotiator yourself. Because only when you think of yourself as a negotiator will the information in this book truly begin to work for you.

In essence, what I'm striving to do in this book is raise your negotiating quotient. In making you more conscious of the countless situations in which you really can negotiate, it's my aim to give you a completely new perspective on the world around you. Not only will you find yourself negotiating in situations where you never thought it possible, but you will also be getting a lot more out of your negotiations.

CHAPTER 2

Free from Fear

Fear cannot be banished, but it can be calm and without panic; and it can be mitigated by reason and evaluation.
—VANNEVAR BUSH

PRETEND FOR A moment that you're on the edge of a dark and thickly wooded forest, one that you've never come upon before. Night is falling. You have no idea of the forest's size, nor of what horrid creatures may be prepared to pounce on you once you venture in. You have no map, no compass, and no flashlight. You're lost. And terrified.

Now imagine yourself in the same situation, except that this time you're better equipped. You have a map, compass, and flashlight, and even though the forest is just as dark and unknown to you as before, you feel better, more relaxed. Why? Because now you've got some direction and a way of shedding light on whatever is out there. Some fears may persist, but they'll be substantially allayed as you become more familiar with your surroundings and realize that your most nightmarish visions aren't going to come about.

So it is with negotiation. If you stumble on it in darkness with no direction, equipment, or familiarity, guided only by your preconceptions, you're bound to be scared. But if the process has been illuminated for you and you have an idea of what to expect, you'll be considerably less anxious. In this chapter you'll get a flashlight, a map, and all the equipment you'll need to expose and defuse your fears of negotiation. I think you'll find that negotiation isn't a forest at all. In fact, you may come to think of it is your own backyard!

Self-Image and the Labor-
Management Myth

Too often when people think of negotiation, they focus on what I call the collective bargaining model; namely, the acrimonious table-pounding battles between labor and management that we see on TV all the time. Judging by the seemingly inflexible stands both sides adopt and the venomous torrent of barbs they fling at each other, it's a wonder to many people that we don't have more strikes. But the fact is virtually all of the insults, table-pounding, and threats are little more than theatrics, a highly effective technique on behalf of the union leadership to rally support from their members, while at the same time demonstrating their toughness in dealing with management. Management, for its part, wants to give the impression that every little concession it makes is given ever so grudgingly.

Only after the grandstanding stops does serious negotiation begin. Only then do both sides roll up their sleeves and set about hammering out an agreement. But because we don't see the real negotiation that goes on behind closed doors, we're left with the grandstanding phase as our image of negotiation.

An angry, distasteful, intimidating process—it's this perception of negotiation that makes many of us cringe at the thought of joining in. Why? Because it doesn't jibe with our self-image. We figure we're simply not hardened or nasty enough to play a game that seems to place such a premium on those qualities. We have a feeling that there's something dishonorable about the whole process and, by association, the people who engage in it. I wish I had a nickel for every time I've heard one of my students say:

> "I'm not like that."
> "That's not me."
> "I'm not cut out for it."
> "I'm not stubborn enough."
> "I give in too easily."

The truth is that almost all negotiations are of an entirely different cast than the collective bargaining model. You don't need an iron will or a hot head to be an effective negotiator; all you need, as we'll see in subsequent chapters, is the ability to decide what you want and a knowledge of the proper approach and of the numerous strategies and tactics to employ in order to get it. Once you begin to grasp the ins and outs of negotiation, you'll come to see the fallacies of the collective bargaining model and realize the process is not the dangerous, forbidding endeavor it seemed to be from afar.

You'll also realize there is nothing dishonorable about it. Negotiation is nothing but an interaction between people for the purpose of fulfilling needs, and what's so dishonorable about that? We've been conditioned to believe that there's something "not nice" about standing up for ourselves and driving a hard bargain. But if we don't stand up for ourselves, who will? Certainly not the person on the other side of the table. So don't allow yourself to be put off from negotiation because of an erroneous perception of what the process entails. Just because you're willing to negotiate for yourself doesn't automatically brand you a nasty person; it merely brands you a person with the knowledge and self-respect to negotiate for—and get—what you deserve.

Opponent vs. Enemy

Recently a student of mine, Bill, told of a negotiation he had had for a car he wanted to sell. It was an old, rust-eaten Volkswagen. He advertised the car for $325, never dreaming he'd get it. A young college student (we'll call him Paul) came to see the car, and he and Bill immediately established a good rapport. They talked about sports and college and the atmosphere could hardly have been more cordial. When the discussion turned to the car, Bill made a brief sales pitch and readied himself for the negotiation. "I guess you have to have $325 for it, huh?" Paul inquired meekly. "Yeah," replied Bill. End of negotiation. The car was sold for $325.

If the college student could've brought himself to say, "That's a little more than I was looking to pay," Bill surely would've come down. Instead, the buyer completely undercut his own position, beginning and ending the negotiation with one very timid question. What made Paul behave this way? Why did he leave himself no chance of shaving some bucks off the price? He was afraid of switching hats, that is, of exchanging the nice white hat of friendly banter for the evil black hat of give-and-take bargaining. Paul was probably thinking, "Here's this really nice guy—how can I all of a sudden square off against him and start driving a hard bargain?"

Paul, like many of us, failed to make a critical distinction. He confused the concept of enemy with the concept of opponent. Everyone we negotiate with is an opponent for that negotiation—not an enemy, just an opponent. When we play tennis or chess, we have no trouble with the concept of the opponent. We square off, we play hard, and we play to win; and if we succeed, we don't make an enemy in the process. The same is true of negotiation. We're out to win and we give it all we've got, but when it's over, that's it. As long as we don't pull out any dirty tricks, there's no reason in the world that a negotiation should engender any bad feelings or result in any ongoing enmity.

Keep this in mind the next time you're about to enter a negotiation. Remind yourself that you're not looking to alienate, antagonize, or injure anyone, as an enemy would. You're merely attempting to fulfill your own needs, a process that requires playing the part of the opponent for the duration of the negotiation. If you have any persistent problems with a fear of switching hats, think back to Paul and how silly he appeared in bending over backward to accommodate his fear. That should cure you once and for all.

Tough Bargaining Earns Respect

Sarah is a young working woman who attended one of my seminars shortly after taking a new job. When I asked her how she did with her salary negotiation, she replied, "Well, I didn't. I was offered $14,000 and I took it.

"Why didn't you negotiate?" I asked.

"Because I didn't want to make an enemy right off the bat. I didn't want to start off my new job on the wrong foot."

Let me respond to that case by relating another. A friend of mine is an administrator who interviews and hires a lot of people. He told me a story once about a woman he was about to hire for a middle-level management position. After interviewing a number of people for the position, he was quite sure she was his top choice. But he added that he couldn't be certain until he had a final interview with her. "Why?" I asked.

"Because I want to see how she handles the salary negotiation. I'll have serious doubts about her if she just takes what I offer. If she doesn't have it in her, if she doesn't think enough of herself to push me at least a little, my attitude is that she probably isn't the best person for the job."

"So you don't get annoyed or think of people as ingrates when they negotiate with you?"

"Not at all. On the contrary, it indicates a self-assurance and confidence that I value very highly in my employees."

There we have it, right from the mouth of someone who hires lots of people. Whether we're negotiating with an employer, a landlord, or anyone else, we've been brainwashed into believing that if we stand up and bargain for ourselves, we'll make enemies. This fear is particularly potent when we're going to be involved in some kind of ongoing relationship with a person. We tell ourselves we don't want to get things off on the wrong foot or make a bad impression and ruin any chance of getting along.

Well, all those awful things will not come to pass. It simply isn't true that we'll make enemies by negotiating. As my friend the administrator showed us, negotiating for ourselves doesn't reflect badly on us in the least. All it reflects is a sense of self-worth, a positive approach toward life that tells people, "I'm not just going to sit back and take what comes. I'm going after what I feel I deserve." Now the person you're negotiating with may not be willing to write you a blank check, but just because you've made a case for yourself doesn't mean he will take an instant dislike to you. If I had made enemies out of even half the people I've negotiated with, I would have been run out of the country a long time ago. I negotiate and I negotiate firmly, but the opponents I deal with still like me and respect me. Maybe they would prefer to be dealing with a pushover, but they're not, and they've just had to accept that fact.

Also keep this in mind: First impressions die hard. Once we've been tagged as patsies, it can be awfully hard to shake the label. Consequently, people come to expect us to be putty in their hands, to ask for a little and give up a lot. The more firmly entrenched we get in the role of a patsy, the harder it becomes for us to break out and stand up for ourselves. Two people I know, Henry and Jennifer, live in different apartments in the same building. They moved in around the same time, and each made an under-the-table payment of $100 to the superintendent to win his good will and make sure nobody else was given their apartments. But there was one big difference: Henry asserted himself from the start, making clear that in exchange for the money he expected the superintendent to perform some occasional services such as fixing broken light sockets, and leaky sinks, and the like. Jennifer, on the other hand, just handed over her money and said nothing at all. So what do you think happens now? When Henry needs a minor repair done, the superintendent does it for nothing. When Jennifer needs something done, he'll do it, but never without leaving with at least a couple of bucks in his hand. Henry stood up for himself from the start, and it paid off. Jennifer did not, and it's paying off . . . for the superintendent.

Don't worry about making enemies when you negotiate. It won't happen. Instead, establish from square one that you are not a pushover. You'll be thanking yourself forever after.

Upsetting the Applecart

Sally works for a small weekly newspaper. She likes her job and her employer, Donald. She doesn't get paid much, but Sally feels the satisfaction she gets from helping to produce a newspaper is more than enough compensation. Her only problem on the job is that she's being asked to shoulder an increasingly large share of the responsibilities around the office. If there's a late-breaking story that has to be covered or a photo that has to be taken or a page that has to be laid out again, the job always seems to fall in Sally's lap. She feels she is being taken advantage of; everyone knows they can rely on "good ol' Sally" in a fix. She's confused about what to do. She doesn't mind helping out, but she does mind being exploited and carrying the load for others. Her problem is she's afraid that if she speaks her mind, she may jeopardize the cordial relationship she enjoys with Donald. She doesn't want to do that, so she bites the bullet and never broaches the subject. "There are a lot worse jobs out there," she rationalizes. "I should count my blessings."

There may in fact be a lot of worse jobs out there, but that isn't the point. The point is that Sally stopped herself from negotiating with Donald because she, like so many of us, was afraid of upsetting the applecart. She had a good rapport with her boss, and she was afraid she'd destroy it if she suddenly changed her style and began asserting her own needs. For his part, the boss probably reinforced her fear by continuously talking about "team effort" and how wonderful it was that "we're just one big happy family."

If you find yourself in a like predicament—where you're worried that you might spoil a perfectly good relationship with someone you deal with regularly by changing your attitude and negotiating for yourself—try to step back and put it all in perspective. Are you really out to wreck this person's world? No. Do you really want to upset the whole applecart? No. All you want are the apples you deserve. Your opponent, of course, may try to "*guilt-peddle*" you into thinking that you *are* upsetting the whole damn applecart, hoping to make you retreat from your position. Don't pay any mind. Stand firm. Don't listen to any bunk about how you're being selfish or unreasonable or to any willpower-sapping questions such as "What's gotten into you?" or "How can you do this to me?" Once you firmly establish that you're not backing off, your opponent will be forced to negotiate with you. He may not be happy about it, but did you expect him to be? The nature of your relationship may change as your opponent realizes you're no longer a pushover, but the change will be a positive one. Because the end result will be a relationship based on mutual respect, not one-sided manipulation.

Fear of the Unknown Reaction

None of us live in a vacuum. We interact with other people all the time, and our self-image is strongly influenced by the ways others react to us. I may think I'm the nicest person in the world, but if everyone treats me as if I've got the plague, I'm going to begin to wonder. People's reactions and opinions, consequently, are paramount to us. We want to be liked, thought of as nice, and make a good impression. So much so, we'll sometimes turn ourselves into yes-men and yes-women just to win the approval of others.

Yes-people will seldom negotiate; *they're too busy doing what other people want them to do*. But the rest of us—those who do negotiate—must deal with how others will react to our standing up for ourselves. This isn't always easy because we can never be sure what their reactions will be. If your goals are received—and acceded to—cheerfully, you've got nothing to worry about. If your goals are resisted—as they may well be, since you're after something your opponent may not be wild about giving you—it's another matter. That's when you're open game for any number of reactions, all designed to make you back off like a scolded puppy. And that's when you must redouble your efforts to stand firm.

What might you expect in the way of reactions? Most common are shock, condescension, scorn, anger, hurt, silence, disapproval, and, in some instances, outright rejection (which, as we shall see, should never be considered an irreversible position; there are countless ways to get around a rejection). You also might be accused of being greedy, selfish, unreasonable, naïve, foolish, or insensitive. What do you do when you're subjected to all this? How do you withstand your opponent's reaction—be it stunned silence or terrible tantrum—plus your own churning stomach and pounding heart, yet remain adamant in your position?

The first important thing to keep in mind is where your opponent is coming from. He would much prefer that you didn't make any demands. *It's a lot easier to deal with a pushover.* Thus his first reaction is often a way to test your resolve, to try to make you backtrack. Think for a moment about these sample reactions you might be confronted with:

"Five hundred dollars! This car's in mint condition. I'm making a huge sacrifice offering it for a thousand!"
"I'm surprised at you."
"That's the most ridiculous thing I've ever heard."
"What do you think, I'm made of money?"
"Don't you think you're being unreasonable?"
"I thought we had an understanding."
"What about the others? They work hard too, and you don't see them asking for whopping raises."
"I guess I had you all wrong."

The list goes on and on. The point is, by reacting in these ways, your opponent hopes to get you to buckle under. Don't! There will be plenty of time later for making concessions and working out an agreement, but if you falter this early, you're probably finished. Once you say, "Well, maybe I was a bit excessive in my demand," you're on the run, and if your opponent is sharp, he won't let you slow up for a minute.

Detaching yourself from the situation, getting some perspective, is enormously helpful in dealing with others' reactions. Take a step back and ask yourself, "Is what I'm asking for really going to alter the course of human events? Does it really matter that my opponent gets disturbed for a short while? Won't he get over it before long?" By objectifying the negotiation this way, you can be more comfortable with your demands and assuage your insecurities about making them.

It also pays to remember that the other person—not you—is solely responsible for the way he happens to feel. That he may be sullen or angry or whatever is not your doing. He will likely attempt to make you think it is. But it isn't. You must never forget that when you negotiate, all you're doing is trying to fulfill your own needs—nothing more, nothing less. If the opponent chooses to react adversely, so be it. It's no big deal. As we've seen, all it probably means is that he was expecting you to be a pushover, and he's distressed to find that you're not going to be so accommodating. If you like, think of it as a trade-off; you're swapping some short-term discomfort—and perhaps unpleasantness—when your opponent reacts to your demands for some long-term respect when he realizes that you are an individual who is not easily pushed around. By any reckoning, isn't that a swap you'd be willing to make?

A Four-Letter Word to Beware of

We interrupt this book to bring you students of negotiation an urgent all-points bulletin: There is a word out there that should be considered armed and dangerous. It seems harmless enough, but that's why it's so deadly. Don't be fooled. Stay as clear from it as you can. If you don't, the little devil will completely undermine your negotiation. *Beware of "Fair"!*

Of all the emotional potholes that dot the road of negotiation, the concept of "being fair" may be the deepest and most hazardous. If you fall into it, it's extremely hard to pull yourself out. In this section we're going to see how to avoid it, so that our journey can continue, safely and comfortably.

"When I negotiate," a client once told me, "I have two basic fears. One is I'll lose and look like an idiot. The other is much worse: I'll win a deal that's great for me but unfair to my opponent."

For many people the fear of being unfair is the granddaddy of all fears of negotiation. It is more responsible than anything else for a reluctance to drive a hard bargain. The thought of being pushy or greedy at the expense of someone else is completely abhorrent to us. From the cradle we've been inculcated with a host of fair-related tenets: "Be nice," "Be polite," "Share your toys," "Give your friend the biggest piece of pie," "Guest gets best," and on and on. I'm not saying there is anything inherently wrong with these ideas; obviously they're rooted in admirable intentions. The trouble is, as a result of our conditioning, we tend to go way beyond the objective idea of fairness and carry it into an emotional realm where it gets all tied up with guilt. We become so obsessed with guilt (I'm a bad person because I played with the dump truck and stuck poor Harvey with the blocks), with a nagging worry about not being good, that we begin to overcompensate. We come to believe that the most vile thing we can do is assert what *we* want. Who of us hasn't been stung by that pejorative word "selfish"? It's probably the last thing in the world we want to be called. So we bend over backward and stop our demand far short of the area that might be defined as selfish.

This deep-seated fear of being unfair prompts us to make certain trade-offs. We decide to be polite instead of pushing for what we deserve. We decide to be nice and cooperative and accept what is offered instead of asking for more. We decide to be reasonable instead of getting entangled in a negotiation. For many of us, the slightest hint from our opponent that we're being unfair is all it takes for us to put our heads in the sand. And there are a lot of people out there who know it. The shrewd negotiator is well aware that we're all saddled with this notice of fairness and will play on it for all it's worth. It's not hard to do: A little guilt-peddling here ("I'm surprised at you"), a hurt look there, a snide statement about being concerned with personal goals rather than the group effort, and other such insidious propaganda are all ways of playing on our fear of being unfair and making us feel guilty for having the gall to make demands.

Habitually low demanders—that's what the fear of being unfair and its bedfellow, guilt, turn us into. Low demanders, if they have the temerity to demand anything at all, negotiate so tentatively and reluctantly that their main goal would seem to be not to step on their poor opponents' toes.

The essence of our discussion of fairness is this: Don't permit yourself to be duped into not negotiating for fear of being unfair to others, for wanting to watch out for the other person first and yourself second. That's not to say I want to convert everyone into a selfish monster and do away with basic human decency. Hardly. We don't want to be monsters, but neither do we want to get so carried away with fairness that we don't do justice to ourselves.

Also remember this: Fairness is a very relative concept. If you start negotiating by fixing yourself at a position *you* think is fair, who's to say that your opponent's idea of what's fair will be the same? We all have our own values, beliefs, and mind sets; what you may think is fair in a given negotiation may not even be close to what I think is fair. What if a settlement your opponent thinks is fair results in your getting ninety percent of what you wanted, whereas what you had thought to be fair prior to the negotiation would have netted you only fifty percent of what you wanted? By asking for only what you think is fair—instead of for all you want, you can end up a substantial loser.

Indeed, part of the very purpose of negotiation is to decide what is fair in a given situation. Negotiation is a process of probing, and you must assume that your opponent is fully capable of probing for himself. People don't need their hands held; you're not taking candy from a baby, you're negotiating. Obviously, if you're dealing with a child or a handicapped individual who, for whatever reason, enters the negotiation at a distinct disadvantage, then it's a different story. But in virtually all cases you negotiate with people like yourself, who are looking out for their own interests, just as you are looking out for yours. Remember, too, that people are not compelled to reach agreement with you. They always have the option of walking away. If you and another adult agree to a negotiated settlement, then that's fair by definition. You cannot allow yourself to be preoccupied with his interests. You'll have your hands full watching out for your own.

Furthermore, if, when you've completed a deal, you genuinely feel your sense of equity has been violated, that your opponent has really gotten the short end of the stick, you're always free to backtrack and give him or her a gift, a little something to even things out. There is such a thing as too good a deal, especially when you will have cause to negotiate with that person in the future. But the time to grapple with the question of equity is after the deal has been made, not before or during the negotiation. Because if you worry about fairness before a settlement is reached, and then *you* end up getting the short end, who can guarantee that your opponent will be equally ethical and willing to reopen the negotiation?

Trust me. Throw off the yoke of fairness. You'll still be as nice and considerate and wonderful as ever, and you'll be a helluva lot better negotiator.

Summing Up

In explaining, exposing, and demystifying our basic fears of negotiation, my intention has been threefold: (1) to reassure you that you're not alone in your fears—all of us are besieged by some of them at some point; (2) to illustrate why those fears are not valid; and (3) to show why we must not let them stop us from negotiating.

Not that I expect that your fears have now been summarily dispelled. We are not machines; we cannot cleanse ourselves of unwanted feelings simply by pressing a magic mental button. The aim here has been to spotlight our fears, to become more aware of them and where they come from, so that we can negotiate effectively in spite of them. *We don't have to feel differently. We only have to act differently.*

How might you learn to act differently? Try this for starters: The next time you sense your fears taking over, tell yourself, "This fear is just a feeling inside me. It won't be with me forever; it probably won't be with me five minutes from now. I would rather cope with this feeling for a short while and go through with the negotiation to try to get what I'm looking for than let this fear shackle me to the point that I'm unable to stand up for myself. By negotiating, I am not looking to make enemies. I am not looking to upset the applecart. I am not being selfish or greedy, and I am certainly not being unfair. I am not attempting to wreak havoc on my opponent's life. I am only trying to fulfill my needs."

Once we're able to hold our fears of negotiation in check, once it has been de-emotionalized, negotiation begins to seem a lot less ominous. We begin to see it for what it truly is—a reasonable, comprehensible process; a process that contrary to our image of the deep, dark forest, is like a well-marked trail. It can be followed by anyone who takes the time to learn its markings and follow them closely.

The forest is behind us. Let's embark on the trail to successful negotiation.

PART II

Setting the Stage

CHAPTER 3

An Overview of Negotiation

WE'VE DEFINED NEGOTIATION as an exchange between people for the purpose of fulfilling their needs. What exactly does this mean?

It means that every negotiation is a trade. You give something to get something in return. If I have apples and you have oranges and we each want some of each other's fruit, then we'll sit down and negotiate a deal, each of us doing some giving and some getting. This give–get exchange, as I call it, is the activating force behind each and every negotiation. What you will learn from this book is how to negotiate in such a way as to gain the most advantageous give–get exchange for yourself that you can.

When Does a Negotiation Take Place?

Two conditions must be present for the give–get exchange of a negotiation to take place. First, you have to identify a need, that is, something you want and/or wish to accomplish; in short, what you want to get out of the negotiation. It may be more money from your boss or less noise from your neighbor across the street; it doesn't matter, so long as you perceive it as a need. Second, you have to involve some person or persons to fulfill your need. If I want a chicken sandwich, I don't have to negotiate. I'll just get up and make it. I have a need, but since nobody else is involved, it isn't negotiation. But what if I want a sandwich and ask you to make it for me? Aha! Now we have a potential negotiation.

Why do I say "potential"? Because whether I have to negotiate with you depends on your response. Look at the accompanying diagram. We've identified our need and we've

WHEN DOES A NEGOTIATION TAKE PLACE?

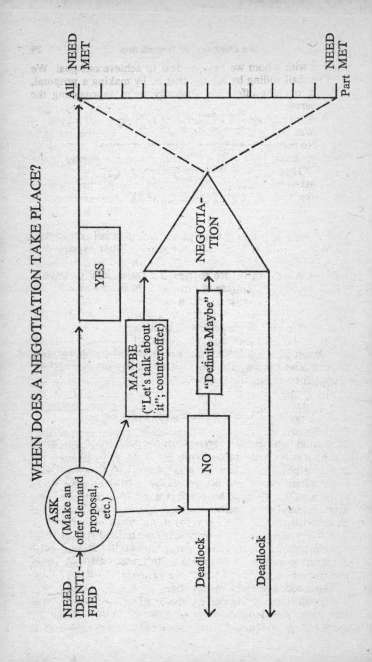

decided with whom we have to deal to achieve our goal. We start the ball rolling by asking; that is, by making a proposal, demand, opening offer, etc. Basically we're approaching the other person and saying, "We want this." Then what happens? We can get one of three responses: yes, no, or maybe.

If we're absolutely certain the answer will be positive, great! No need to be concerned with negotiating.

"Hey, how 'bout some of those oranges you've got?" "Sure." "Thanks a lot."

We asked and we got. How nice! Would that life were always like that. But alas, it isn't, and whenever there's a chance the answer won't be yes, when there's even the slightest possibility that we'll get a no or a maybe or any other response short of total acceptance of what we're looking for, then we have to begin preparing for a negotiation. We'll see just how we prepare later. But first we must interrupt this book once more to alert all negotiators to another dangerous word to beware of.

No and the Negotiator

Too many of us are frightened away by the terrible omnipotence of the word "no." We were brought up to be terrified of it and to accept the unalterable finality of it. It could not be questioned or misconstrued. "Mommy, can we go to the amusement park?" "No." Case closed. Those two letters, as we were taught them, were completely nonnegotiable.

In the context of negotiation, however, the concept of "no" is seen in an entirely different light. Because, contrary to what we've been conditioned to believe, no is an opening negotiating position. It is what I call a "definite maybe." Few negotiations would ever get off the ground if no were taken at face value. A story I once heard tells of two men who were negotiating a major business transaction. Each man stated what he wanted out of the deal. "Your offer is ridiculous," the seller said. "I could never accept it." "Your price is ridiculous," countered the buyer. "I could never accept it." At which point they parted and both said, "We'll talk again tomorrow."

The good negotiator won't take no for an answer. The good negotiator is always on the lookout for ways to get around it. A woman I know recently had trouble with her landlord, who continually refused to attend to the substantial repairs her apartment needed. She heard "No" at every turn. But she did not give up. She contacted the local board of health office, and within days the landlord's work crew showed up at her door. Or take the case of the distraught little girl who lost her balloon. Did she take no for an answer? No way! She kept on negotiating—crying her little eyes out—until her need was met. So the next time you hear that dangerous little word, remember: No is an opening negotiating position. I can't guarantee that you will always find a way around a no, but the point is you can't let yourself be put off by it from the start. Later, when we explore specific strategies and tactics, you'll learn how we can change it to a yes. For now, just keep in mind that no isn't the end of the negotiation. It's just the start.

Knowing Your Goals

Earlier we discussed how we have to have some need in order for a negotiation to take place. We assumed that we had our need clearly identified, that we had thought it all through, before going ahead and asking. That's a large assumption to make, so let's go back briefly and make sure we've pinpointed our need(s) as best we can.

Sometimes careful thought is necessary to know what you really want. If I hadn't taken a moment to think about what I felt like eating, if I had just said, "I'm hungry—will you fix me something to eat?" my chances of getting the chicken sandwich, which deep down is what I truly wanted, would have been slim indeed. One fundamental fact about negotiation is that we have to know what we want to get out of it. We must clarify our goals; if we don't, the chicken sandwiches of the world will almost always elude us. Sound easy? Sometimes it is, like when we're looking to get a raise or a good deal on a new car. Then our goal is money, plain and simple. There are other instances, however, when clarifying our goals is not so easy.

A woman who has written a couple of successful cookbooks was approached by a public television station to do a series on cooking. When I discussed the station's proposal with her, the goals she mentioned were almost solely financial, that is, to make as much money as she could. But as we continued to talk and as she probed her ambitions more thoroughly, she began to realize that the money was secondary,

that her primary goal was actually to use the program to gain as much exposure as she could for herself and her books. So much so, in fact, that while she would try to get as much as she could for the series, she would be willing to do it for nothing if it came down to that.

If she hadn't bothered to clarify her goals, she might have gone ahead and negotiated for the wrong thing. In doing so, she would have run the risk of losing the whole deal because of a secondary issue—money. Entering a negotiation without well-defined goals is like preparing a gourmet dish without a recipe; you're bound to omit a key ingredient, and chances are the whole thing simply won't turn out the way you had hoped.

When I began writing this book, I took great pains to clarify my goal, namely, to systematize the negotiating process in a way that's comprehensible to everyone. If I hadn't done that, I might well have written thousands and thousands of words without ever really zeroing in on the message I wanted to convey. I wouldn't have known where I was going. If you enter a negotiation without clearly identifying your goals, you won't know where *you* are going.

When to Go Ahead and Ask

"Ask, and it shall be given . . ." the Bible says. "Don't ask, and ye will never know," I say.

Asking is the starting point of every negotiation. In the simplest of negotiations, when the stakes are low and the issues relatively minor, there's no sense wasting time getting things going. Just ask! In these situations you needn't worry about strategies, tactics, or any elaborate preparations. It simply wouldn't be worth the effort. Just go ahead and pop the question. If you get a no or a maybe, then you can either negotiate from there or forget it if the matter is very small. But I think you'll be surprised how often the answer is yes. Asking is a lot like fishing. As long as you've got your line in the water, there's no telling what you might reel in. But if the line is in the boat, you're never going to land a thing.

Take my word for it: There's an awful lot to be had by fishing around. Some years back, when I was living in New York City, I bought a security grate to cover a skylight in my apartment. I was walking upstairs with it when I happened to run into my landlord. "I just picked up this grate for $40," I said. "I'm installing it myself, and it'll be a permanent fixture for your building. Would you mind reimbursing me for it?" "Not at all," the landlord replied. I had my line in the water, and it paid off nicely.

Another example: A student of mine was in a muffler shop talking price with the sales manager. My student had recently paid the shop $20 for a minor muffler repair, and now he needed a whole new unit. "Can the $20 be applied toward the cost of the new muffler?" he fished. The sales manager paused. "All right," he said. A little triumph.

Another student of mine was shopping for a television at a small appliance store. He was about to pay by credit card when an idea flashed into his head. "How 'bout taking off $15 if I pay you in cash?" he asked. The storeowner agreed. Fishing paid off once more.

Of course, not all of your needs will be met simply by asking. But what's the harm in trying? The worst that can happen is that you'll get a no, and that's not the end of the world. If you want to follow it up from there, fine. If not, if you think it's just not worth it, you've lost nothing for your effort. Even the best fishermen come up empty-handed sometimes, and so it is when you ask. *But at least give yourself the chance to succeed.*

Introducing the Settlement Range

Dropping a line in the water is great for simple low-stake negotiations. You've got everything to gain and nothing to lose, as long as you view the negotiation in question as small potatoes.

But what about when it's not small potatoes? What if you're dealing with bigger potatoes, with a raise or buying a house or something else that really is of considerable importance to you? In such instances you've got to be more sophisticated in your approach. You've got to take a little extra time to get yourself off on the right foot and to structure your negotiation in such a way as to enable you to get the very best agreement you can. How? By devising a Settlement Range for your negotiation.

The Settlement Range is the most critical concept in this book, the foundation that we will return to time and again on which everything else we discuss will be built. Simply put, the Settlement Range is the range of all possible settlements you would be willing to make in a given negotiation, from the very best to the very worst. The bottom end of the Settlement Range—the end we call the Least Acceptable Result (L.A.R.)—is the rock-bottom point at which you'll make a deal and still feel that you've negotiated to your advantage. We'll talk about how you arrive at your Least Acceptable Result shortly; for now just think of it as a safety net, the end of the Settlement Range that prevents you from getting ensnared in a deal that is to your detriment.

The other end of the Settlement Range—the Maximum Supportable Position (M.S.P.)—is what you're aspiring to ideally get out of the negotiation. It represents a one-hundred percent fulfillment of your needs. It's your opening position in the negotiation, a position that your opponent probably won't agree with but one you nonetheless bolster with everything you've got in the hope of achieving a settlement as close to it as possible. We'll talk about the Maximum Supportable Position in much greater depth, too, but right now let me give you an example to illustrate simply the use of Settlement Range.

Let's say I'm selling an electric office typewriter, and you come over to take a look. It's just two years old and in very good condition, so I decide before I even begin talking to you that there's no way I'll let it go for less than $500. So that's my Least Acceptable Result; anything less than that I've determined would be worse than not selling it at all. Bear in mind, of course, that my Least Acceptable Result is hush-hush; the last thing I want you to know is how low I'm willing to go. I also decide that I will open my bargaining with a Maximum Supportable Position of $900. Hell, it's practically a new machine and the new ones go for over $1,000.

You, on the other hand, have a completely different Settlement Range in mind. You've done a little checking around and have decided that if it's really in tip-top shape, you're willing to go as high as $600 for it. Thus, $600 is your Least Acceptable Result; but you have also decided, since you never know what might be wrong with a used typewriter, that you'll set $250 as your opening stance (Your Maximum Supportable Position).

Okay. The negotiation has been set up. Will there be a settlement? Yes, because there is an overlap in Settlement Ranges, that is, in our Least Acceptable Results. You're willing to go as high as $600 and I'm willing to go as low as

$500, so we should be able to cut a deal. It's not my intention to get into the specifics of how I would go about nudging you upward or how you would try to nudge me downward; that comes later. The key point here is this: *Your ultimate success in any negotiation, in using all the strategies and tactics laid out for you in this book, can be measured by how well you can move your opponent toward your Maximum Supportable Position and reach a settlement at or near his Least Acceptable Result.* The better you're able to do so, the better settlements you'll achieve. It's as simple as that.

CHAPTER 4

The Settlement Range: The Best Friend Your Negotiation Will Ever Have

YOU'RE HEADED FOR a negotiation. It's important enough to you that you're not just going to dive in and ask and hope you get a yes. You're going to approach it rationally and methodically. You've thought through what you want and you know with whom you have to deal to get it.

You have cause to believe that your opponent will greet your demands with a "No" or a "Maybe" or a "Let's talk about it" or perhaps even a concrete counteroffer. Now it's a contest between what you want and what your opponent wants. You know you want to set up a Settlement Range to secure the best possible settlement. But how do you actually do it?

The answer is that you have to establish two all-important guideposts for your negotiation—a Least Acceptable Result (L.A.R.) and a Maximum Supportable Position (M.S.P.). One guidepost, the *M.S.P.*, is *the absolute most you can ask for in your opening position without leaving the realm of reason;* the other, the *L.A.R.*, is *the point at which you would be better off walking away and forgetting the deal rather than accept less.*

Right now, these two vital poles probably seem like purely theoretical concepts with little bearing on your real-life negotiations. But, believe me, once you see how indispensable the Settlement Range they form is to getting what you want, they'll be the two best friends your negotiation will ever have. Let's examine the two guideposts in depth to find out why they're so critical and how to go about determining them for any given negotiation.

Least Acceptable Result

We've discussed the importance of zeroing in on your goals for a negotiation and how you leave yourself little chance of being satisifed if you don't. But since you're assuming your demands will *not* be totally accepted (and thus, your goals not fully achieved), you also have to determine how far you'll back down from your demands. This is precisely what determining your Least Acceptable Result (L.A.R.) accomplishes. It is your bedrock, the point at which you would decide you'd be better off chucking the agreement. Think of it as a cutoff line below which any deal you make would leave you in worse shape than you were in. As long as a proposal is above your L.A.R. and you feel it's the best deal you can get, it's in your best interest to accept it.

"What deal can I make that will leave me at least a little better off than I am now?" The answer to this pivotal question is your L.A.R. It's the least you'll settle for; anything less, and you would be negotiating to your detriment. The L.A.R., in essence, is a reality exercise. It tells you, "I'd like to get more out of this negotiation, but if I can't and push comes to shove, this is as far as I'll back down."

If you prepare nothing else for your negotiation, prepare your Least Acceptable Result. Because knowing it guarantees you that you'll never accept a settlement to your disadvantage. It's an awfully nice guarantee to have.

Finding Your L.A.R.

To calculate your Least Acceptable Result, you have to build it, piece by piece, from the ground up. You've got to sit down and do some serious probing of your state of mind, your state of wallet, and your degree of need in this particular negotiation. The L.A.R. is both objective and subjective, a combination of the facts surrounding the situation and the value you place on them.

For example, two people could be selling the exact same car, in the same condition and with the same mileage, and yet they could have two entirely different L.A.R.'s. Say you're selling the car and you've already got a new one in the driveway. The old one is just taking up space, and you don't need the money terribly much, and you simply want to unload it. In this scenario, your Least Acceptable Result may be, or you might even be willing to pay someone to tow it away so you don't have to deal with it anymore.

But what if I've got the same car and I happen to need $500 to make a down payment on the new one I want to buy? No down payment, no new car. Well, if you come along and offer me $300, I'm going to refuse it because that much money won't do me any good. I'm better off holding out for what I need. Why? Because I've calculated my L.A.R. to be $500, and by definition, any settlement below that and I'd be better off not settling at all. If, however, I've just received a check in the mail for $200 from my Aunt Tillie, it's very possible that I may accept your $300 offer. My situation would have changed; therefore, my Least Acceptable Result would have changed.

The point is that there is no magical formula for determining your Least Acceptable Result. What I set as mine may be totally untenable for you. You must search for a true idea of what the deal is worth to you and at what point you'd be better off scrapping it.

Also be sure to wipe clean your mental slate of expectations, of preconceptions, and, most importantly, of what you want. *The L.A.R. is not what you want!* It's the least you'll accept, the point at which you'll settle and still feel the negotiation has been beneficial in some way.

Confusing what you want—your wish point, as I call it—with your Least Acceptable Result can be deeply hazardous, if not fatal, to the health of your negotiation. If I decide I *want* $500 for my car and set that as my artificial L.A.R. when my actual L.A.R. may be a lot lower, I'll probably end up rejecting some deals which, even if they were less than I hoped for, would still have been to my advantage to accept. Don't fall into this dangerous trap! Keep your hopes and expectations out of the picture entirely when calculating your Least Acceptable Result. Don't forget: Your L.A.R. is your meat; your wish point is gravy.

For further clarification, let's take a look at a discussion I had in a seminar with Susan, a beginning free-lance photographer who was preparing to negotiate a fee for a job.

Mike: What's your minimum price for this kind of work?

Susan: Well . . . $450.

Mike: Okay, $450 is your Least Acceptable Result. Anything less, considering your time and costs, and you will be worse off than if you don't do the job, right?

Susan: Yes.

Mike: Are you really sure? Remember, the definition of the Least Acceptable Result is not what you would like to get. It's that point at which it's just barely worth it to you to do the job. In developing the L.A.R., you must be totally honest with yourself; otherwise you might end up refusing a deal that really would be in your best interests. Now let's try building your Least Acceptable Result from scratch. What's the cost of your materials?

Susan: About $100.

Mike: Okay, do you have another job you could do during this time?

Susan: No.

Mike: How long will this job take you?

Susan: About twenty hours.

Mike: What price do you put on your labor? To say it another way, below what price would you rather just go to the movies or to a museum?

Susan: At no point.

Mike: You mean you'd work twenty hours for nothing?!

Susan: No, I guess not.

Mike: So there is a point. Would you work twenty hours for $40?

Susan: No.

Mike: Would you work twenty hours for $100?

Susan: Yes.

Mike: For $75?

Susan: No.

Mike: Would you say the least you'd work twenty hours for is $100?

Susan: Yes.

Mike: Okay. So your Least Acceptable Result for your fee negotiation is actually $200—$100 labor and $100 for costs. Now that you've calculated your *actual*

L.A.R., you know the cutoff point below which it's just not worth bothering to do the job.

This is a good example of the thought processes you have to employ to accurately assess your L.A.R. By stripping away her hopes, casting aside her wish point, and doing some hard thinking about just how low she could go, Susan was able to locate the worst deal that would still be to her advantage to accept.

A Sure Offer

One case where you can look *outside* yourself in figuring your L.A.R. is when there's a sure offer bearing on the negotiation. If you have a sure offer in hand and it's an improvement over your L.A.R., you can safely slide your cutoff point upward to the level of the offer. Let's return to the used-car case. The person who had previously been willing to go as low as $0 has now done some shopping around at used-car dealers and has received an offer of $250. Now what? Well, $250 becomes the new Least Acceptable Result because the person knows it would be to his disadvantage to settle for less. On the other hand, the $250 sure offer wouldn't amount to a hill of beans to the guy whose L.A.R. was $500, since he's already determined that's as low as he can go.

A sure offer doesn't eliminate the need for building your L.A.R. because you still have to build it to know whether the sure offer is higher or lower than it. So long as the sure offer is higher, plug it right in and peg your Least Acceptable Result at that level. If you go looking for a job, for instance, and you've got an offer of $15,000 for a like position in hand, you can use $15,000 as your L.A.R. and negotiate upward from there. But if you had previously figured that, with your mortgage and another kid on the way, you could not accept an offer for less than $20,000, clearly the $15,000 offer will have no impact on your L.A.R.

While a sure offer can give a dramatic boost to your Least Acceptable Result, be aware that in many negotiations there won't be a sure offer better than your L.A.R. Take the photographer, Susan, for instance. She had no sure offer, so she was left to her own devices to calculate what her time was worth and what the rock-bottom deal she would agree to was. If she had another offer that would have paid her $12 per hour, say, she could have jacked her L.A.R. up to there. A sure offer can give you the luxury of setting a higher floor to your negotiation. But be certain that the offer you're adopting as your L.A.R. is one hundred percent sure, not something that merely seems likely to pan out. Because if you reject some settlements on the basis of the "sure" offer, and the offer turns out to be not so sure, then you've missed the boat completely.

Changing Your L.A.R.

It's important to realize that your Least Acceptable Result may change during the negotiation as other factors come into play and offers and counteroffers are exchanged (indeed, a basic strategy we will discuss later is how we go about moving our *opponent's* L.A.R.). Susan's L.A.R. initially was $200, but what if her opponent offered her $150 with a written promise of $2,000 work in the next month? She would have to reassess her L.A.R. and decide whether the revised offer would leave her in a better position than she is in presently. Similarly, if I'm negotiating to buy a car and I've decided my L.A.R.—the most I'd be willing to pay—is $1,000, wouldn't I have to think about changing my L.A.R. if my opponent asked for $1,100 but agreed to throw in four new radial tires and a C.B. radio in the bargain? You bet.

This is not to say that you should change your L.A.R. easily or quickly. Do so only when new developments warrant it, and even then, only with great care. Remember that the whole reason for having a Least Acceptable Result is to insure that you don't wind up with a settlement that isn't of at least a little benefit to you. It's your guarantee of successful negotiation; you set it out at the beginning so that, in the heat of back-and-forth negotiating, you don't get pushed into a corner you don't want to be in. If you start playing around with it when nothing substantive has changed, it's going to be a lot less valuable.

It isn't always easy to unearth exactly what your Least Acceptable Result is. It takes some digging, particularly in the absence of a sure offer. But believe me, whatever effort it takes is effort well spent. It's an indispensable element in successful negotiating, because knowing it sends an unequivocal signal to you when you're in the danger zone . . . the danger zone of negotiating a settlement that's not to your advantage.

Maximum Supportable Position

We've looked at the bottom of your Settlement Range and seen how it protects you from getting trapped in undesirable deals. But just because you *would* settle there if worse came to worst doesn't mean that's what you're shooting for. What you're shooting for—your Maximum Supportable Position—is at the other extreme of the Settlement Range.

It may be helpful to imagine the Settlement Range as a big flagpole. You can't fly the flag unless the pole is firmly anchored in the ground. That's where the L.A.R. comes in; it's your anchor, your base. Once you've got that set, you can run the flag as far up the pole as you can—right to the top—to your Maximum Supportable Position. Simply put, the M.S.P. is the point furthest in the direction of meeting all your goals that can *justify in some way, shape, or form*.

The One-Trip-to-the-Well Principle

Let's say you're interested in buying a house. The real estate broker shows you one, quoting a price of $60,000. Two days later you call him to begin negotiating the price. But before you can make an offer he says, "The price has been increased to $61,500." What do you know on the basis of these contacts? You know almost for certain that the owner would at least be willing to accept $60,000 for the house—the original offer—and quite likely, less. Why? Because that's what he first asked for, and if he wouldn't have been delighted to get $60,000, he never would have asked for it.

The point? In any negotiation, you get only one opportunity to state your opening position. It's your only trip to the well, and it's vital you make the most of it. In going for as much water as you can, you leave yourself the option of pouring some back. But if you limit your demands from the outset, you're stuck. Put another way, it's almost impossible to reverse directions and ask for more if you belatedly realize your M.S.P. is too low. If I advertise a car for $2,000 and the next day thirty people are banging down my door for the right to buy it, I've clearly blown it; I've asked for much too little. I'd have been better off asking for $500 more, having only three people show up, and winding up selling it for $2,-350. John Masefield, the English poet, was right on the mark when he said, "Success is the brand on the brow of the man who has aimed too low."

Don't undermine your only trip to the well. Come back hauling as much water as you can. If you spill some along the way, don't fret, because you'll still be far better off than if you'd just filled the bucket halfway and not spilled a drop.

The Big "M" of the M.S.P.: Why the Maximum Is So Important

The best settlement you can secure in a negotiation is, by definition, at your opponent's Least Acceptable Result; in other words, at the very bottom of your opponent's Settlement Range. You can't hope to do better than that because beyond that point it's in your opponent's best interest to deadlock rather than cut a deal. Thus, if you want to get as much as your opponent is willing to give and settle at or near his L.A.R., you've got to make sure your opening demand, your M.S.P., is at least at, and preferably beyond, his L.A.R. If you fail to truly maximize your opening position, you'll fall short of your opponent's L.A.R. . . . and of the best settlement you could have attained.

To make this clearer, look at the accompanying diagram. Let's suppose we're selling a stereo system. We advertise it and have a potential buyer. We decide to be "reasonable" in setting our asking price (M.S.P.) at $250. The least we will accept, we decide, is $200. Lower than that, and we've determined we'd be better off holding on to it.

Now it just so happens that our potential buyer is a good negotiator. She's not afraid to shoot high, and she has carefully calculated her Settlement Range. She has decided that her Least Acceptable Result—the most she would pay for the system—is $300. She has also decided, by checking the used-stereo market at several dealers, that she can just barely justify offering us $100 for our stereo.

Let's analyze Diagram 1. Will the system be sold? Yes, because there's an overlap between our Settlement Range and hers. If her L.A.R. had been $150, there would have been no sale, but since it's $300, and our L.A.R. is $200, we've got

only three people show up, and we're one up? Selling it for $350, John Fornield, and... ...es right when he sell... ...the offer to...

SELLING A STEREO SYSTEM

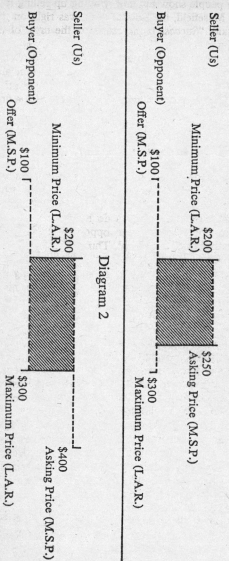

Diagram 1

Seller (Us)
Minimum Price (L.A.R.) $200
$250 Asking Price (M.S.P.)

Buyer (Opponent)
Offer (M.S.P.) $100
$300 Maximum Price (L.A.R.)

Diagram 2

Seller (Us)
Minimum Price (L.A.R.) $200
$400 Asking Price (M.S.P.)

Buyer (Opponent)
Offer (M.S.P.) $100
$300 Maximum Price (L.A.R.)

 = Overlap in Settlement Ranges

some common ground. The sale will occur at some point in the overlap.

But do you see what we've done by being "reasonable"? We've shortchanged ourselves. We've negotiated stupidly! Can we possibly hope to hit her top price of $300? No way, not with our asking price (M.S.P.) of $250. Will we even get that much? Well, if we're absolutely unyielding we may, but we don't even know what her top price is. All we know is what she offered ($100), and when we said we thought that was pretty low, she started talking about the dealers she had talked to and their prices and seemed determined to get a low price herself. She's going to try to make us believe we'll have to come down from our $250 asking price to sell it at all, and the likelihood is that we'll end up selling it for closer to $200 than $250, given her shrewd M.S.P. of $100, which has successfully made her seem like she's making major concessions just to come up closer to our $200. Our M.S.P. was not really a maximum at all, and as a result, we've eliminated any chance of securing the best deal she was willing to make.

Okay, now let's run through it again, except this time we're going to be smart, too. We conclude that we can just barely justify asking $400 for the stereo. Look at Diagram 2. There's still an overlap in the Settlement Ranges. But what a difference! The most we can get from this buyer is still $300 (though we don't know that yet), but now that we're out beyond her L.A.R., we have a real shot at settling there. We now stand a much better chance of coming as close as we can to the most she would pay. By moderating our demands, as in Diagram 1, we excluded that possibility. But with our good ol' M.S.P. in Diagram 2, we've given ourselves a fighting chance and, at the very least, a lot more room to play around before getting back down toward our Least Acceptable Result.

Diverting Attention Away from Your L.A.R.

Another key advantage of the M.S.P. is that it shifts the focus of the negotiation far away from your Least Acceptable Result. Even though you would be willing to settle at your L.A.R., you never want to let your opponent know that. You want to keep the action as far from your L.A.R. as you can and convince your opponent that the only settlements agreeable to you are those at or near your M.S.P. Look at Diagram 2 of the stereo example. What we did by setting $400 as our M.S.P. is whisk the focus of the bargaining away from our $200 L.A.R. and thus tilt the whole negotiation to our advantage. Now we've got our opponent thinking along entirely different lines and made it much harder for her to uncover the whereabouts of our bottom line.

Concealing your Least Acceptable Result is essential to the success of your negotiation. And nothing accomplishes that better than establishing as high a Maximum Supportable Position as possible.

Creativity and the M.S.P.

In basketball, one of the greatest assets a player can have is peripheral vision. By seeing the entire scope of movements on the court, the player has many more opportunities to play creatively. The same is true when you're determining your Maximum Supportable Position. You have to see the whole court of possibilities and look beyond the obvious. Be creative when you figure your M.S.P., so as to make it as all-encompassing as it can be. Let me show you what I mean.

Barbara, a student of mine, is a classical violinist who often performs on ocean cruises. She was having a lot of trouble negotiating because the people who run the cruises tended to be very inflexible about wages. So I asked her, "Why limit your demands to wages? Why not look at other things? What about first-class accommodations? First-class dining privileges? What about publicity—getting some billing in the ship's brochures and advertisements? What about advertising and arranging classes on the boat so interested people could take lessons from you?"

Barbara's negotiating problem was that she was suffering from a bad case of tunnel vision. She was looking at only the wage issue instead of broadening the scope of her demands to include other forms of compensation that could be valuable to her.

In pure buy-sell negotiations, your M.S.P. will often come down to dollars and cents. But the point is that in many negotiations that isn't the case. Open your eyes so you can establish a truly maximum M.S.P.

Not only does a broad-based Maximum Supportable Position give you a chance of getting more out of the settlement, it also supplies a way to maneuver around any major stumbling block to the negotiation. Take the case of Jeanne, a student of mine who works for a market research firm. She was negotiating with her boss for a raise and was told flatly that it was impossible because of the company's established salary range for her position. End of negotiation? No. There are ways around a salary limitation. How about a car? A bonus? Better benefits? A better pension plan? A profit-sharing arrangement?

By entering a negotiation with as all inclusive an M.S.P. as possible, you greatly enhance your chances of a good settlement. Don't get trapped by the obvious. Avoid tunnel vision. Take in the whole array of negotiating possibilities and set yourself a first-class, A-1 Maximum Supportable Position. It will do wonders for your negotiation.

Saving Face

Allowing the opponent to save face is an important element in negotiation, and the M.S.P. aids you in that regard as well. By getting beyond the opponent's L.A.R., you leave yourself room to back down and still settle at or near his L.A.R. Think about how *you* feel when you negotiate. If the most you would pay for a car is $2,000 and the seller is asking $2,200, won't you feel good about being able to move him down to $2,000? Sure! Because it makes you feel like you've negotiated well. It's the same for your opponent. If you establish a high opening position, your opponent can exact some concessions from you and wind up feeling much better about the bargaining. Meanwhile, you don't lose a thing because you started with an M.S.P. which was beyond the opponent's Least Acceptable Result. So you still get the best settlement possible, and the opponent gets the satisfaction of having talked you down.

Don't underestimate the importance of the opponent having a positive feeling about the negotiation. It's critical, especially when you know you'll be negotiating with him in the future. If someone feels like he's been burned, if you don't give him room to save face, it's going to be awfully hard to get him to negotiate with you the next time.

The Big "S" of the M.S.P.: Why Having a Supportable Position Is So Important

Okay. We've looked at why you should maximize your initial offer. But the question remains, how maximum is maximum? How far can you go with it?

The answer is that you should go as far as you can and still have justification for your demand. Why? Because if your opening demand is so outrageous that it's beyond all reason, then you've completely undermined your credibility and drastically impaired your chances of reaching a settlement. Credibility is vital in negotiation; once you lose it, it makes life much more difficult.

If you're selling a solid walnut living room set and I offer you $15 for it, obviously you're going to be very wary of negotiating with me, if you bother to talk to me at all. My M.S.P. is way out there, all right; so much so that I've served notice to you that I am not a reasonable person with whom to negotiate. But if I come up with an offer I can back up with some sort of rationale, however flimsy—some way of saying "This is why I'm asking that"—the situation changes completely, even if my offer is well below what you're looking to get. By being within the bounds of credibility, I force you to take me seriously.

The justification for your M.S.P. need not be ironclad. It only has to be a little bit credible, to put you in the furthest reaches of the ballpark but still in the ball park. In the case of your living room set, perhaps I can fix my M.S.P. by finding out what a dealer would pay you for it. Or I might shop around at garage sales and flea markets to find the lowest price for a similar set and use that figure. Or maybe I'll chop my price down further by making deductions for the nicks and imperfections I can find in your set. The particular method doesn't much matter, so long as I can somehow throw out a Maximum Supportable Position on which I can hang some rationale to get the negotiation rolling. As long as I have some rationale, I make it impossible for you to dismiss my M.S.P. outright.

A Case Study: The M.S.P. in Action

Alice is an office secretary who wanted a new typewriter. The one she had was an old clunker and terribly inconvenient to use. To get the new machine, she had to make a proposal to her boss. There are lots of different typewriters that do lots of different things, so Alice had to decide what kind of proposal to make. She could've said, "I'd like a new typewriter," and left it up to her boss to decide if she'd get one and what kind, or she could've priced some machines, chosen the least expensive one (she doesn't want to alienate the boss, right?), and proposed that one as the replacement.

Well, we discussed the issue at one of my seminars, and Alice came to see the simple truth: If she asked for very little, she would get very little . . . or nothing at all. So she decided to locate her M.S.P. and approach the negotiation in an entirely different way. First, she checked all the typewriters on the market. She didn't worry about what her boss might say about the tight budget or the tough times or anything else; she simply asked herself, "Which typewriter do I want the most?" At first thought, her top choice was a correcting machine, costing about $1,000. But after further consideration, because she typed lots of form letters and reports, Alice concluded that what she would really like was a typewriter with a memory unit that cost $5,000. Great! She had taken the first critical step; instead of worrying about what she *might* get, she identified her true goal.

The next question Alice asked herself was, "Can I somehow justify asking for the memory typewriter? Can that be my opening position, my M.S.P.?" Sure, if she could come up with some rationale for it. So she did some figuring. Assuming it lasts five years, the machine will cost $1,000 a year. Now Alice had to show her boss that the machine would save enough of her time, which could be put to other productive use, to warrant the $1,000-per-year expenditure. She did just that. She calculated how much time she would save by using the memory unit and outlined alternative projects and duties she could attend to with her newfound spare time.

Alice has put herself in a position to get what she wants. Her maximum position is supportable; she's got a way to respond if the boss should say, "Why are you asking for the most expensive machine going?" She had entered into a serious discussion with her boss on the merits of her proposal, her justification, and the clear need to replace the existing equipment. At this writing, the jury is still out; Alice's boss has agreed to lease the expensive machine for six months to see if it's really worth buying. Even if she doesn't wind up with the $5,000 machine for good, Alice has set up her negotiation very well. Her opening position was both maximum and supportable. She made the most of her one trip to the well. She shifted the focus of the negotiation far away from her L.A.R. (which was any new machine) and left herself plenty of room to fall back if her boss balked at her M.S.P.

The I-Can't-Ask-for-a-Lot Syndrome

How are you feeling about all this? If you're like most people, I'll bet dollars to doughnuts that you're thinking, "All this M.S.P. stuff is well and good, but I can't do it because I feel funny asking for so much." In all my years of teaching people how to negotiate, the Maximum Supportable Position has consistently been among the biggest stumbling blocks. The reason, as we saw in Chapter 1, is that most of us have been conditioned very strongly to moderate our demands, to limit our wants, and, if we do have the gall to ask for something, to be reasonable and ask for just a little rather than be greedy and ask for it all. As a result, we end up getting crumbs instead of our share of the pie.

What we mustn't forget, however, is that there are a lot of people who are *not* afraid to make demands and who are looking to walk away with as much of the pie as they can. If you're afraid to make demands, people will pick it up very quickly. They will do everything they can to exploit your hesitancy and keep you on the diet of crumbs.

The point is that if you don't join in with gusto and vigor, you'll simply get a lot less, and nobody is going to pat you on the back for being so nice and reasonable. If you're comfortable with that, fine. But if you're not (and I'm sure you're not if you've read this far), then you're going to have to overcome your reticence and force yourself to make demands—not little ones, but big ones—because the simple fact in life is that *if you don't ask, you won't get,* and if you ask for a little, that's exactly what you'll get, a little.

Low demanders get themselves into a lot of trouble in negotiation, most commonly with a couple of conflict-avoidance techniques I call prenegotiating and giving away the store. When you prenegotiate, you decide before you even meet the opponent to scale down your demands to what you think is the "fair range." Running the negotiation through your head, you determine what your initial demand will be, figure out how the opponent might counter, and finally settle somewhere in between. Say you're selling a car and you think you can get $300 for it. Instead of setting a high demand, say $700 (Horrors! That might be unfair!), you moderate the asking price and zero in on a figure—for instance, $400— that's much closer to what you expect and fits nicely with your concept of what's fair. Some chap comes along and offers $300, and you end up selling the car for $350. Presto, you've succeeded in avoiding much conflict and fooled yourself into thinking you've negotiated effectively. But in reality, by prenegotiating—fixing an asking price so close to what you *expected* to get—you denied yourself valuable negotiating room and in all likelihood sold yourself short. Remember, there's nothing inherently unethical or unfair about aiming high. All you're doing is testing the market, and if people don't want to negotiate with you, because they think what you're asking is out of line, then they won't.

Giving away the store is beginning a negotiation by presenting your opponent with a range within which you expect an agreement to be reached. A writer I know, for example, recently needed some editorial assistance on a book he was working on. He found someone he liked and when they sat down to discuss financial terms, he said, "I'm prepared to pay between three and five thousand dollars." What do you think his assistant ended up with? Five grand. By giving away his upper end, he sealed his own fate. He gave away the store because he was afraid that a flat offer of $3,000 might've been construed as unfair.

Once you let your opponent know how high or low (depending on whether you're buying or selling) you're willing to go, the ball game is over. Once my father, a rare book dealer, and I were negotiating with a Frenchman who was selling lithographs. After the Frenchman told us he was willing to sell them for between forty and forty-five thousand francs (a better offer than we had expected), we returned the following day and said, "Fine, we'll buy at forty thousand francs." He tried—in vain—to nudge us upward, but because he'd already given away the store, he had no ground to stand on.

Remember, your fears and hesitancies are *only* feelings. They can be pushed aside for a little while. The discomfort you feel when asking for a lot won't last forever. Try to keep the negotiation in perspective. You're not bargaining out of greed or selfishness or to trample someone else's rights. You're bargaining only to stand up for yourself and fulfill your needs, and there's no reason to feel guilty about that. Other people stand up and negotiate hard; why shouldn't you? You have everything to gain—respect at least, much-improved settlements at most. And all you stand to lose is the reputation for being a pushover.

Aim High, Settle High

Extensive research has been done on the psychology of negotiating, all of it pointing to one indisputable fact: People with high aspiration levels reach better settlements much more often than people with low aspiration levels. In other words, if you aim high, you'll do much better than if you aim low. The Maximum Supportable Position turns on a mental switch that tells you you're expecting a lot out of the negotiation, and when you expect a lot, you strive harder to get it. The M.S.P. presents a challenge, and invariably you rise to meet it, as two professors discovered some years back when they designed an experiment.* Pairs of students were separated so they could not see or hear one another. Negotiations, offers and counteroffers, were conducted by passing notes under the table. Each bargainer was instructed the same way and told to get as much as he could, but some were told they could feel good about reaching a $7.50 settlement and others that they could feel good about reaching a $2.50 settlement. Neither group was given any advantage; they bargained on equal footing. The result? Time and again, those who sought $7.50 got $7.50, and those who sought $2.50 got $2.50.

You do yourself a big favor when you aim high.

---

* Sidney Siegel and Laurence E. Fouraker, *Bargaining and Group Decision Making* (New York: McGraw-Hill Book Co., 1960).

Lowering Your Opponent's Expectations

When it comes to expectations, the Maximum Supportable Position is a gilded double-edged sword; while it raises yours, it lowers your opponent's. Think about how you react when you find yourself negotiating with someone who starts right in with high demands. If you're like most of us, you immediately start thinking, "Gee, I'll be lucky to get out of this with my shirt." By coming out high, you leave your opponent with a firm impression that his greatest hopes will probably not be realized and transfer the bulk of the anxiety load ("I don't think I'll get what I want") off your shoulders and onto his.

In Diagram 2 of the stereo case, for example, the woman who was buying it from us had to have serious doubts about settling near her $100 M.S.P. when we came out with our opening position of $400. Her expectations were lowered because we had some rationale for a figure that was beyond even her Least Acceptable Result, and as a result, the overlap in the Settlement Ranges tilted in our favor.

Scaling down expectations is particularly valuable in those frequent cases when the opponent has only a wish point and not a genuine Least Acceptable Result. A good M.S.P. in these instances will help make him reconsider the situation and come to grips with what his real bottom line is, which, of course, is exactly what you want.

Summing Up

Not long ago, I ran into a former student of mine. "You know," he said, "the Settlement Range really works. For the first time I feel like I'm in control of things when I'm negotiating."

He hit the nail on the head. We've spent an entire chapter looking at all the benefits, both practical and psychological, the Settlement Range provides—from safeguarding you against deals not to your advantage to getting the most you can out of any given negotiation. But perhaps the biggest benefit you get from the Settlement Range is a feeling of control over the negotiation. It gives you a system, an approach, that you can easily apply to every negotiation you enter. Instead of viewing negotiation as a big, blurry mess, it reduces things to a simple, well-defined structure, a top end and a bottom end, that keeps even the most complex negotiations in sharp, reassuring focus. As long as you have a Settlement Range, negotiations will never seem intimidating or unmanageable again.

CHAPTER 5

Coping with Tension

LET'S GO BACK to the negotiation you and I were having over the typewriter. Each of us has determined our individual Settlement Ranges. Having thought about what the machine is worth to me and how much I need the cash, I've decided that $500 is my L.A.R.; anything below that, and it's simply not worth my while to make the deal. At the other end, I've decided that in view of the machine's mint condition and how little it has been used, I can credibly set my M.S.P. at $900.

You on the other hand have calculated that $600 is your absolute limit for a machine of this sort and that if I insist on more, you're going to say, "So long, Schatzki." You've also checked around the used-typewriter market and come up with $250 as an opening position you feel you can reasonably justify—at least enough to get things going.

Since there's an overlap in the bottom ends of our respective Settlement Ranges—$500 and $600—an agreement should be reached in this negotiation. But neither you nor I know that because we don't know each other's L.A.R.; all you see is my asking price of $900, and all I see is your opening offer of $250.

This disparity entangles us in a web of uncertainty and creates what I call the tension dynamics of negotiation. Inevitably, you feel tense when you sit down to negotiate. Not only is it an uncomfortable feeling, but it can also sap your willingness to bargain. Because acute tension tends to make you opt for the path that will eliminate it as soon as possible. "When I negotiate," a student once told me, "my main goal is to end it as soon as I can." Remember the guy I told you about who was looking for a used car and would not answer any ad that said "Make an offer"? It was the expectation of feeling tense that so stifled him.

Much as with your fears, an understanding of the sources of tension in negotiation can go a long way toward reducing that uneasy feeling. Let's examine what those sources of tension are.

Can You Make a Deal?

You're about to negotiate with me for the typewriter. You've received my opening position of $900 and you know it's quite a distance from your Least Acceptable Result of $600. You figure I'm willing to come down some, but you're not sure and don't know whether it would be far enough anyway. You don't know me from a hole in the ground. I might be completely unreasonable and start ranting and raving at the mere suggestion that my precious typewriter is not worth what I am asking. You're feeling tense. Why?

Because at this point you're not at all sure that a deal is even possible. You want the typewriter, but with my opening position $300 higher than your Least Acceptable Result, it seems highly doubtful that you'll get it. Your tension springs from your uncertainty about being able to reach an agreement.

Let's assume we continue negotiating and you manage to get me down to $600. Suddenly you feel a great sense of relief, right? By bargaining me down to a spot that falls inside your Settlement Range, you've eradicated your source of tension because you now know a deal is at least a possibility. Then what happens? Well, if you're like a lot of negotiators, you're so relieved to have reached this point and to be rid of your tension that you'll settle at your Least Acceptable Result and be done with it. As an opponent, naturally I'm delighted that you're thinking along such lines. This is just the way I want you to feel about the negotiation—that you've expended so much time and energy just to get me to your Least Acceptable Result that you're willing to cash it in and forget about exacting any further concessions from me. After all, I'm still $100 away from *my* Least Acceptable Result, so I'm feeling quite good about the situation.

But what if you decide not to bow out just because you've achieved a marginally acceptable settlement? What if you decide to hold out for a better deal? Enter a new sort of tension.

How Good a Deal Can You Make?

Before, you were worried about whether you could even make a deal. Now that you know you can and have decided to try to do better, the question foremost in your mind is, "How *much* better can I do?" It's like the predicament a game-show contestant is put in: He already has the refrigerator and the range; should he risk losing them in the hope that there's a car behind Door No. 3? Suddenly you're bombarded with a whole new wave of uncertainties: Where is the opponent's Least Acceptable Result? What are your chances of pushing him there? How long should you hold out? How much do you need the deal and how much can you afford a deadlock?

In the case of the typewriter, let's say you've negotiated brilliantly and have moved me from my opening position of $900 all the way down to $525. Even though the price is already well within your Settlement Range, you hold out because you feel like you've got me on the run. You don't know where my bottom line is, but you've thought things through and decided that, since it won't kill you if you don't walk away with the typewriter today, you'll roll the dice and see what happens. You offer me $450 for it. "I'm sorry," I say. "Well, $450 is the best I can do."

What has happened? Well, in this scenario you've paid the price for gambling. You've held out for the best deal you could get, but in the process you've made it impossible for me to agree to the deal, since my Least Acceptable Result was $500. The result is a deadlock. Had my L.A.R. been, say, $400, you would have walked away with a typewriter for a helluva price. But it wasn't, so you didn't. Like I said, you win some and you lose some.

There's no right answer to the question of how long you should hold out in a given negotiation. It depends on the circumstances surrounding it; on how much you need the deal, on how much you can afford losing it altogether, and on the sense you get of your opponent's need for it.

As a general rule, the more you hold out for a better deal, the better you will do in your settlements but the more often you will deadlock along the way. Negotiation is like a game of chicken. It's safer to back off early and accept agreements at the bottom end of your Settlement Range. On the other hand, if you're willing to take a few more risks, you stand to gain bigger and better deals by staying in the game to the end.

One word of caution to you high rollers: Don't allow yourself to become so wrapped up in the game of chicken that you lose sight of what you're negotiating for. It's one thing to hold out for a better deal because you think you've got a good shot at getting it; it's quite another to take risks indiscriminately to prove how tough you are or to show up your opponent. Keep your ego out of it; negotiation is difficult enough without contending with that too. Don't play games just for the sake of playing games. You've set up your Least Acceptable Result for a reason—to distinguish between settlements that are satisfactory to you and those that aren't. By definition, a deal that is above your L.A.R. is in your best interests to accept. If you choose not to accept it and to hold out for something better, do so only because, after careful consideration, you've determined there's a strong chance your opponent still has not been pushed to his Least Acceptable Result, not because you want to show the world what you're made of. Do that, and *you*—not your opponent—will wind up the big loser.

Summing Up

Feeling a certain degree of tension when you're negotiating is inevitable. It flows from two separate concerns. First, you're worried about the question, "Can I make a deal with this opponent?" or, in the parlance we've been using in this book, "Can I get my opponent to a point that is at least at the bottom of my Settlement Range?" If you can't, if your opponent's position never overlaps with your Least Acceptable Result, then an agreement is out of the question. When you have successfully moved your opponent to somewhere within your Settlement Range, the second kind of tension enters the picture. It raises from the question you naturally ask yourself at this point in a negotiation, "How *good* a deal can I make?" or, to put it another way, "How long should I hold out before agreeing to a deal and how far should I try to move my opponent in the direction of my Maximum Supportable Position?"

There's no correct answer to the question of how long you should hold out. It depends on the feeling you get from your opponent as to how much he needs a settlement and how much he would be willing to bend to get it. It also depends, of course, on how much you need a settlement. If you need it desperately, then that's going to seriously impair your willingness to engage in an all-out game of chicken. If you don't need a deal that much, you're in a position to gamble a bit more. Whatever you do, heed the caution we passed along earlier: Don't let your ego rear its ugly head when you're negotiating. Don't get into the gamesmanship of negotiation to the extent that you always take a hard line, regardless of the circumstances, just so you can walk away feeling tougher and stronger than your opponent. Base your decision on how much to gamble solely on your assessment of your realistic chances of achieving a better settlement.

In any case, knowing that it's perfectly natural to feel these kinds of tension and knowing where they're coming from will lessen them considerably once you actually begin negotiating.

CHAPTER 6

Meeting Your Opponent: How Will He React?

BEFORE YOU SIT down at the bargaining table with your opponent, you want to ask yourself two fundamental questions: "How is he likely to respond to my wanting to negotiate with him?" and "If I get what I want out of this deal, what kind of position will it leave him in?"

By putting the negotiation in this kind of context and getting a handle on how your opponent's likely to react to you, you do your negotiating cause a world of good. Because, as we'll see a little later, how you go about getting what you want is strongly influenced by your opponent's initial reaction. Now let's see what his reaction will be in any given negotiation.

I have broadly classified negotiations into three categories, each one embodying a specific reaction on the part of your opponent. They are

1. Oh-Boy Negotiations
2. Show-Me Negotiations
3. Oh-No Negotiations

Let's take a look at each.

Oh-Boy Negotiations

Thus far, most of the examples we've been discussing have been Oh-Boy Negotiations. By this I mean those negotiations in which both sides have the expectation of coming out ahead. Both you and your opponent have certain needs, you're negotiating to meet them, and you're basically happy about it. The attitude on behalf of you and your opponent is "Oh boy, let's negotiate" for the simple reason that you both stand to gain something from it.

Like most buy-sell situations, our typewriter negotiation is an example of an Oh-Boy Negotiation. You need a typewriter, I need the money, and we're glad to have the opportunity to fill our respective needs. In a sense, we have a cooperative approach to the negotiation; to the extent that it fills both our needs, our negotiation can be looked on as a joint venture. This is not to say there isn't a competitive side to the negotiation. We're each trying to secure the best deal for ourselves that we can. But this fact doesn't prevent us from seeing the overall picture, which is that between my typewriter and your money we can negotiate a deal that will be to our mutual advantage.

Negotiating for a job is another example of an Oh-Boy Negotiation. Both sides stand to benefit from an agreement and, generally speaking, enter into the negotiation eager and hopeful of having their needs fulfilled—on one hand, the need for a good, steady job; and on the other, the need for a good, steady employee.

Suppose I'm a manufacturer who has developed a new line of tummy-trimming exercise equipment that's destined to take millions of flabby pounds off of America's collective midsection. My problem is that I need someone to sell it to retail outlets, so I call you, a manufacturer's representative specializing in sporting goods. You're going to be very receptive to my inquiry because if the stuff is all I say it is, your wallet— as well as mine—is going to get fat while America gets slim. A vintage Oh-Boy Negotiation. In sum, any time your opponent greets your desire to negotiate with him with open arms, you're involved in an Oh-Boy Negotiation.

Show-Me Negotiations

A Show-Me Negotiation is slightly different. In a Show-Me Negotiation, one side has a demonstrable need to be filled, but the other side is more or less indifferent. What transpires as a result is that the side with the need attempts to create a corresponding need on the other side. Let me show you what I mean.

Say I'm a door-to-door vacuum-cleaner salesman. I have a clear need (assuming I'm interested in making a living), which is to sell vacuum cleaners so I can collect nice fat commissions. I knock on your door. "Geez, another salesman," you're thinking as you search for a graceful way to tell me to get lost. You don't have a need (at this point) for a vacuum cleaner, and that's my problem. So what do I do? I give you my very best spiel, which is designed to *create* a need in you for one of my machines. I swear this is a revolutionary machine, destined to change forever the way America cleans.

"It'll save you hours of time and energy," I hype. "It goes upstairs by itself, moves furniture by itself, wraps up its own cord and even puts itself back in the closet." You're getting interested. "If it's as good as he says, maybe it would be worth it to have one," you begin to think. The seeds of a need have been sown. At first, you had no interest in me, my needs, or my machine. But in this classic Show-Me Negotiation, I have shown you that you do in fact have a need, and being a nice guy, I'd be more than happy to fulfill it. Of course, if I hadn't had to create a need in you, if you had answered the door and said, "Great, I've been meaning to get a new vacuum cleaner for years," then we would've had an Oh-Boy Negotiation on our hands. But whenever you have a need and initially encounter indifference on the part of a would-be opponent and must convince him that he really does have a need, too, then you're involved in a Show Me-Negotiation.

When you stop and think about it, all advertisers are really engaging in Show-Me Negotiation. After all, what are they doing? They're trying to convince you and me and the mass of consumers out there that we do have needs—needs to smell nice, to be clean-shaven, to eat right, to have a germ-free house, to shop in the nicest store—needs, in short, for whatever they're selling. If the campaigns work and they succeed in creating needs in us, then we all march out and spend our money to make them rich.

A while back I was thinking about buying a camera, so I went out to do some comparison shopping. I did not have a pressing need to buy a camera at that point; I was merely looking to see what was available at what price. But I walked into one store and came upon a salesman who performed his job brilliantly; in giving me his sales pitch, what he did, in essence, was show me that I did, in fact, have a need to buy a camera that day. He talked me into negotiating with him and, as a result, had *his* need—selling a camera and picking up a commission—fulfilled.

Suppose you approach me, the tummy-trimmer manufacturer, to propose taking over the distribution of my product. I already have a distributor, so I don't have any great stake in negotiating with you. Your task, therefore, is to show me that I do have a need for your services, that your outfit has the capability of taking my goods to broader and more lucrative markets. You have a need, and if you succeed in arousing one in me, you may be able to get yours fulfilled. That's the essence of Show-Me Negotiations.

Oh-No Negotiations

Have you ever been in a situation where your opponent has wanted nothing whatever to do with you, where he put on his sneakers and headed for the door the moment he saw you coming? If so, then you've been involved in an Oh-No Negotiation.

In Oh-No Negotiations, your opponent's attitude is that he has nothing to gain—and a lot to lose—by negotiating with you. Consequently, he'll try to avoid you at all costs. And if he can't avoid you altogether, he'll probably try subjecting you to harassment, anger, intimidation, and other such histrionics in the hope of getting you to go away. You have to force the issue in an Oh-No Negotiation because if your opponent has his way, there will be no negotiation at all. Complaint situations are classic examples of Oh-No Negotiations. Feeling like you've been taken, you go back and confront the person who did the taking. Maybe your opponent is a salesman who sold you a bum car or a plumber whom you paid $75 to fix your sink only to wake up the next morning to find your pipes spouting like Old Faithful. Or maybe he's your former employer who owes you $500 in back wages, which you still haven't gotten even though "the check was in the mail" ten days ago. Whoever your opponent is in an Oh-No Negotiation, he's content with the status quo and he's not going to be pleased that you're coming along to try to change it.

The way to handle a reluctant opponent is to give him what I call a backhanded need, that is, a need for something not to happen. For instance, I once had a difficult time getting a security deposit back from a landlord. When it became clear to me that he would not deal with me willingly, I came up with a backhanded need; I told him that if he wouldn't negotiate with me regarding the deposit, I would not vacate the apartment and force him to intitiate eviction proceedings, usually a long and costly ordeal that a landlord would like to avoid if at all possible. By injecting a backhanded need into the picture, I changed his thinking and gave him an incentive to negotiate with me, which he did.

Put another way, what you're doing in an Oh-No Negotiation (assuming you're the one initiating the action) is coming up with some kind of threat that, if enacted, would be a bigger negative in your opponent's mind than negotiating with you. In the context of the give-get exchange we talked about earlier, your opponent is agreeing to negotiate to give you something which he really doesn't want to give you in exchange for getting something—agreement not to carry out your threat. What you're doing is changing your opponent's balance of priorities. Before you come up with a backhanded need—what your opponent wants very much not to happen—he simply tells you to get lost; but once you confront him with a rather unpalatable alternative, he changes his tune, deciding that negotiating with you is the lesser of two evils.

Suppose, for instance, that rap I gave you about the vacuum cleaner was a bunch of malarkey. The thing won't go upstairs unless you carry it. It's a lemon, I knew it, and now you know it too. Fortunately for you, I left my card and you're able to track me down at the office. You approach the negotiation anxiously because you're not sure how I'll react and because you know you're going to ask me for something I'm not going to be wild about giving you—a new machine or, perish the thought, a refund. It's distinctly possible, of course, that if I worked for a reputable company I wouldn't be put off in the least by your request; indeed, I would be pleased to deal with you squarely in order to maintain the company's credibility in your eyes. Large, well-known firms respond this way often. For the sake of good public relations, they'll forsake a few cents here and there and respond to a consumer complaint with extreme good will. A friend of mine once got nine Lifesavers instead of ten in a pack. He wrote a letter to Beech Nut, and two weeks later he received a very apologetic letter not to mention six cases—thirty-six rolls—of Lifesavers.

Let's assume, however, that I am not employed by such an

accommodating firm. I work for a schlock outfit with no credibility to maintain. So what does seeing your grimacing face in my office mean to me? Nothing but trouble. Do I want to negotiate with you? No way. All I want is for you to go away. So you search for a backhanded need. What do you think that I, as a vacuum-cleaner salesman, want to avoid? Maybe you could threaten to write a letter to the president of the company or to my immediate boss. Or you might tell me that you'll report me to the Better Business Bureau if I don't cooperate and give you a refund. Perhaps you'll even threaten to mount a townwide campaign, alerting people not to buy machines from me.

Whatever course you choose to try to make me negotiate with you, you've got to convince me of two things. First, you must show me you are *willing* to carry out the threat, that this matter is important enough to you to follow up on; and second, you must show me you are *capable* of carrying it out. Because no matter how willing you are to make my life miserable, if I don't think you have the clout or wherewithal to do it, I probably won't lose much sleep over your threat. Obviously, it's not hard to write a letter, and if I want to avoid having my company president get a letter from you saying how unscrupulous I am, then I'll probably succumb to that backhanded need and deal with you. But if you tell me that your nephew went to high school with the news director of a local television station and that you're going to get him to do a series on my reprehensible sales ploys, I'll likely let you go ahead and try.

A friend of mine recently told me a story that's a perfect example of how to handle an Oh-No Negotiation. The issue centered on $1,300 in bonus money, which my friend's boss had promised to him for outstanding service to the company. Not long after, my friend left the job to go back to school. He made several polite inquiries about the bonus money, but when he received nothing after three months, he wrote a firm, pointed business letter to his former boss requesting that the money be given to him promptly. The reply from the boss was that the bonus was for "services yet to be rendered," and therefore my friend was not entitled to it since he had left the company. Subsequent attempts to get the money proved fruitless; the boss wanted nothing to do with the matter.

Well, my friend did some thinking about a backhanded need he could come up with to make the boss negotiate with him. What he came up with was a letter to the stockholders of the company who, my friend happened to know, were already down on this guy and would love to have had an excuse to get rid of him. My friend told his former boss about his plan to send the letter, and it worked like a charm. The check came through within a week.

Summing Up

Whether you're approaching an Oh-Boy, Show-Me, or Oh-No Negotiation, you'll be much better off for having some idea beforehand of how your opponent will react. By viewing the bargaining in the context of the two questions: "How will my opponent respond to my wanting to negotiate?" and "If I get my needs met, how will it leave him?" you give yourself a big boost in launching your strategic and tactical approach to the negotiation. If a Show-Me Negotiation is upcoming, for instance, you'll know that your opponent will react rather flippantly and that it's incumbent on you to come up with a compelling case to show him that he does have a stake in negotiating with you. If it's an Oh-No Negotiation you're looking at, you give yourself time to come up with a backhanded need that will induce your opponent to bargain with you, even though he'd much rather not. When it's an Oh-Boy Negotiation ahead, on the other hand, you know you won't have to prove anything to your opponent or threaten him to bring him to the table; on the contrary, he's likely to roll out the red carpet, since you represent an opportunity for him to meet his needs. Unencumbered by any hurdles, you can start right in setting up your Settlement Range and thinking about how you can go about getting the best deal you can.

Particularly when you suspect the negotiation will be of the Oh-No ilk, knowing in advance how your opponent will react also helps reduce your anxiety. Forewarned is forearmed. Most people respond badly when they're confronted by a negative reaction from an opponent, but if you were expecting it all along, you won't be nearly so fazed by it. Anticipating your opponent's resistance gives you a chance to gear up psychologically. You become more resilient. It sends you a message saying, "If this guy doesn't want to cooperate and deal with me reasonably, well, I'm just going to have to give him an incentive to cooperate."

Of course, it's possible for all of us to misjudge a situation. Who knows, the opponent whom you expected would be fleeing for the hills at the sight of your face may be entirely decent and accommodating, and you may not need to drop any bombshells at all. So much the better. But it's best to be prepared for any eventuality.

Back to the vacuum cleaner. You may walk into my office, and I may be an absolute angel. "Oh, I'm sorry it didn't perform as I said it would. Please accept another new machine, or would you prefer a refund?" On the other hand, if I say, "That model carries no guarantee. There's nothing I can do for you," and you're not prepared to come back at me, you'll be caught flat-footed with no recourse to make me negotiate with you.

Step inside your opponent's shoes before racing headlong into a negotiation. Try to think about what he's thinking about bargaining with you. If what he's thinking is, "Why the hell did this guy have to show up and make my life miserable," at least you'll be braced for his reaction, feel less anxious about it, and have your bombshell waiting in the wings. And in any case, no matter how he reacts, your forethought will enable you to see much more clearly what tasks await you at the bargaining table.

PART III

Mapping Out Your Action Plan

CHAPTER 7

Strategic Forces: Your Springboard to Successful Negotiating

LET'S GO BACK to our typewriter negotiation. You'll recall that we said that my Maximum Supportable Position was $900; that's what I've offered the machine to you for. You've countered with an M.S.P. of $250. We also said that your Least Acceptable Result (the most you'll pay me for the machine) is $600. Okay, now let's stick in a new twist. Let's say that, for this one negotiation, you've discovered what *my* Least Acceptable Result is. An unimpeachable source close to me has told you that, if worse comes to worst, I would be willing to part with the typewriter for $500.

What does this piece of information do for you? Aside from making you very happy, it completely eliminates your need to map out strategies and tactics. Why? Because the whole purpose of your strategies and tactics is to enable you to secure the best agreement you can, but you already know what the best agreement you can get out of me is. It's $500. Presto, no more tension! You know not only that you can make a deal (because $500 is within your Settlement Range) but also how good a deal you can make. If every negotiation were like this, you could put down this book right now.

In fact, very few negotiations you will ever be involved in will be like this. When was the last time you were bargaining with someone and he said, "I want $900, but if you really back me up against the wall, I'll go as low as $500"?

Because we cannot bank on such candor—and stupidity—on the part of our opponents, we *do* have to be concerned with finding a way to reach the best settlement we can in a given negotiation. And that means we have to be concerned with strategies and tactics.

Before we go any further, I would like to draw a distinction between strategies and tactics for you. There is but a fine line between them, but it is a line nonetheless, and it's important to be aware of it. Because being able to distinguish between the two will enhance your overall comprehension of what negotiation is. Setting up a negotiation is a lot like building a house. You start with a foundation, your Settlement Range. From there you have to establish some kind of floor plan, an overall blueprint for action. That's basically what the Strategic Forces are . . . your blueprint for action for your negotiation. Once you've got that down, then it's time to haul out the tools and supplies, the hammer and nails and boards, etc., and that's really what the tactics of negotiation are—the actual implements you employ to carry out your blueprint for action. Now let's turn to the drawing board and design that blueprint.

Achieving a Settlement at Your Opponent's L.A.R.

There are two basic Strategic Forces Concepts involved in designing a plan of action. The best and simplest way to think about these two Strategic Forces is in terms of your opponent's Settlement Range. Even though he probably hasn't thought it through as thoroughly as you have, your opponent nonetheless has some kind of range within which he wants to settle. If he's smart, he has thrown out a Maximum Supportable Position that exceeds what he expects to get but that gives him some room to make concessions and still make a reasonably good deal. At the other end, he has a bottom line that he'll back down to if he must but that he won't go beyond. *Your aim in any negotiation is to get your opponent to settle at that point—his Least Acceptable Result.* And that's precisely what these two Strategic Forces, working in tandem, are designed to do.

Strategic Force No. 1: Raising Your Opponent's Doubts About Getting a Better Settlement

Your opponent's Least Acceptable Result, by definition, is literally the *last* place he desires to settle. In fact, he's doing everything he can to settle as far from there as possible. In view of this, what would make him abandon all his high hopes for a superior settlement and retreat all the way back to his last resort? Quite simply, if he believes it's either settling there or not settling at all. If your opponent thinks that a deal at his L.A.R. is the best he can do in that negotiation, then he's going to settle there. Put another way, he'll settle at his Least Acceptable Result if he is convinced that that point is also *your* Least Acceptable Result and that he has no hope of getting anything more out of you.

But what if he is *not* convinced of that? What if he thinks that you are *not* backed up to the wall and that he can get a better agreement from you? He's going to hold out for more. Think about your typewriter negotiation (without the twist— you don't know my L.A.R. anymore). Your Least Acceptable Result is $600, but will you shake hands on a deal there if you think you can nudge me lower? No way. You're going to push me until you believe I have no more room to give. The more uncertain your opponent is of his chances of securing a better agreement, the less likely he is to hold out for it. Now let's see how you go about increasing that uncertainty by setting your first Strategic Force in motion.

Building Credibility of Your M.S.P.

I've laid out for you my opening position of $900 for the typewriter. You've countered with an offer of $250. Before we get very far into the negotiation, I flash some impressive information, information that I hope will impress on you the fact that I'm taking my opening stance seriously. "I think I'm being quite reasonable," I begin. "Go ahead and check around at the used-typewriter shops in town. I have. You won't find this make and model machine for less than $1,200. Plus, this model's got the best repair record of any electric typewriter made in the last ten years. I've got the *Consumer Reports* issue that says so right here if you'd like to see it. As you can see, I've kept the machine in impeccable condition. It's been regularly cleaned and maintained. Here are the work receipts if you'd care to see them." I go on and on.

What are you thinking as you hear all this stuff? Probably something like, "Geez, this guy's really serious. He really does want $900 for the machine. I know I can't afford that much, but even if I can talk him down, I don't know how far. I have a feeling I'll be lucky if I can get him down to my L.A.R. of $600."

See what I've done? By building credibility for my Maximum Supportable Position, I've injected a bundle of uncertainty into your head and shifted the whole negotiation in my favor. Already I have you thinking not about how you can get me to the vicinity of your M.S.P., but about whether you'll even be able to convince me to settle at your L.A.R. You're on the run. You're thinking negatively, rather than positively, about your prospects for the negotiation. I have dramatically increased your doubts about whether a better deal than $600—if that—is possible. And as a result, you're now much less likely to hold out for something better.

What if I hadn't bolstered the credibility of my opening position this way? What if I'd just thrown out the $900 figure without much to back it up? You would've commenced your bargaining with much more gusto. You would've felt much more confident about your ability to move me lower and to reach an agreement not merely at your L.A.R. but close to your M.S.P.

Do whatever you can to enhance the credibility of your M.S.P. in the eyes of your opponent. Fuel his uncertainty about getting a better deal. By launching your negotiation in this fashion, you take a giant step toward realizing Strategic Force No. 1.

Masking Your True L.A.R.

The flip side of building credibility for your M.S.P. is hiding the true location of your Least Acceptable Result. Because what does the credibility-building do? It sends a message to your opponent saying, in effect, "My L.A.R. is damn close to my opening position, so don't even bother trying to talk me down very far." Look at it this way: Since the last thing you want your opponent to know is how far down you can be pushed, you want to move the scope of the bargaining as far from your L.A.R. as you can. And the best way to accomplish that is by making your opponent believe the bottom of your Settlement Range is in very close proximity to the top. When I gushed forth that torrent of information supporting my M.S.P., it immediately got you thinking that I wasn't going to be budged too far from $900. It's like I draped a big blanket over the bottom part of my Settlement Range and told you, "Don't even dream about trying to bargain with me down there. That's miles away from what I'll accept in this negotiation. The only place we're going to bargain is right up here near my Maximum."

Concealing Your Need for the Deal

Another effective way of throwing the big blanket over your true L.A.R.—and thus increasing your opponent's doubts about getting a better settlement—is by concealing your need for the deal. If your opponent thinks you haven't much at stake in the negotiation, he's going to get the distinct sense that you aren't going to bend very much in the bargaining. The more you need a deal, the more you'll be willing to back off from your opening position and accept any settlement that is at or above your Least Acceptable Result. If your opponent picks up on this, then all your efforts to raise his doubts about getting a better deal will be for nought; he's going to do exactly what you don't want him to do—hold out.

To illustrate the critical role need plays in negotiation, come with me for a moment on an imaginary trip halfway across the globe. Suppose you're stranded in the Sahara. You have no provisions, save the tattered clothes on your baking body. It's 115 degrees in the shade; the only problem is there's no shade for hundreds of miles. The sizzling sun is frying you up like bacon in a pan, and you swear you can hear your blood boiling within. You'd gladly give an arm for a shot glass of water.

Crawling up yet another dune, you feast your eyes on what is either the miracle to end all miracles or the cruelest mirage a parched mind has ever concocted: There, in the middle of the Sahara, is a lemonade stand. It is no mirage. A vendor stands behind a sign advertising freshly squeezed ice-cold lemonade for fifty cents a glass. An astute—if unscrupulous—businessman, the vendor sees your dire condition and quickly retracts the sign. "A glass of lemonade," you gasp, handing over half a buck.

The vendor balks. "It's $20 a glass. Take it or leave it," he says defiantly. "There *is* another stand . . . forty miles east of here." You're being swindled unmercifully, but what to do? You fork over the twenty, with pleasure. There won't be any negotiating over this transaction; you and the vendor both know he's got you over the barrel. You have a glaring need, and he's exploiting it for all it's worth.

But suppose you aren't stranded in the desert, that you just happened to be passing through in a jeep, felt a bit thirsty, and decided to stop at a duneside stand for refreshment. Then what? Well, the vendor probably wouldn't pull any shenanigans in the first place, being content to pick up his usual fifty cents. But if he did try to jack up the price, you would hold out for something better, and if he refused to bargain, simply wait forty miles and get your lemonade there. Not having such an acute need, you're in a much stronger position to stand firm, rather than backing off to your Least Acceptable Result.

Suppose you're an executive with a rapidly expanding company. You have a number of new openings, and I come in for an interview. Now it just so happens that I lost my job a month ago and that I have a wife, two kids, and a mortgage . . . and a swiftly shrinking bank account. Clearly I have an urgent need for the job, but I do my best not to let on. I explain that my dismissal from the previous position was due to circumstances in the company beyond my control and proceed to tell you, politely but firmly, what strengths I feel I can offer your company. I inquire about salary structure, job responsibility, promotion policy, benefits, etc., making it seem as if all these factors will contribute mightily to my decision whether to join your firm or not. Inside I'm thinking, "You gotta give me this job," but outwardly I'm behaving as if this is just one of a number of career opportunities I have and that it isn't a life-and-death issue to me. By being an actor and concealing the degree of my need, I have put myself on much firmer negotiating ground.

By contrast, how would you as an employer respond if I came in there and sent you not-so-subtle signals that I was on a one-way express to the poorhouse? What if I made no inquiries about the nature of the job, showed no self-respect, and generally made it clear that I would accept the job—any job—under any conditions. Apart from correctly judging that I was one horrendous negotiator, you'd probably be thinking, "I wonder what's wrong with this guy? He seems reasonably well qualified, but he's acting like this is the last job on earth and he hasn't an option in the world." You're going to think twice about me. And even if you do eventually hire me, you can bet it'll be for a lot less money than if I had effectively concealed my need for the job.

Another example: Two schoolkids—we'll call them Johnny and Bobby—are out on the playground during recess. Johnny has a basketball, and Bobby would like to borrow it. But Bobby isn't merely interested in shooting baskets. It seems he has a bad case of the heartthrobs for a cute little girl named Cindy, who happens to be standing near the basketball court. Being a pretty fair basketball player, Bobby figures this is a great shot for him to make *the* big impression. He's prepared to buy Johnny a candy bar every day for the rest of the week to get the ball, but he's cool and doesn't let Johnny know that. Bobby casually approaches Johnny.

"Can I borrow your basketball for a few minutes?"

"Maybe. What's it worth to you?"

"How 'bout a stick of gum?"

"How 'bout a whole pack?"

"It's a deal!" beams Bobby, who dashes off to the court to do his dazzling. He had a bad need, but because he was able to hide it, he made off with the ball for next to nothing compared to what he would've been willing to part with to get it.

Sometimes you'll find yourself in situations where it's not possible to completely conceal your need, even with an Oscar-worthy acting job. When you were in the desert, for instance, the vendor knew he had you dead to rights. He knew you had a dire need for drink and, as a result, knew your Least Acceptable Result was so far down it was practically nonexistent; that is, you'd do anything to get a glass of lemonade. But often when you can't conceal your need, you can at least take measures to minimize it. My co-author Wayne Coffey told me of an experience in which he did just that. He was driving down Second Avenue in Manhattan when suddenly his car sputtered, gagged, and finally died altogether just as he pulled into a service station. He was at the mercy of the mechanic, who promptly told him he needed a new carburetor that cost $160. "I had a new carburetor put in a month ago," Wayne told him. "Ain't no good," replied the mechanic.

Somewhat skeptical to say the least, Wayne took a calculated risk. He waited a while, managed to get the car started, and even though it was bucking like a bronco, he decided he'd try to drive it to another station. He rightly figured that if he could drive into a station, he would be in a lot less vulnerable bargaining position. Having reduced the degree of urgency, he stood a better chance of being dealt with squarely.

Well, he nursed the car into another station, told the mechanic the car was running very roughly, and asked him to take a look at it. After a few minutes of checking, the mechanic removed the gas filter, cleaned it, and presto, the car was running like a top.

"Your gas filter was completely clogged," the mechanic said. "That'll be $5." It was five bucks happily spent . . . and $155 happily saved.

Conceal your need for the settlement whenever possible. In our negotiation for the typewriter, for example, what if I say, "It'll sure be nice when this machine gets sold. The phone's been ringing off the hook for two days now," or perhaps, "I'm sorry, but I can't spend much more time with you right now. I've got two other people coming over to see the machine at two o'clock." By letting you know that you have some competition and that I've got other options, I'm downplaying my need for you or your deal. Hell, the next guy who comes along may snap up the machine for $900. So do you really stand much of a chance of talking me down? No—or at least I want you to believe you don't.

Okay, now let's put the shoe on the other foot. Now you're the one who is concealing the need and masking your true L.A.R. "Well," you say as you put on your coat, "you've got my offer of $250. Here's my number. If you think we can do business, give me a call." If I have all the options I said I had, then your walking away probably won't faze me. But if I don't and I have more of a need for a settlement than I've let on, then I'm going to try to make you stay put by backing off from my opening position. So I might say, "I can't accept $250. The machine is simply worth a good deal more than that. But you're here now and I'd just as soon sell it and be done with it, so I'm prepared to let it go for $700." I'm not in your Settlement Range—yet—but you're tugging me in the right direction.

As you can readily see (and as we've already noted), bluffing is an important element in many negotiations. Not in every negotiation, mind you; there are situations, which we will explore in greater depth later, when it's in everyone's best interest to be completely up front. As a general rule, this is true when you expect to have an ongoing relationship with the person you're negotiating with. A friend of mine, for instance, who was working on a book project was negotiating a collaboration agreement with a writer. For his own self-interest, the last thing my friend wanted to do in this case was bluff, take a hard line, and hold out for the best deal he could secure from the writer. Why? Because it would've been foolish to run the risk of alienating the writer or making him feel as though he had gotten a raw deal when the two of them would be working very closely together for the ensuing year. Lingering ill-feeling about the negotiation could've jeopardized not only their working relationship but also put a damper on the writer's enthusiasm for the project and his willingness to give it his best professional effort.

But when you're engaging in what's called share-bargaining, that is, when you're negotiating to determine who gets what share of the pie—as you and I are with the typewriter—being an actor is a valuable asset indeed.

In a share negotiation, regardless of what you're feeling inside, do your best to hide your true need for a settlement. Try to generate competition. Make your opponent think you have options and that settling with him is not of earth-shaking importance to you. It'll lead him to believe that he won't be able to get you too much lower than your Maximum Supportable Position and mask the bottom of your Settlement Range. But most important of all, concealing your need, along with building the credibility of your M.S.P. and hiding your bottom line, will give a huge boost to Strategic Force No. 1—heightening your opponent's doubts about getting a better settlement from you.

Strategic Force No. 2: Increasing Your Opponent's Need to Settle

Like the first Strategic Concept, Strategic Force No. 2 is designed to achieve a settlement at your opponent's Least Acceptable Result. But whereas the first strategy accomplishes it by increasing his uncertainty about his prospects for a better deal, the second works by increasing his very need for the deal.

From our discussion of the role need plays in negotiation,

it should be clear that the more a negotiator needs to settle, the less he'll be willing to hold out for something better. The less he needs to settle, the more he'll be willing to hold out. It's as simple as that. Need in negotiation is a double-edged sword; the more you know about your opponent's need, the more you can hold out and increase the pressure on him to settle. And the more he knows about yours, the more he can hold out and increase the pressure on *you* to settle. What you want to do, consequently, is try to find out as much as you can about the extent of his need for settlement while at the same time concealing your own. It's a bluffing game, and he who bluffs best will get the better of the bargaining.

But regardless of how well you bluff, your opponent's need will inherently put pressure on him to cave in the moment he gets an offer inside his Settlement Range. Given that, wouldn't it be nice if you could *increase* his need still more and make him even more inclined to cave in? You bet, and you can do just that by unleashing Strategic Force No. 2. By increasing your opponent's need, Strategic Force No. 2 not only adds to his pressure to settle but also to actually *move* the bottom of his Settlement Range, thus making even better settlements possible for you. Need, after all, is embodied in the Settlement Range; the more he needs the deal, the lower he'll set his Least Acceptable Result. Of course your opponent will hide the bottom of his Settlement Range, so you won't see tangible evidence of its movement. But be aware that you're moving his L.A.R. just the same and exerting pressure on him to settle *where you want him to*. Now let's look at the two components of the second Strategic Force that actually make it work.

Goodies

Back to the typewriter. You've bargained me down to $600 (your Least Acceptable Result), but it hasn't been easy, and you're not at all sure you can do any better. You might settle there of your own accord, but I really don't want to get any closer to my L.A.R. of $500, so I'm going to give you an added incentive. We continue to talk, and I happen to mention that I have two dozen carbon ribbons and a service contract good for eight more months at the Main Street

Typewriter Repair Shop. "The ribbons won't fit the new machine I'm getting, and I'll get a manufacturer's warranty on my new typewriter, so I'll throw in the ribbons and the contract for no charge."

What have I done? By sweetening the pot with some goodies—goodies of little or no value to me but of substantial value to you—I've made the deal more attractive to you and thereby increased your need for it. "Carbon ribbons go for $3 apiece, and that contract is a nice thing to fall back on in case the machine screws up on me," you say to yourself. Without changing my Settlement Range (since the goodies are of no real value to me), I've succeeded in changing yours. Perhaps you'll attach a value of $100 to the goodies, thus moving your Least Acceptable Result from $600 to $700. And since you're getting more for your $600, your incentive to settle is greater. I've made it harder for you to refuse the deal.

Here's another example of how goodies exert pressure on the opponent to settle. A friend of mine was running a garage sale and negotiating with a potential buyer over a sofa. He asked for $250 and subsequently backed off to $225, still an attractive settlement in my friend's eyes as his L.A.R. was $150. Not wanting his opponent to try to do any better, my friend came up with a goody for him. "I've got a neighbor with a pick-up truck I can borrow to deliver the sofa to you later this afternoon." At no cost to himself—save a little time and muscle—my friend had come up with an effective sweetener which made the agreement more appealing to his opponent. We don't know for certain, but it's distinctly possible that going into the negotiation the opponent's L.A.R. was $200. In any case, with the addition of a valuable goody, he agreed to buy it for $225.

Tom, an executive with a truck-leasing firm, was negotiating a large volume sale with a food distributor, whom we'll call Al. After extensive discussions, Tom happened to learn that Al's drivers were complaining about having to take their trucks back home at night. Being refrigeration units, the trucks had to be on at all times, which made a lot of racket and provoked complaints from the drivers' neighbors. Al couldn't do anything about the problem since his company had very limited parking space, but Tom could. His firm happened to have a huge parking lot with plenty of extra room, and he tossed that goody into the negotiation. It worked like a charm. Al had such a pressing need to resolve his parking headache that the deal, on almost any terms, was too good to refuse. Tom's goody enabled him to secure a settlement extremely close to his Maximum Supportable Position.

In all these cases, by offering something not initially on the table, the goody-dispensers dramatically increased their opponents' needs for settlements. They changed their opponents' Settlement Ranges without changing their own. They enhanced their offers in a way that made the opponents change their thinking about the deals because, with the goodies, the opponents saw they were getting more value in exchange for what they were giving.

Goodies, of course, are effective only insofar as they fulfill a certain need of your opponent's. If they don't do that, they aren't goodies at all; they're immaterial to the negotiation. In order to come up with enticing goodies, you have to do some exploring of your opponent's situation, of his possible hidden needs. Put yourself in his position. Be creative and try to come up with things you can offer with little sweat which might plug one of those needs and thus make your opponent much more inclined to settle—where you want him to. Sometimes it's easy, like in the case of the sofa. It didn't require a lot of profound thinking on my friend's part to figure that the guy interested in the sofa might be strapped for a way to get it home. Tom, on the other hand, had to do a lot of probing of his opponent and, even then, was very fortunate to have learned of Al's truck-parking problem.

Timing is a key factor in making effective use of goodies. Don't throw them into the bargaining too early because then they'll seem like routine concessions and, worse, will usually be taken for granted. To maximize the impact of your goodies, inject them into the picture later on when they can curtail whatever ideas your opponent has to hold out and induce him to say, "That clinches it—I'll settle here."

And remember, it's not important how valuable the goodies are to you, but how valuable they are to your opponent. One person's garbage may be another person's gold. To Tom, the parking lot was just a big hunk of asphalt. To Al, it was the solution to a long-standing hassle. Don't project your values onto your opponent. You may have a goody in your hip pocket that may be just the incentive your opponent needs to sign on the dotted line . . . and provide you with a settlement much to your liking.

Threats

Threat is definitely not a nice word. It smacks of meanness, of a base human impulse to hit below the belt when nothing else will work. The dictionary defines it as "a statement or expression of intention to hurt, destroy, punish, etc., as in retaliation or intimidation." But no matter what negative images the word conjures up, there's no way around the fact that threat plays a central part in many negotiations.

A negotiating threat, however, is not designed to hurt, destroy, or punish the opponent. It is merely designed to create a backhanded need for a deal. In other words, when a threat is put on the table, it makes the opponent reevaluate his position and see that agreeing to settle is better for him than not settling and having the threat carried out.

Threats do double duty in negotiation. As we've seen already in our discussion of Oh-No Negotiations, they can be used as a means of inducing an opponent to negotiate with you when, in fact, he wants nothing to do with you. Here we're talking about how threats work in a negotiation in process and help you set your second Strategic Force in motion . . . and get a settlement at your opponent's L.A.R.

Like goodies, threats have the effect of increasing your opponent's need for a deal. And like goodies, they change his Settlement Range because their very presence in the bargaining forces your opponent to consider settling at points that were outside his initial Settlement Range. But whereas goodies accomplish these things by fulfilling hidden needs of your opponent's and making the deal more enticing, threats accomplish it by exploiting hidden fears of your opponent's and making the consequences of deadlock more foreboding.

Put another way, goodies work because they increase what your opponent has to lose if the agreement is not achieved, while threats work because they increase what your opponent fears might happen if the agreement is not achieved. Either way, they both work to heighten the opponent's need, which in turn makes him less willing to hold out for something better than his Least Acceptable Result.

Now, some examples of threats in action. Several years back, I purchased a $250 pocket dictating machine from a leading manufacturer in the field. The rewind mechanism did not work properly, so I called the salesman, who cheerfully agreed to exchange the machine for a new one. Well, the new one didn't work right either. I got back on the horn with the salesman, but this time he wasn't so accommodating. "I'm sorry," he said, "but company policy allows only one exchange per customer." He did agree to send a repairman over to fix my machine, but that turned out to be a charade, the repairman trying to convince me that the machine was fine when I knew full well it was screwed up. I phoned the salesman once more, only this time I was fortified with what I hoped would be a backhanded need for him to give me a new machine. I told him, "I represent a number of institutions which are valuable clients of your company. I don't think you would want me to tell these clients that your firm doesn't deal in good faith and doesn't stand squarely behind its products." In other words, "Look, pal, give me a new machine or you're gonna lose a pile of business."

Did it work? Regrettably, it did not. I was trying to hit a nerve of the salesman's, but obviously I missed, since he told me in so many words that he didn't give a damn if I badmouthed the company to the clients. Like any negotiator worth his salt, I persisted. I went looking for another nerve . . . and this time I found one. I asked the salesman for the name of the company president, who, I told my recalcitrant opponent, would be getting an irate letter from me detailing my intense dissatisfaction and notifying him that I intended to let my colleagues know about my distress. The salesman gave me the president's name but, in fact, did not seem terribly worried by my threat.

Five minutes later, however, my phone rang. On the other end was one panicked pocket dictating machine salesman. "Don't write the letter," he implored. "I've discussed your case with the regional sales manager and gotten authorization to issue you a new machine or, if you prefer, a full refund." Clearly, my letter threat sent shock waves through the chain of the command. For a reason still unbeknownst to me, the regional sales manager in that particular company had a dire need for the company president *not* to get an angry letter from this customer. It was in his self-interest in this case to waive the policy and accede to my demands. Avoiding the consequences of not making the deal—i.e., the threat—was more important than adhering to company policy.

A threat worked nicely for me when a dry cleaner lost one

of my shirts. The storeowner promised to try to track it down, but when it didn't turn up within a month, I asked him to please compensate me for the shirt, which was worth $15. "No problem," he said. I waited a couple of weeks, then went into the store and told the manager I had been more than patient and I wanted a settlement then and there. He proceeded to call the owner of the store, who, acting as though he'd never heard of the matter, began barraging me with questions about receipts, proof that I had in fact brought the shirt in to be cleaned, and other nonsense.

I thought about the situation and decided that dealing with the owner was probably less fruitful than dealing with the store manager, who, I figured, would be able to wrest a check away from the owner if I provided him with a backhanded need to do so. I walked in one day and told the store manager that I was going to small claims court to resolve the matter and that I was going to subpoena him as a witness to verify the facts of my claim. What resulted was an angry stream of invective . . . and a $15 check within the week. Clearly, his desire to avoid getting hauled into court superseded his desire to give me the runaround.

An important thing to keep in mind when you're planning on using a threat to increase your opponent's need to settle is that it is only as good as its credibility. If your opponent doubts either your willingness to or capability of carrying the threat out, he probably won't bat an eyelash. Say, for instance, that you confront your boss with a raise demand and make it clear that if none is forthcoming he'll have to get himself a new employee. Well, if this is the seventh time you've threatened to quit if you didn't get a raise and you come back each time with your tail between your legs and settled for a third of your original demand, your quitting credibility is going to be nil. If, the eighth go-round, you insist you really mean it, is there anything you can do to enhance the credibility of your threat? Sure. Go out and get yourself a better job offer—in writing. When he makes some crack about you being Joe Quitter, matter-of-factly drop the offer on his desk. He'll get the message in a hurry that your threat is not merely idle banter and that this time you mean business.

By the same token, if you're on the receiving end of a threat, do everything you can to verify its credibility before knuckling under to it. A lot of nasty-sounding threats are nothing more than empty words concocted on the spur of the moment. Ask yourself if your opponent actually has the willingness and capability to follow through. If you're a talented copywriter working for my advertising agency and we happen to have a serious difference of opinion concerning one account and I tell you, "You better do it my way, because if you don't, you'll be outta here and I'll see to it that you won't work in the field again," perhaps you can safely laugh in my face. Advertising is a highly competitive business, and you know there are all kinds of agencies who would love to hire you.

Also, before giving in to a threat, make sure, even if your opponent can and will in fact carry it out, it's something you genuinely want to avoid. Sometimes horrid-sounding threats can be relatively innocuous at second glance. I know a computer programmer who was constantly feuding with his boss. Even though the programmer was indispensable to the company's operation, the boss was disgusted by the way he continually flouted office procedures and angered by his independence and refusal to cater to her every whim. One day she called him into her office, requesting that he immediately begin work on a new program. "I'm just wrapping up a project that's extremely important," he said. "I'll get to this new one when I'm done with it." The boss was livid. She told him she was going to file an insubordination report with the personnel department if he did not do as she ordered. It sounded nasty at first but, after thinking about it, the programmer realized that since everyone in the firm's top echelon knew of his value to the company and of his predilection for working independence, a bad report from personnel wouldn't amount to a hill of beans. So he told his boss, in effect, "Go ahead to personnel." She did, and all it cost him was a very mild caution from a vice-president to find a more gentle way to say no to his boss.

Don't be afraid to put a threat on the table when there's no other means to secure the settlement you want. But I caution you to use threats selectively and only as a last resort. Once you confront your opponent with a threat, you're serving notice that you're playing hardball, and often his response will be to play hardball in return. The tougher you negotiate, the tougher the resistance will be, so don't drop your bombshell and expect the opponent's white flag to be automatically hoisted.

Summing Up

When you strip it down to its essence, negotiation is a tug of war between Settlement Ranges—your's and your opponent's. You're trying to move your opponent as far down in his as he's willing to go, and he's trying to do likewise. Your ultimate goal is to achieve a settlement at your opponent's Least Acceptable Result, which, by definition, is the absolute best you can do.

To accomplish this end, you want to unleash two Strategic Forces, the most powerful tools you have. By heightening your opponent's uncertainty about getting a better deal on the one hand and increasing his need for the deal on the other, they exert a double-barrel pressure on your opponent that will do nothing but good for *your* negotiating cause. You'll discover this for yourself when you put them to work in your next negotiation.

CHAPTER 8

Making a Better Deal Possible

A COUPLE OF years ago, a New York real estate developer proposed a land swap to city officials: a city-owned playground at First Avenue and Forty-second Street in Manhattan in exchange for two parks in Tudor City, an elegant residential complex owned by the developer. City officials were hesitant to make the swap, primarily because they did not want a high-rise apartment complex built that would obstruct and detract from the United Nations Building, one of the splendorous hallmarks of the New York skyline.

When negotiations bogged down, the developer took the bull by the horns and boarded up his two Tudor City parks, turning an exquisite retreat into an appalling eyesore and creating a widespread media uproar in the process. Upon learning that their landlord had taken such action, the enraged tenants of Tudor City—some of the most affluent and influential people in New York—immediately put the arm on their friends in city hall, saying, in effect, "Do something about this or we'll make your lives unpleasant." Confronted with an angry mob of people—the sort of people you don't want angry at you—the bureaucrats and politicians sprang into action. And by the time the last ripple of the tidal wave of political pressure from the denizens of Tudor City had been stilled, the city had agreed to the swap. The developer had taken a big step toward getting what he wanted—the hunk of earth to build his apartment building on. (At this writing, subsequent court actions and the opposition of a powerful city agency have left the status of the swap in much doubt. But regardless of the outcome, the developer's negotiating ploy was highly effective.)

Strategic Force No. 3: Changing the Circumstances Surrounding the Negotiation

What the real estate developer did is a good illustration of a third Strategic Force you can draw on in negotiation, what I call changing the circumstances surrounding the negotiation. In our discussion of Strategic Force. No. 2, we talked about how you can alter your opponent's Settlement Range by increasing his need for the deal. Using Strategic Force No. 3, you're also altering his Settlement Range, but in a different way. Here you're doing it by throwing a new element into the bargaining that changes the situation and pressures your opponent to change the location of his Least Acceptable Result. With the newly expanded negotiating room, you're able to secure settlements that weren't even possible (i.e., outside your opponent's Settlement Range) before.

I'm not going to make a case for the ethics of what the developer did. But he did do a helluva job in changing the circumstances surrounding the negotiation. By creating such an uproar by so many politically influential folks, he exerted pressure on the city to accede to his wishes. He opened up a Settlement Range where previously there had been none at all. With the new element—the political pressure—injected into the negotiation, the city officials felt compelled to alter their Settlement Range and consent to the swap. Now let's look at some other examples of Strategic Force No. 3 in action.

Arthur has been the editor of a fledgling weekly newspaper for eight months. When he was hired, the publisher of the paper, Garrett, made it clear to Arthur that, though the operation was starting small, there were big plans for it in the near future. In the meantime, Garrett said, Arthur would have to be less of a conventional newspaper editor and more of a jack-of-all-trades, selling ads, doing some promotional work, and solidifying the paper's contacts in the community. That was fine by Arthur at first; the challenge was attractive to him. But as the months passed, Arthur began to feel frustrated by what he viewed as an absence of growth and progress in the paper. He felt his eighty-hour work weeks were doing little but beating him into the ground.

Periodic discussions with Garrett proved unsuccessful. The

publisher urged Arthur to be patient and said that progress was in fact being made, that the future for the paper was as bright or brighter than ever. Arthur wanted to believe that and went on plugging away as long as he could, until he decided that, publisher willing or not, something had to be done.

Arthur had a great deal of working autonomy; the publisher was not a part of the paper's daily operations. Taking matters into his own hands, Arthur went out and hired, on a provisional and commission-only basis, an advertising accounts manager, someone who would go out and solicit the ads the paper needed to survive. Freed of that onerous burden, Arthur felt he could then devote his full energies toward improving the editorial content of the paper.

Arthur kept his little secret for a month, long enough to prove to him that it was an unqualified success, both in the ledger and in the paper's editorial quality. Then, with ledger in hand, he confronted Garrett with his surprise. "I'd like to propose making the accounts manager a full-time, salaried employee," Arthur said. "He's proved that he's very capable and, after only a month of part-time work, has already been a significant boon to our financial outlook."

Before coming up with his plan, Arthur knew that very shortly he would have to try to negotiate with Garrett to get an accounts manager for the paper; Arthur just could not go on doing it all himself. He also knew that Garrett, judging by his past performance and overall inertia, would not be at all receptive to the idea. So he went ahead with his plan, armed himself with irrefutable evidence documenting its effectiveness, and presented the publisher with a *fait accompli*. By doing so, he was able to confront Garrett, not to ask "Can we do this?" but to state, "I've done this, it's worked, and it's in our best interest to continue it."

What did Arthur, as a negotiator, actually do? He found a way to make the publisher recalculate his Settlement Range and move his L.A.R. in a direction favorable to Arthur. Although he had no definitive proof, Arthur had every reason to believe that if he had merely asked Garrett to hire an accounts manager, the response would've been a resounding "No." In other words, hiring an accounts manager would not have been in Garrett's Settlement Range. Indeed, Garrett probably would have had no Settlement Range at all and would have simply dismissed the proposal altogether. But by taking the initiative and forcing the action, Arthur opened up possibilities that weren't there before and effectively created the room to get what he wanted. And he did, by the way, get what he wanted; the accounts manager was put on salary and hired full time.

Say you're a departmental manager in a mid-sized company. You enjoy a reasonably cooperative and cordial working relationship with Phyllis, who manages the other department on your floor and with whom you work on a number of important projects. The problem is that she always seems to get the better of things when the two of you sit down to negotiate the nuts and bolts of your joint ventures. You always wind up with the bulk of the work, and she always winds up with the bulk of the credit. It's not explicit, but you get the impression that she thinks you're more of a plodder and plugger and she's more of a thinker and innovator. You want the situation to change, particularly before you begin negotiating the next project—the big one—next week.

Much of the problem, you decide, stems from her aptitude in the game of company politics. She seems to have or at least acts like she has more clout with the higher-ups, and she doesn't hesitate to make you aware of it. She stops short of being condescending, but you know she thinks you're a relative lightweight with no ins to the right people, like C.R. Chandler, a rapidly rising director and resident company *wunderkind* who, everyone knows, has become a right-hand man to the president.

Determined to do something about it, you lay the groundwork for your plan. When she walks into your office for your weekly Friday lunch date, you casually inform her, "Oh, I'm sorry, Phyllis, I guess I forgot to tell you. I've got some rather important things to go over with C.R., so I'm having lunch with him today."

"C.R.?"

"Yes, you know, Chandler."

The following Monday, you walk into Phyllis's office to work out the details of the big project. Rather than wait to hear her thoughts on the subject, you outline *yours*, which entail using much less of your department's resources than in the past, and make it clear that, this time, the two of you will jointly submit the final project proposal to the higher-ups, even though she has always made the presentations in the past.

She comes back with plans of her own, but you don't get the feeling she's trying to go one up on you the way she always did in the past. And that's because you have changed the circumstances surrounding your working/negotiating relationship with her. Having lodged in her head the notion that you do, in fact, have connections—and with the best person imaginable, Chandler—you've enhanced your credibility in her eyes, forced her to take you more seriously, and, most importantly, expanded the scope of your negotiating opportunities with her.

As another example, take the case of Phil, a labor leader. In his past dealings with management, Phil has had difficulty negotiating labor contracts. He knows the reason only too well: The union has a history of infighting, and while the different factions are vying for supremacy, management consistently wins at the bargaining table.

Phil wants to change that pattern for the upcoming contract negotiation. He goes before the rank-and-file and tells them the settlements they want will never be realized until the internal squabbling stops. "If you give me your unqualified support, we all stand to gain," he says. Several weeks before the talks begin, the membership stages a big rally at which they conduct a ceremonious voice vote, giving Phil an overwhelming vote of confidence. Management cannot help but take notice.

Phil goes before management and lays the union demands for the new contract on the table. Management takes its usual hard line, but Phil senses that their negotiating resolve is not what it was. A new element has entered the negotiation; for the first time, management must weigh the possibility of a strike if the newly united workers are not satisfied with the agreement. By convincing his membership to line up squarely behind him, Phil has changed the circumstances of the talks. With the specter of a possible strike looming in the background, management is now compelled to expand its Settlement Range to include possibilities they previously would not have considered.

Whenever you hear of a group drumming up support for its particular cause or grievance, that, too, is a case of changing circumstances. During a severe winter several years back, for example, the residents of certain neighborhoods in Queens were outraged by the city's woeful performance in removing the snow from their streets. After repeated attempts to get the situation righted were unsuccessful, they staged a large demonstration in their snow-covered streets, attracting extensive media coverage. The ensuing public outcry on behalf of the snowbound souls exerted pressure on the city to dig them out and, after future storms, keep them dug out. "Going public" with their gripe enabled the residents to change the circumstances surrounding their negotiation with the city and induced the city to alter its Settlement Range. Before the uproar, remember, the city seemed unresponsive to the residents' problems; quite likely, they had no Settlement Range at all and simply hoped the issue would fizzle out. The uproar assured that it wouldn't fizzle out and made the city deal with it.

When you have a grievance of your own, filing a law suit is often a highly effective way of changing the circumstances of your negotiation. Whether you plan to represent yourself in small claims court or hire a battery of lawyers to do it up big, you inject a new element into the situation merely by taking the initiative of filing. Not only does it show your opponent that you mean business, it also makes him question how much he wants to expend the time, energy, and money that dealing with the courts entails, particularly since he's extremely uncertain of how much the judge will award you should you win. These prospects frequently result in an altered Settlement Range . . . and an out-of-court settlement. A friend of mine who was burned out of his apartment recently filed suit against his landlord, charging him with negligence. (The cause of the fire has been determined to be faulty wiring in the building.) My friend was seeking damages of $10,000. Prior to the filing of the suit, the landlord flatly refused to compensate my friend for his losses. Apparently the landlord had no Settlement Range; his negotiation position was simply "No." That changed shortly after the filing. Suddenly the landlord was willing to talk. By introducing a new element into the negotiation, my friend was able to secure an out-of-court settlement for $6,000.

Overhauling the Circumstances

Sometimes you cannot only change the circumstances surrounding a negotiation; sometimes you can *overhaul* them and obviate the need to negotiate at all. What overhauling the circumstances basically does is pull the plug on the negotiation by making what your opponent wants impossible.

Say, for instance, that you are an employer who is being driven up the wall because of a chronic problem with employee vacation time. More and more, the workers have opted to take vacation days here and there, rather than for whole weeks at a time, and the situation is playing havoc with your work scheduling. You have the power to prohibit the practice, but you're not comfortable confronting your workers about it.

So you make an end run. You convince the personnel director to issue a policy prohibiting vacations of less than one week with a proviso that all exceptions to the policy must be approved in advance by personnel. Your maneuver has altogether eliminated the need to negotiate the issue.

As another example, take the case of Joe, a hospital administrator recently hired by the hospital's governing board. Being a hospital administrator is a high-pressure, high-risk job because it almost inevitably involves a power struggle with the hospital medical staff, each side fighting to have the last word on the institution's policies and operations. Having suffered through a string of ineffective administrators, the board is delighted to have a tough, hard-driving guy like Joe at the helm. They want very much for Joe to have the clout to deal effectively with the doctors; consequently, the board agrees to Joe's demand for a clause in his contract stating that if he is fired before his contract has expired, he will receive a settlement of $400,000.

When Joe began making decisions and implementing policies that were highly unpopular with the doctors, they went running to the board, demanding his resignation. To which the board replied, "Sure, we'll fire him, but *you* will have to come up with the $400,000 he's entitled to." Not being willing to part with that kind of cash, the doctors had little choice but to live with him. The negotiation ended before it had even begun. By agreeing to Joe's demand, the board overhauled the circumstances of the negotiation. They wanted Joe on the job, and by accepting the $400,000 buy-out clause, they were virtually assured he would stay there.

The opportunities you may have to overhaul the circumstances of your negotiations this way may not be that common. Nonetheless, it's important to be aware that, on occasion, they will be there. Particularly when you're dealing with a thoroughly intractable person, sometimes overhauling the circumstances is your only recourse to achieve your needs.

Summing Up

The purpose of Strategic Force No. 3 is to move your opponent's Least Acceptable Result to expand your negotiating room and make better settlements possible. The irony of it is that, in many cases, no matter how effectively you change the circumstances and no matter how many new elements you give your opponent to consider, you still cannot be absolutely certain that you have, in fact, altered his Settlement Range. The reason is that unless you're negotiating with a simpleton, you don't know for sure where his Least Acceptable Result is. Go back to the case of Arthur, the newspaper editor. He did not have concrete proof that the publisher would've rejected the idea of hiring an accounts manager if Arthur had simply approached him about it. Who knows, maybe the publisher's Settlement Range did include hiring an accounts manager—not likely, but not impossible either. The point is that in the absence of proof Arthur just had to make a calculated guess, based on the publisher's attitude toward such things in the past. And that guess dictated his strategy: Change the circumstances and expand the possibilities of the publisher's probable Settlement Range.

It's a given in negotiation that you don't know where the bottom of your opponent's Settlement Range is. It doesn't matter if you don't know for sure whether you've changed it. The most important thing is that, by changing the circumstances and tossing in new variables, you are putting pressure on him to settle at a place that's advantageous to you. You don't know if your opponent has actually changed his L.A.R., but you do know that you've increased the pressure on him to back down, and that's the transcending value of Strategic Force No. 3, just as it is with your other two Strategic Forces.

Putting pressure on your opponent is the unifying thread of all your Strategic Forces. Whether you're raising his doubts about getting a better deal from you, increasing his need for the settlement by throwing in goodies and/or threats, or changing the circumstances that impact on the bargaining, the key is that you are *exerting pressure on him to settle where you want him to*. And that pressure, ultimately, is what's going to enable you to get what you want out of your negotiation.

CHAPTER 9

Pulling Your Bargaining Levers

Wow, HAVE YOU got a problem. Somehow, between the time you went to bed last night and the time you awoke this morning, a massive, five-hundred-pound boulder has mysteriously appeared in the middle of your backyard. What's worse, it's sitting squarely in the middle of your badminton court, and you have a big game coming up this afternoon for neighborhood bragging rights.

"Oh, shuttlecock!" you moan. "What am I going to do now? It's so firmly implanted I don't think four people could budge that thing." Taking a moment to gather your wits, you suddenly flash upon a thought that would do your high school physics teacher proud. "It's a terrific idea," you say to yourself with all immodesty. "I'll set up a lever and pry it out. Once it's loose, a couple of people can lift it off the court with no sweat."

With a cinder block for a fulcrum, you take a crack at the rock, using a two-foot-long board as a lever. The boulder barely moves. You try again, this time with a four-foot board. You rock it a little, but not nearly enough. Undaunted, you fetch an eight-foot board, wedge it under the rock, rest it on the fulcrum, and push down. Just like that, the boulder seesaws out of its self-made crater. Your badminton cronies help you roll the dislodged hunk off to the side. Bring on the game!

You may be wondering what badminton and boulders have to do with negotiation. Very little. But levers have *everything* to do with negotiation. Think of your opponent's Settlement Range as the boulder. You already know you want to move it, but how? By using negotiating levers to exert pressure, just as you used the board to exert pressure on the rock. Negotiating leverage increases your means of accomplishing some purpose, namely getting your opponent to settle at a place most beneficial to you.

You derive the bulk of your negotiating leverage from the three Strategic Forces. Without them, you stand as much chance of achieving the settlement you want as you do moving a hundred-pound boulder with a toothpick. With them, you've got yourself a long, sturdy lever that's primed for some serious prying. But there are ways you can further enhance your negotiating leverage, ways to make the lever longer and sturdier still. In this chapter we're going to discuss several additional strategies which, by prying right along with the Strategic Forces, significantly improve your ability to move your opponent's Settlement Range to where you want ... even if it's the Rock of Gibraltar.

The Leverage of Options

One of the few immutable truths in the negotiator's world is the more options you have, the more leverage you have. As long as you have options, you know you can take your negotiation elsewhere if the proposed settlement is not to your liking. If you have no options, on the other hand, your negotiating room is drastically reduced, particularly if you need the deal badly. With no place to turn, what choice do you have but accept any settlement that comes along, even one in the pits of your Settlement Range?

Options provide you with leverage in two basic ways. First, they afford you the luxury of "shopping" comparatively. If I have five people coming to look at my typewriter today, that gives me the flexibility to pick and choose among the various offers. By the time you show up, I may already have received an offer for $600. With that to fall back on, I can play the waiting game to see if you can do better—and wait without the slightest trace of anxiety. Having options is never more valuable than in raise negotiations. If you show your boss a written offer for $3,000 more than you're presently making, you are implicitly telling him, "Pay me or lose me." Even if the new offer is otherwise unattractive, your negotiating leverage is greatly enhanced. "You know how much I enjoy the working environment here, Jack," you might say to him. "But don't you agree it's only fair that I be given my true market value?"

The second way options give you added leverage is by increasing your opponent's doubts about your willingness to bend in the bargaining. As we saw in our discussion of the role of need in negotiation, your opponent is going to feel highly uncertain about his prospects for a better deal if he sees you have options but don't have any pressing reason to negotiate with him. You don't need an ironclad offer to generate this uncertainty; all you need to do is show your opponent that you have other irons in the fire. Such a display is frequently all it takes to induce your opponent to forget about holding out and settle where you want him to. Some years back, I was being courted by several potential employers. Though I had not received firm offers from any of them, the feelers were sufficiently serious to allow me to report back to my own employer and say, in so many words, "Look, I'm a pretty hot commodity right now, and if you want to keep me, you had best come up with a nice incentive for me." I was able to parlay those options into a significant salary increase.

A literary agent I know recently used options in a similar fashion to improve his negotiating leverage on behalf of one of his clients. The agent sent some of the writer's novels to an editor at a publishing house who promptly replied that she would be extremely eager to receive a proposal from the writer. To which the agent said, "Well, he'd like to do a proposal for you, but he's got a lot of other things going now [read options], and he wants to be sure it's worth his while to pursue this opportunity." With the leverage of options working for him, the agent subsequently negotiated the largest contract in the writer's career.

You won't be able to come up with options in *every* negotiation. If you're trying to redress a grievance, for instance, you have no choice but to negotiate with the person who wronged you. What was I going to say to the dry cleaner who lost my shirt, "You better give me the $15, or I'll take my complaint elsewhere!" The guy probably would've kissed me. But in those negotiations where you are *not* locked in to dealing with a single opponent, do everything you can to give yourself options. Leave yourself negotiating room. If you're selling something, line up as many opponents as you can. If you're buying something, see if you can get a better price elsewhere and use the offer as a means to talk another opponent down. You can never have too many options. The more people you can get to compete for what you're offering—whether it's money, goods, or services—the better will be your negotiating leverage.

Remember, too, that the next best thing to having options is making your opponent *think* you have them. Do your best to conceal your degree of need for the deal. Give your opponent the impression that you have no great stake in settling with him, that you have other alternatives if things with him fall through.

By the same token, be aware that your opponent is probably trying to convince you that he, too, has options. He very well might. Then again, he might be bluffing. Probe your opponent. Test his resolve. See if he in fact does have as little need to reach an agreement with you as he's leading you to believe. Recall in our typewriter negotiation that I told you my phone was ringing off the hook, a piece of information calculated to make you think, "Gosh, I've got lots of competition. If I want this machine, I'd better do something about it now." Well, if you don't have an urgent need for the machine, you might test me with inaction. "I'm gonna give it some thought," you say. "Maybe I'll give you a call if I think we can work something out." If I truly have the options I've made you think I have, then your walking away probably won't faze me. If I don't, I'll be taking your coat out of your hands and saying, "Oh, I think we might be able to work something out. This is a damn good machine, and there's been a lot of interest in it, but to tell you the truth, I would just as soon get it off my hands. Your offer is low, but if you can improve it some, I think we'll be in the ball park." If I talk like that, it's a safe bet that I don't have many options at all. By finding that out, you've curtailed my leverage and added to yours.

The moral: Make your opponent believe you have options, whether they're real or illusory. But don't get so preoccupied in doing so that you neglect to test your opponent's options. They may not be all he's cracking them up to be.

I'm reminded of a cartoon I once saw about a man looking to buy a house who was on his way to see the umpteenth real estate agent. Tired of hearing the same sales hype everywhere he went, he walked into the agent's office and handed him a printed card. It read: "Yes, I know I have good taste. Yes, I know fifteen people had already been to see it by seven o'clock this morning. Yes, I know it's priced to sell, and that it's a brand new listing. Now that we understand each other, would you please show me that overpriced, rundown shack that you haven't been able to unload for two years?"

The Leverage of Allies

Let's go back to my negotiation with the pocket dictating machine salesman. After I got nowhere with my initial threat to inform several of his important customers of my dissatisfaction, I went looking for another threat. I didn't know what would work. I was stuck and doing nothing but shooting in the dark when I came upon the idea to threaten him with a letter to the president. Obviously I was on target with that one. Without even knowing it, the president was an indispensable ally to my negotiation. I needed help, reached out, and found a friend, who enabled me to get what I wanted from the salesman.

Some years ago, my father purchased a Japanese-made television set that went on the blink shortly after the warranty had expired. Over $125 in repairs later, it was still on the blink. Complaints to the repair service and to the manufacturer itself achieved nothing. My father was stuck until, in a moment of inspiration, he got the notion to call the Japanese consulate in New York City. Within two days, the matter was resolved to his complete satisfaction. He, too, reached out and found a friend for his stalled negotiation.

These examples are not uncommon. There are times when, no matter how brilliantly you've negotiated, there's simply a limit to what you can accomplish on your own. Those are the times to enlist an ally for your negotiation. You can't always muster enough leverage by yourself. When you can't, get help. There's lots of it to be had.

My wife Jeanne and I once had steam damage in our apartment inadvertently caused by a plumber who was attempting to fix the radiator. After some creative (but not baseless) calculations, we estimated the damage to be $450. The insurance company sent over an adjuster who checked out the damage and said we would be hearing from the company. Weeks passed. Not a word. Nice letters got us nowhere. Follow-up phone calls got us nowhere. Ditto for irate letters and calls. We needed an ally. A friend of Jeanne's is a lawyer, and she asked him if he would write a letter to the company on our behalf. Not only did he demand a settlement in the letter, he also made it abundantly clear to the company that he was a close friend of ours—a critical point, since no lawyer would normally pursue a $450 case. Of course, we never would have asked him to do anything but write the initial letter, but the insurance company didn't know that. Five days later, our lawyer ally secured for us a $400 settlement offer that we happily accepted.

Not only are there allies out there who can help you, sometimes they are even *programmed* to help you. When Jeanne and I moved into our house, we were told the water was going to be turned off the next morning because the water company had not been able to get in to take an initial meter reading. When I expressed my displeasure, the company said, "We're sorry, but you're not our customer yet. What can we do?"

I immediately picked up the phone and raised hell with the state public utilities commission. The state called the water company, launching what I'm sure was a cascade of ripples down the chain of command until some guy in the local office caught the flak—"Why are you creating a stir that's getting the state involved?" At eight o'clock the next morning a meter reader was knocking at our door. The water was not turned off. Another triumph for the allies.

Then there was the time my auto insurance policy was due to expire. I called my agent, inquiring about what my new premium would be if I chose to renew it. He said he would find out and get back to me but never did. Months went by, and finally I heard from him . . . in the form of a bill with a retroactive premium hike of $200. I was flabbergasted. What gall! I had never agreed to any increase; I hadn't even been able to find out what my premium would be. I gave my agent an earful, but he pleaded helplessness. "It's in the company's hands. I can't do anything for you." The company was completely intractable. "It's policy," they said, "to issue bills on a semiannual basis, and the fact is that the premium on your policy went up $200 for the last pay period."

"You want to talk about facts?" I replied. "How about the fact that nobody ever told me my premium was practically being doubled?"

"We're not at liberty to change your premium, sir. Please remit the full amount shown on the bill."

I was having none of that. So I reached out for an ally, the state insurance commission, which received from me a letter detailing my complaint. Once more the ripple effect came to my rescue. Within ten days the company abandoned its effort to get the extra $200 out of me.

These examples illustrate the myriad ways in which allies can increase your bargaining leverage. There are allies out there for almost every conceivable negotiation. Sometimes, they're very easy to find. A friend of mine who is self-employed was having a lot of trouble convincing a landlord to let him move into an apartment. The landlord was concerned about my friend's uncertain financial standing. My friend resolved the problem by enlisting an ally, a well-to-do friend who was willing to co-sign the lease.

But when an ally is not so readily apparent, you have to be more creative in your search. Analyze your situation and think about who might be able to help you. A governmental agency? A consumer group? An elected official? A friend in the business? A community group? The media? There are plenty of allies out there. All you have to do is pinpoint the one that's right for your negotiation. Once you do, your negotiating leverage will take a giant step forward.

The Leverage of Timing

Two youngsters were discussing the fine art of getting money out of their parents. One of them seemed to have much better fortune.

"How do you do it?" the other one asked.

"Friday."

"Not when. How?"

"The when is the how. Payday is Thursday, bill-paying day is Saturday, so I always make sure I hit them up on Friday."

A good sense of timing is a vital asset for a negotiator. The world is a fluid place. What's not negotiable today may very well be negotiable tomorrow and vice versa. No matter how well you've constructed your negotiation, it can all come tumbling down with a single misfire in timing.

Timing cannot really be taught. You have to feel it. You have to develop a sense for when the forces are going your way, when the time is right for you to get the most you can out of the negotiation. A moment's hesitation or a moment's haste can be your undoing. Trust your instincts. You know better than anyone else when the momentum of the negotiation is swinging toward you or away from you.

Say you're planning on asking your employer for a raise.

Your timing should hinge on several variables. What's the current financial shape of the company? If the most recent earnings report showed a record in the red, it would probably not be a good time to visit your boss. How about your standing in the firm? Have you been performing very ably or are you coming off a major success? And what about the way your employer has responded to your raise requests in the past? Is he generally fair with you or do you have to pull the money out of him? You have to juggle all these factors. If you've been doing a good job and your boss has rewarded you justly for that in the past, then it's likely a good time to talk raise, regardless of the firm's financial picture. If it's bad, after all, it's no doing of yours. If, on the other hand, your boss is a habitual tightwad, you might want to consider a bolder move such as bringing up the raise issue while you're in the middle of a project that your boss has a lot at stake in. If your boss is a hardballer, sometimes the only way to make him negotiate is to play his game. You need not necessarily give him an ultimatum: the raise or else; but the timing of your request should make it abundantly clear to him how serious you are about it. Again, the important thing is to trust your instincts. They'll let you know when the forces surrounding the negotiation are with you.

Of course, the forces are never with you more than when what you're offering is in high demand. Back in the early spring of 1978, a friend was thinking about selling his car. The gas shortage struck, and suddenly cars with massive gas tanks and four-hundred-mile cruising capacities became hot items. My friend's car had both, and he told me he got some $300 more for the car because of it. Rick Cerone, the New York Yankees' catcher, struck when the forces were with him when he negotiated a contract prior to the 1981 season. Coming out of by far the best season of his career in 1980, Cerone sought to cash in on his skyrocketing market value, asking for a five-year contract for a reported $3.5 million. The Yankees balked at that demand, knowing full well that, from their standpoint, the timing could not have been worse to negotiate a long-term deal with Cerone, who wound up with a one-year pact for $440,000. It should be interesting to see what happens in the future. If Cerone tails off in 1981, I would wager that the Yankees would then be extremely eager to talk to him about a long-term deal in the hope that they could retain his services comparatively cheaply by baseball standards. Cerone, on the other hand, probably would prefer another one-year agreement, banking on a solid 1982 season to boost him back into the megabucks class. In any case, the point is to time your negotiation, if you can possibly swing it, to coincide with a high demand for what you have to offer.

If you're on the receiving end of goods or services, try to time your negotiation to coincide with a low degree of need. When you need something in a hurry, you forfeit leverage and are bound to pay more for it. If your refrigerator seems to be on the wane, don't wait for it to die completely before looking for a new one. Shop around while you've got some negotiating room, while you're not pressured into getting your hands on the first cold box you see and getting it home before all the food rots. Sometimes you'll be caught flat-footed and will have to negotiate, regardless of whether the timing is wrong. Try to avoid that eventuality whenever you can. Try to time your negotiation so (and let your opponent know) that it's discretionary, not necessary.

Timing is everything in negotiation. You may walk into a car dealership on the fifteenth of the month and find a salesman who is unwilling to make even minor concessions in price to you. Go back at the end of the month, however, when the salesman has a monthly quota hanging over his head or when he's dreaming about that bonus for his xth sale for the month, and you may find a new salesman with a much keener interest in bargaining with you. Needs, fears, circumstances, all the things that impact on negotiation, are subject to change at any given moment. Don't negotiate as if you lived in a fixed world. That guy who flatly rejected your $80,000 offer for his house last month might just be willing to listen to you this month. Keep yourself open to the possibility of changes. Keep a finger on the pulse of the forces which may have a bearing on your negotiation. And when it *feels* right, when the momentum is in your corner, jump on the opportunity. Tomorrow may be too late.

CHAPTER 10

Tactics: Your Tools for Getting What You Want

YOU'RE ABOUT TO enter into a negotiation, so you open up your chest of negotiation tools. You look them over, picking up a few and getting a feel for the wide assortment of negotiating implements available to you. While they're all fashioned with the same purpose in mind—to work on your opponent so as to enable you to achieve the best settlement you can— it's important to realize each one goes about it in its own way. They're not infinitely interchangeable; they won't all work in every negotiation. Just as a hammer won't help you turn a screw, some of these tactics won't help you turn the tide of a specific negotiation in your favor.

What you're presented with here is a smorgasbord of tactics. You have to pick and choose and decide for yourself which one or ones are appropriate and likely to work for your negotiation. Experiment. Get comfortable with them. Some of them, just in the reading, will make intuitive sense to you. Others may require testing in an actual negotiation before you fully grasp how and why they're effective.

And another thing: Just because this is a smorgasbord, don't feel obliged to digest everything all at once. Refer back to it, come back for seconds and thirds; the spread will still be here. Nor should you feel obliged to use a certain number of them in a negotiation. One good, well-applied tactic is worth a lot more than five bad ones. Use them selectively. Try them one at a time. Measure your opponent's reaction. If it works, it may be all you'll need. If it doesn't, no sweat. You've got a bounteous supply, and you can always come back for another.

Straw Men

This tactic involves padding your high-priority goals in a ne-gotiation with goals that are of little or no priority. Then, when you get on in the bargaining, you can give away the chaff in exchange for some extra wheat from your opponent. What straw men are, in essence, are the fluff of your opening position. Not that you let your opponent know that; on the contrary, you want him to believe that your straw men are an integral part of what you're negotiating for. Then, when you grudgingly concede them, the impression is that you're giving away some items of genuine significance. The hope is that your opponent, seeing the sacrificial strides you're making toward settlement, will be obliged to make a concession, a bona fide one, of his own, an exchange which leaves you with a better deal than you had before.

Say you're a labor leader negotiating a new contract with management. You lay out your demands: an eighteen-percent salary hike over three years; a cost-of-living adjustment clause keyed to the rate of inflation; more rigid and more fre-quent safety inspections of the plant; and a provision to pro-tect your workers' jobs in the face of new, labor-saving, high-technology machinery. In the dark recesses of your scheming mind, you know you don't really care about the safety inspections. True, a few of the rank-and-file have sus-tained injuries on the job in the last few months, but privately you know that they were the kinds of accidents that even ev-eryday inspections could not have prevented. Still, you persist with the demand, all the more so because it's a touchy and emotional issue with management, which feels bad about what happened to those workers and studiously wants to avoid getting a reputation of disinterest in the workers' wel-fare. Finally, in the waning hours of bargaining, you reluc-tantly concede on the issue in exchange for a significantly improved cost-of-living provision. Your straw man, bless his heart, has worked like a charm.

One caveat about straw men: To be effective, they must be credible. Your opponent has to think they're things you're zealously pursuing, or he won't be inclined to match them with concessions of any meaningful advantage to you. In our example, for instance, you would've had one helluva time convincing management to give in on the salary question in exchange for your willingness to abandon your quest for a new and bigger soda machine.

Good Guy/Bad Guy

If you're a fan of police shows or movies, you've probably seen good guy/bad guy in action. A suspect gets hauled in to headquarters where he is promptly accosted by a surly and abrasive officer, who treats the suspect with all the respect of a convicted murderer. Ranting, raving, and browbeating the suspect relentlessly, the officer makes life as miserable as he can for him. Enter the good guy—calm, reasonable, and understanding. What a relief, the suspect is thinking. He's so relieved, in fact, at being treated like a human being again that he divulges much more than he should about his role in the incident. In essence, the suspect is making a subliminal trade-off: the comfort of dealing with someone civil in exchange for facts about the crime.

Nick and Sal are negotiating with a buyer for their storefront restaurant. They decide on $60,000 as their asking price, though they're willing to go as low as $52,000 to make the sale. Taking the bargaining initiative, Sal comes on with all the charm of a rat. The buyer offers them $54,000, and Sal all but laughs in his face. "We priced it at sixty because it's worth sixty," Sal snaps, in the most intimidating tone he can muster. Having sold the buyer on his utter uncivility, Sal stomps out and gives way to Nick who is all smiles and sweetness. He speaks soothingly to the cowering buyer. "Look, don't mind my partner. He just gets carried away sometimes. You let me worry about him. He'll listen to what I say." Gradually, the buyer's guard comes down. It's a pleasure dealing with someone so reasonable. In contrast to his fiendish partner, Nick's mild-mannered way builds his credibility and gains the confidence of his opponent. The buyer wants to bargain with Nick and feels he can trust him. So when Nick says, "I think I can get my crazy friend to agree to $57,500," the buyer gets the sense that not only is Nick doing him a favor offering it at that price, but that it's a special deal that really is as low as they can possibly go. Coming on the heels of the bad-guy routine, Nick's offer seems downright magnanimous and, at the very least, reasonable, to the buyer. Moreover, the buyer is so delighted to be bargaining with Nick that he might not put up much resistance to his proposal. The buyer's willingness to hold out for something better is undermined by the good-guy come-on of Nick who gives him the distinct impression that he's on the *buyer's* side, not his partner's.

The extremes between the good guy and bad guy need not be so far-flung as I've depicted them here. The bad guy doesn't have to be Satan incarnate; all he has to be is intractable and single-minded enough to make the opponent relieved to be done with him and dealing with someone who's willing to bargain reasonably.

On the defensive side, if this tactic is employed against you, take care not to eat out of the good guy's hand. Remember, what he wants is for you to trade part of your Settlement Range in exchange for the pleasure of dealing with him instead of the fanatic in the next room. Keep in mind that just because an offer comes from the good guy doesn't mean you should accept it at face value or that it's the best they can do. The good guy isn't doing you any favors, so don't hesitate to bargain hard with him. Rather than jump at his offer, let him know that he has got to do better. Chances are he can do better and that he's not going to let the deal slip away so easily. Sometimes, too, you can dismantle this tactic merely by letting your opponents know that you know what they're up to. Once, when good guy/bad guy was tried on me, I said, very calmly, to the good guy, "You know, your partner plays one helluva bad guy." You've never seen such a crestfallen negotiator.

The Clout of Cloutlessness

You're getting impatient and rightfully so. I've owed you $5,-000 for some four months now. My back is to the wall, my business sinking inexorably down the tubes of insolvency. I have not a whit of bargaining strength in my upcoming negotiation with you. Or do I? Come to think of it, maybe I do. I'm about to file for bankruptcy anyway, so I figure, what the hell, I'll offer to settle with you for $1,000. You won't like it, but what recourse do you have? Once I go bankrupt, you're not going to get a dime. This is what I call the clout of cloutlessness.

As another example, take the case of my co-author, Wayne Coffey, who, when we first met, was having transmission trouble with his car. He took it to a nationally known repair specialist and was told he had two options: Pay $475 for a brand new transmission with a 180-day guarantee or pay $350 for a new transmission with certain rebuilt parts and a 90-day guarantee. Since the car was in the twilight of its life, the prospect of forking over those kinds of bucks was not particularly palatable to Wayne. "But what can I do?" he asked me. "I guess I've got no choice but to pay the guy the $350.

"Hold it," I said. "Those prices are not immutable. Some guy just threw them out to you over the phone. Sure, that may be what they'd like to get for the work, but they'll play with those figures if they have to. Let's be a little creative. Given the age of your car, is spending that much money on a new transmission a prudent investment?"

"Not really."

"Isn't it at least worth considering selling the car as is, for parts or whatever, taking that money and the money you would've spent on the transmission, and putting it toward a newer and better car?"

"That makes sense."

"Okay, now you've got an option, a negotiating lever you can use to try to move them in your direction. Suppose you call them back and say, 'Look, guys, I appreciate the offer, but I just don't have the money for the work, so if you would just put my old transmission back in, I'll come and tow it away and sell the car for parts.' "

Wayne did just that, and guess what happened? The shop manager said, "Wait a minute, let me check with my boss and see if we can work out some kind of special deal for you." Two minutes later the guy got back on the phone and said, "How much *do* you have?"

"About $175." Which is exactly what he got his new transmission for. Once more, clout springs from cloutlessness. In this negotiation Wayne was immeasurably aided by his very weakness. After all, how far would he have gotten if he had tried to negotiate with the manager outright, if he'd said, "Three-fifty is much too high. How much better can you do?" While he might've received some concession in price, you can safely bet that the service manager wouldn't have backed off all the way to $175. But because of Wayne's cloutlessness, the service manager was forced to see the deal in terms of $175 or nothing at all.

The situations in which this tactic is applicable are not

very common. But the point is, don't assume that your goose is cooked just because you're negotiating from a position of utter weakness. Sometimes, as we've seen, there is indeed strength in weakness.

Showing Your Wares

You're thinking about buying a new car. You walk into a showroom. After he learns something about the models you're interested in, what's the first thing the salesman does? He steers you over for an up-close look at that gleaming, alluring automobile that already has you fantasizing about the boundless joy you'd get from owning it. He tells of its latest safety features, boasts about its improved mileage, then stokes your interest even more by giving you a test drive out on the road.

What he's doing is showing you his wares. Before he even thinks about negotiating price with you, he wants to impress you with the quality and value of what he has to offer. He wants to get your mouth watering because he knows if he can sell you on the merits of the product itself and get you to really want it, he's going to have a much easier time selling you on *his* price. Let's face it. When we have a high degree of desire for what we're negotiating for, we're a lot less inclined to hold out for the best settlement possible.

If what you're offering in a negotiation is of high quality, by all means let your opponent know it. Get him thinking of its value to him first, of how nice it would be to have it, before he starts thinking about what it'll cost him. Titillate him with a delectable appetizer and make him want the full-course meal almost regardless of its cost. There's a story told about Mark Twain, and how he went to San Francisco and offered his services free to a newspaper. For three weeks he wrote articles—all very well received—then suddenly announced he was leaving.

"You can't leave!" cried the editor.

"Why not? I'm not even an employee."

Having shown his literary wares, he left the editor no choice but to hire him. Once your opponent sees the quality of what he stands to gain from the deal, it makes him want to settle that much more. So why hold back? Let him see it and let his desire swell to the point that to have it for his own, he'd be willing to settle, even at the bottom of his Settlement Range.

Buying Your Opponent's Objections

"Hey, Dad, can I have the car tonight?" Lee asks.

"Oh, I just washed it today and put it in the garage. Heard it's supposed to rain tonight. It'll get all messed up. I don't think it's too good an idea."

"I promise I'll wash it if it gets dirty, okay?"

"Yeah, but I just gassed it up for my trip tomorrow," Dad says.

"I'll top it off before I come home."

"I don't know, it's been losing some air in the right front tire. I don't want it going flat on you."

"I'll fill it up before I go anywhere."

"The last time you took it, there were cigarette butts and doughnut boxes and all sorts of—"

"Dad, I'm just going to Allison's, and then we're going to the movies. I'll bring it back spotless, I promise."

"All right, all right, take it. Just don't get home too late."

In this negotiation Lee used his father's objections to assume a tacit agreement on his goal of getting the car. By coming out with his objections, his father, in effect, was saying, "I would have no problem with your taking the car except for this and this and this, so I really don't think you should take it. By buying his father's objections, then effectively countering them, Lee was finally able to exhaust his father's supply of objections and wind up with what he wanted.

This can be a very effective tactic in negotiation. When your opponent has a problem with a particular settlement, put his objections to your advantage by using them to get him to agree tacitly to the principle of what you want. When he says, "I can't do this because . . ." you say, "I understand that, but we can get around that this way." Then if he says, "Well, here's another problem," you say, "We can get around that too. Here's how . . ." By engaging your opponent in this type of discussion, just as Lee did with his father, you get your opponent to agree tacitly to the principle of what you want. Eventually he'll run out of objections at which point you can say, "Well, we've dealt with all the problems concerning the settlement, so I assume now that we have a deal." The result, in many instances, will be that you'll walk away with what you were after. If he still is reluctant to settle after all that, you will at least have stripped away the phony stuff and smoked out his real reason for opposition. Here's another example.

A wife approaches her husband about firming up the plans for the vacation they've been talking about for weeks now.

"Why don't we make it a skiing trip? I think going up north would be great."

"No, I don't think so. My back's been acting up—I'd be a waste on the slopes."

"Okay, well how 'bout that island in the Caribbean the Bakers were raving about? That sounded wonderful."

"You know I'm not too hot on the beach. I always get fried the first day and wind up walking around looking like a cherry wrapped in terry cloth."

She persists. "Well, we've been talking about spending time in New York City for a long while. Why don't we head there?"

"You kiddin' me? Haven't you been reading about the crime wave goin' on there? We'd be safer in the Amazon jungle."

She has heard enough. "What's the matter, don't you wanna go on vacation?"

"Sure I do. I'm just not that wild about any of those suggestions."

"So where do you want to go?" she asks.

"Well, I'm not sure, but I've been thinking, and I think it might be a good idea to wait until the summer."

She senses that she's now getting to the real problem. The discussion continues, and finally, reluctantly, he tells her of the beating he's taken recently on some stocks he bought without her knowing. She's upset, sure, but at least the crux of the issue is out in the open, and they can now deal with it accordingly. Maybe they'll postpone for a month or two, or maybe they'll go the low-budget route and visit friends in a nearby state. By smoking out the true bottom-line difficulty, the wife has allowed them to move ahead.

Often in negotiation you'll be confronted with an opponent who either doesn't want to say why he has a problem with the deal or who doesn't have any good reasons but, for whatever cause, is emotionally set against it. By penetrating his smoke screen, you force your opponent to come to terms with the nub of the problem. You may not *always* walk away with a settlement, but by getting past his front, you've at least improved your chances.

Go Along, Get Along

Often your opponent will lay out certain conditions which he wants met if a deal is to be seriously considered. Unless the conditions wreak havoc with your Settlement Range, don't begrudge them. Go along. It'll go a long way toward insuring that you and your opponent will get along.

Say you're preparing to negotiate with me for a car. "Before we can talk seriously about price," you assert, "I want to have the car thoroughly checked out by my mechanic."

"No problem."

"Also, I would like to test drive it on the highway as well as around town. You don't really know what you're getting in a car until you get it on the open road."

"Fine. We can take it on the highway if you like."

"And do you have the repair receipts for the car? I'd like to know what's been done to it and when."

"Yes, I believe I've saved most of them."

Is it any skin off my back to go along with your conditions? Not at all. Indeed, it can only do me good because it helps build a bridge of trust and good faith between us. I may think you're a bit of a fanatic, but that's neither here nor there. There's no reason for me to take your requests as a personal affront. Your opponent has every right to have some skepticism when he's dealing with you for the first time. There are a lot of bad apples in the world, after all.

Don't take umbrage when your opponent sets out conditions. He's just trying to protect himself. Keep your ego out of it. Don't take his conditions as some subtle form of character assassination or behave as though you're making grandiose concessions. You're not. In accommodating him, all you're doing is enhancing your trustworthiness in his eyes, and that will do nothing but enhance your prospects of reaching a settlement with him.

Delay

You're negotiating with an opponent to buy his sailboat. You've checked it out carefully, shown great interest in it, and spent enough time with your opponent to whet his appetite for settlement. "It's a real fine boat," you say. "I'm going to give it some serious thought. How 'bout if we meet again next Thursday?"

Employing the delay tactic can be a very effective way of determining how itchy your opponent is to settle. If, for whatever reason, he needs to sell the boat immediately, he's not likely to let you walk off just like that. Measure your opponent's reaction when you put the negotiation on hold. Does he look like his world has collapsed just because you've suggested resuming the discussion in a few days? If so, that betrays a pressure on him that you may not have picked up on. It also indicates that he probably won't try pushing you too far; after all, if the deal means so much to him that he's deeply distressed over having to wait a little to resolve it, is he at all likely to run the risk of losing it altogether by taking a hard line?

Not only can delay be used to feel out the pressures impacting on your opponent, it also works to stall the bargaining if you're expecting that circumstances are soon to change in your favor. For instance, a community group is up in arms because a developer has purchased a tract of land and is laying plans to build a high-rise apartment building in the neighborhood. The developer's plans hinge on an upcoming ruling by the town planning board, which is set to hold a hearing on the issue at its Thursday night meeting after which they'll render a decision. Some of the members of the community group have learned that a local paper is planning on running a major exposé on some of the developer's shady financial dealings in the past. The group, saying they haven't yet been able to gather all the necessary information for the hearing, asks the board to postpone the decision for a week. In the interim, the exposé sends tremors through the community, thus dramatically changing the circumstances of the matter in the community group's favor.

As another example, say you've begun discussing a raise with a vice-president in your company. But then your boss comes around and tells you to get right to work on a short-term but very important project—one that you're the only person qualified to do properly. You decide to put the raise negotiation on hold. Three weeks later, when you've put the finishing touches on your masterful job, you go visit the vice-president again. By delaying things, you've given yourself an added valuable negotiating tool with which you can prove your worth to the company . . . and your right to a handsome pay hike.

Naturally, if you can swing it, it would be preferable to change the circumstances in your favor before the negotiation begins. But when you can't swing it, be aware that often you can drag your feet *during* the bargaining until the tide turns to your advantage.

Speedup and Deadlines

In many negotiations, no significant movement toward settlement takes place until the deadline is at hand. Labor bargaining is a perfect example; after months of back-and-forth squabbling, the deadline comes, both sides announce they're "stopping the clock," and then at a hastily assembled press conference at four o'clock in the morning, bleary-eyed bargainers announce that a settlement has been reached.

To overcome negotiation inertia it sometimes behooves you to force the action. Try setting a deadline, whether real or arbitrary. See if you can't get things moving. Salesmen use this tactic all the time. "Tell you what, I'll let the car go for $5,650, but if you want it for that price, you're going to have to act fast. The boss is coming back Friday, and he'd have my head if he knew I offered it to you for that." Speedup also has the effect of showing your opponent you're not afraid to deadlock. "We've been going around and around for two days now. If you're seriously interested, you'll have to make me an offer by Saturday." Under no circumstances, however, should you set a deadline in a way that makes the opponent believe you're under pressure to make a deal with him. Because if you say, "You'll have to make an offer by Saturday because I've got to make my mortgage payment on Monday," then he knows you're under the gun and will probably try to hold out until the last possible minute to take full advantage of the pressure on you.

Knowing when to reveal a deadline is a tricky business. Sometimes it'll exert pressure to shake your opponent from the clutches of inertia, other times it'll put the pressure on you. You have to ask yourself, "What would happen if I set a deadline in this negotiation? Who would be more affected, my opponent or me?" Obviously, if it's the thirtieth of the month and a salesman has a quota still to be met, his deadline is the last thing he wants you to know, as it would lay bare his need to reach a settlement with you. On the other hand, if you're thinking about finally making me an offer on the typewriter, it would be much to my advantage to say, "I think you should know that some guy who was here earlier is calling me at six o'clock to make me an offer."

Sometimes announcing a deadline can apply pressure equally on you and your opponent and work for mutual benefit. Some years back I was in charge of procuring major equipment for a hospital. I had $250,000 at my disposal, but not forever; it was state money which would no longer be available if it wasn't spent by the end of the fiscal year. Negotiating with a hospital bed salesman, I let him know of my deadline. It worked on us equally because if we failed to reach agreement by the deadline, I would lose out on some much needed beds and he would lose out on a much needed sale. We reached a settlement and both walked away happy.

Revealing a deadline may or may not work in your favor. The bottom line is how much you need the deal vis-à-vis your opponent. If you get the sense that your opponent's need is minimal and you know yours is high, that he has options and you don't, the deadline will work to your disadvantage. Forget it. If it's the other way around, make your deadline public. If a deadline is likely to impact on you and your opponent evenly, as it did in the hospital bed case, throw it out there, too, if you feel the talks are in need of prodding.

On the defensive side, when an opponent lets you know of his deadline, try to find out if it's real or arbitrary. If it's real—and he can prove it—then it acts as a guaranteed deadlock point that is out of his control, and you'll have to negotiate accordingly. If it's not, test to see how adamant he is about it. Avoid getting strong-armed into a deal just because he says he needs to know by so-and-so time. When the car salesman pulls out the line about his boss coming back, say, "I'm sorry, but we're simply not in a position to make a firm decision by that day. We've got several other dealers to see. How 'bout if we get back to you on Tuesday?" He may—and probably will—offer resistance, but is he really going to let a big, fat commission slip away that easily? Highly unlikely.

After all, he never would've made the offer in the first place if its acceptance wouldn't have left him sitting pretty.

Like delay, speedup also can be used in connection with the circumstances surrounding the negotiation. Say you've begun interviewing for another job when you abruptly learn that a financial calamity has beset your present firm and that, under the new austerity budget, your position may be eliminated. Knowing that your bargaining leverage for the new job would be severely impaired if you were out of work, you discreetly push for a commitment from your prospective employer as soon as possible. "I've got several other opportunities hanging in the balance," you might say, "and I'd like to know how serious you are about reaching an agreement with me." The worst you can do is find out he's not all that serious or not in a position to act quickly. If so, at least you'll know it's time to show your wares elsewhere—and pronto.

Turning the Tables

You're thinking about purchasing a franchise of a fast-food restaurant chain. You sit down to discuss the matter with the regional director of franchising, and before you have time to utter a word, he begins barraging you with questions, all pointed toward learning one thing: Are you worthy of buying one of their wonderful franchises? He asks about character references, credit references, your financial situation, and the extent of your roots in the community. And it kind of makes you wonder, "Hey, I'm the buyer here. Shouldn't they be trying to convince me that their franchise is worthy of my money instead of determining if I'm worthy of buying it?"

This is known as turning the tables. You're absolutely right; in most negotiations the buyer is the one who has to be sold on the value of what he's being offered. But in this negotiation the director has changed all that, seizing the initiative and putting you in the *defensive* position of proving why you deserve to buy one of their franchises so *they* can make more money. What he's doing, in essence, is taking for granted that you want to buy the franchise, basically sweeping that issue right off the table, and undermining your negotiating position by putting you in the position of proving why he should even be talking to you. Is it logical? Not especially. Is it effective? You bet.

Don't get locked into a preconceived notion of what you

expect your position to be in a negotiation. Often *you* can turn the tables and put *your* opponent on the spot to convince you that you should be talking to him. A job negotiation is an ideal situation for table-turning. The conventional interview runs something like this: The almighty employer calls you before him, sizes you up, ascertains your qualifications, and, ultimately, determines whether you're worthy of working for him. I'm not aware that it's written in stone anywhere that's the way an interview must be conducted. Turn the tables. Stand up for yourself. Go in armed with questions of your own, so you can find out what the company has to offer *you*—not only in terms of salary and benefits and the like, but also in terms of future opportunities, promotion policies, financial stability, reputation, etc. In short, make your opponent convince you that you should give thought to putting your considerable skills to work for them. Apart from enhancing your negotiating position, this approach conveys a self-assurance and a sense of self-worth that will separate you from the field of other candidates. Don't worry about coming off as presumptuous or arrogant; if you handle it properly, not a trace of either attitude will be in evidence. All you're doing is saying, "I've told you all about myself. Now I'd like to hear about you."

Turning the tables is not applicable in a good number of negotiations. I mean, I'm going to think you're pretty much of an oddball if you're selling a car and you say, "This car has been my best friend for eight years. I want to make sure the person who buys it will take care of it. May I see if you have any marks on your license? And do you have references?" But when it is applicable, table-turning can be a highly effective negotiating tool, particularly when your opponent doesn't expect to have to sell himself to you. When most people go to a bank for a loan, for instance, their attitude is, "I need money. Would you be good enough to lend me some of yours?" as opposed to, "I'm interested in taking out a loan. Can you show me why I should deal with you and not the bank across the street?" Turning the tables can make a tremendous difference in the outcome of your negotiation.

One More for the Road

Recently I was negotiating to buy a tape deck from an audio dealer. The salesman and I had just about settled on a price when I decided to pull out my one-more-for-the-road tactic. "Throw in a box of cassettes and you've got a deal." And so he did.

Often you can exact one last little concession from your opponent without jeopardizing the deal. What you're capitalizing on is the fact that your opponent isn't going to turn his back on the main event just because he has to give up on an insignificant sideshow. The salesman had all but deposited his commission from the sale in the bank; was he really going to risk losing it for a measly box of cassettes?

Timing is the key to getting one more for the road. You have to make your pitch when settlement is at hand, when you and your opponent have generated a full head of negotiating steam. If you do it too early, it'll be worthless. What would I have gotten from the salesman—other than a weird look—if I'd said, "Your price is too high, but I might be willing to bargain with you if you'll throw in a box of those cassettes"? Keep your last-ditch pitch out of the picture until the deal is almost consummated. Wait until he can practically taste the deal. Once he has gotten a whiff of the full-course meal you're about to serve him, he's not about to let himself go hungry just because you want the Jell-O.

Playing the Crazy

A student of mine recently told me of a negotiation he had with a local outlet of a nationwide service center company. He had a $180 repair done on his car and pulled out his credit card to pay for it. But after running a routine credit check, the clerk reported, "I'm sorry, but your account is already $50 past due. We cannot accept your card this time."

"That's impossible. I paid the $50 balance last month."

"I'm sorry, the computer records show that you have not kept up with your payments."

After a discussion with the store's proprietor was unavailing, my student decided some craziness was in order. Ranting and raving like a man possessed, he vowed to go as high as he had to to resolve the problem. "This is absurd," he railed. "I do a helluva lot of business with your company, and believe me, they're gonna hear an earful from me about this. The manager was apparently convinced. Initially stonewalling the matter ("I've got a lot of other customers to take care of"), suddenly he found time in his hectic schedule to place a call to company headquarters to get to the bottom of the matter. Ten minutes later, a subsequent credit check revealed that my student was in fact telling the truth. He was permitted to use his card.

Particularly in Oh-No Negotiations such as this, playing the crazy can be a very effective tactic. Sometimes it takes more than simply and calmly revealing your threat to set an opponent in motion; sometimes it takes fireworks. By acting up, you visibly demonstrate your emotional commitment to your position and significantly enhance the credibility of your threat. If plain words won't stir your opponent, perhaps a vituperative song and dance will.

Playing the crazy can also be used as a preemptive measure to stop a negotiation you don't want to start. Say, for instance, you're upset about the possible transfer of the most valuable worker in your department. A little histrionics ("Over my dead body! If I lose Tricia, my whole operation is going to go down the tubes!") may be all it takes to dissuade your opponents from trying to push you on the issue. At the very least, it will heighten their uncertainty about implementing the transfer.

Finally, when you achieve the settlement you wanted, acting a little unbalanced can provide your opponent with a good way to save face. Suppose your ranting has convinced a store manager to waive a policy and give you a cash refund for an item you bought. Your opponent doesn't have to look far to justify his giving in—"That guy was out of his mind." Don't underestimate the importance of giving your opponent a rationalization for a settlement. Because if he can't justify it in his own mind, he may not settle.

Avoiding the Pigeonhole

Let's eavesdrop on a hypothetical skull session between two of my opponents. "We know that to get our proposal enacted," says one, "we've got to go through Schatzki. How should we approach him?"

"We've dealt with him plenty of times before. We know what he's like. The guy just doesn't like to take risks. As long as we broach it in a way so he sees that his basic interests are covered, he's not going to push us on it. That's just not his style."

What have I done wrong in my negotiations with these chaps? I've clearly been too predictable. I've allowed them to pigeonhole me, to get a fix on my negotiating style, and the upshot is that they don't have to contend with much guesswork when dealing with me. They know how to handle me, and from my point of view, that's a bad situation to be in.

Try not to let this happen to you in your ongoing negotiating relationships. Avoid the pigeonhole; don't let yourself get into a negotiating rut. Vary your style and keep your opponent guessing. If you find that you usually bow to confrontation, initiate a negotiation, even a minor one, in which you feel more comfortable taking a hard line, regardless of the resistance you may encounter. If you're usually the meek and mild type, try playing the crazy every now and then. If you think your opponent has come to bank on your always making the first big concession, hold out, give grudgingly, and try to make him to concede something first. On the other side, if you get the sense that your opponent thinks of you as the master negotiator, the guy who always calls the shots and gets what he wants, you might want to arrange a deal where he can savor the feeling of defending his own cause successfully. In this way, he won't be so intimidated by you that he'll make every effort to steer clear of negotiating with you.

The whole point here is to increase your opponents' uncertainty about your style. Get them to start thinking, "Gee, maybe I had this guy figured wrong." By avoiding the pigeonhole, you'll make their task a good deal more difficult because they won't have the luxury of relying on a set plan in negotiating with you.

Linkage

Often in negotiation you can take advantage of your opponent's desire on the main issue by linking it to another issue and demanding that they be settled simultaneously. Suppose you're interested in buying a wood-burning stove listing for $800. You say to the salesman, "Before we get into the specifics of price, we have to discuss the issue of a service contract. I want to make sure I'm adequately protected in the event of an emergency." Your opponent may not be wild about your complicating the bargaining, but if he really wants the sale, he doesn't have much choice but to deal with the two issues as a package. From your point of view, it's much better to do your linking early, so as to get maximum leverage out of his need for a settlement. If you bring it up after the principal issue has been, or is close to being, resolved, he doesn't have nearly the same incentive to go along with you. You make it much easier for him to sweep the secondary issue under the carpet.

As another example, say you've just received an astounding job offer. Obviously this company really wants you. You say, "I'm flattered by your offer, but I'm not really in a position to make a final decision on it until we've reached agreement on what my budget will be and what my reporting relationship in the firm will be." Your opponent may attempt to separate the matters ("We can resolve the minor stuff later, can't we? Let's first firm up whether you want to work with us.") but by linking them to an issue they clearly have a great stake in, your coming aboard, you dramatically decrease his ability to do so.

Keep linkage in mind. It's a great way to bring important issues to the bargaining table in a manner that makes it difficult for your opponent to resist.

Humble and Helpless

In real life, in the movies, on television, you've seen it played out hundreds of times. Having been found guilty, the convicted party poignantly beseeches the court with a final desperate plea, "I have seen the errors of my ways and deeply regret that I have inflicted harm on others. My transgressions cannot be undone and I do not expect to be forgiven, but I beg you, your honor, not to throw a life away because of one wrong turn. Give me a chance to redeem myself, and I promise, so help me God, to prove to everyone here that the court shall not regret its mercy. But whatever fate you determine for me, your honor, it will be nothing compared with the sentence I'm already serving—having to live with myself after what I've done."

In fact, this approach will sometimes work quite well. In situations where one side is all powerful and the other utterly defenseless, the power-brokers frequently show surprising magnanimity. All of us, at one point or another, are caught in a weak or defenseless negotiating position. When you are, try appealing to your opponent's mercy and compassion. If you've screwed up, admit it. Bare your soul. Be humble and helpless. Your entreaty might just sway his thinking and leave you in a better position than you thought possible.

A while back, a student of mine had a fire in her apartment and lost everything she owned. In the ensuing period of confusion and depression, she neglected to keep up with her bills. The utility company, having issued her a number of warnings, finally disconnected her service, referred the matter to a collection agency, and informed her she would not be taken on as a customer in the future unless she made a substantial deposit. After much anguish, she finally arranged a meeting with an executive in the billing department. "I don't have any excuse," she said. "All I can say is that I have always been a customer in good standing, but it's just that I was burned out of my apartment and ever since then, well, everything has been so unsettling—you know, moving from place to place, dealing with insurance companies, replacing everything I lost—I guess I've just let things slide that I shouldn't have." The result? Suffice it to say that she never made the deposit . . . and she didn't live in the dark.

Suppose you're in danger of losing an important customer for your company. Instead of waiting for your boss to walk in one day and give you holy hell, go to him first. "Nothing I'm doing is working. I really feel miserable about it. I know what a blow it would be if we lost them. You're the promotion wizard—do you think you might be able to give me some suggestions that might help me turn things around?"

While most people will be responsive to such appeals, do exercise caution in whom you are humble and helpless with. If you suspect you're dealing with a cold, heartless type, best to keep your humility and helplessness to yourself and struggle on as best you can.

Divide and Conquer

In search of a refrigerator, a husband and wife are talking with a salesman in the large-appliance section of a department store. As the wife wanders off to explore other models, the salesman swoops in on the husband, who is looking longingly at one particular refrigerator.

"This is a real nice one, isn't it?" leads the salesman.

"Sure is. It's sleek—not blocky like a lot of the others. How's it work?"

"I'll tell ya, this one outsells every other one on the floor by two to one. It's designed so that it'll hold fifteen percent more food without taking up any extra floor space."

"That's handy," replies the husband. "We've got six hungry mouths at home."

"Well then, the automatic ice-cube maker should be great for you. Never run out of cubes, plus it's built right into the outside of the door, so you don't have to waste energy opening and closing it all the time."

"Oh yes, does it come in green—a darkish shade? That's what I've done my kitchen in."

"Sure does," says the salesman. "Here's the color chart."

By the time the wife comes back, hubby is sold. "I've found the refrigerator of our dreams," he beams. "It's got everything we were looking for." What has happened here? The salesman has subtly inserted a wedge into their united negotiating front. Having already sold one of them on it, he has divided the team and enlisted the husband's help in convincing the wife that this is the one to buy. The couple's negotiating strength has been significantly weakened.

Another example of divide and conquer in action: A manufacturer's representative is peddling a new line of surgical equipment. Instead of dealing directly with the hospital's purchasing department, he makes his appeal to other vitally interested parties—the doctors, who, after checking it out, get all excited at the prospect of having new equipment to use. Mission accomplished: Doctors sold. Next, the rep goes to purchasing, which, not surprisingly, is already feeling pressure from the doctors to buy the stuff. The pressure plays right into the hands of the rep, who knows very well that the money-minded folks in purchasing are trying to keep a tight rein on expenditures. Having sold one part of the team, he has left himself in much better shape to sell the other.

If you're having trouble making headway negotiating with a team (a team being two or more people), try appealing to one member or faction. If you can get one segment to want to settle with you, you will have tilted the tenor of the bargaining in your favor. Because, in essence, now the reluctant segment must negotiate not only with you, but with its compatriots as well.

Springing a Leak

Joe had an upcoming raise negotiation with his boss. Although a prized employee, Joe never fared very well in getting raises—at least not as well as he thought he should have. The problem, he decided, was that the boss took for granted that he'd always be there to count on. Rather than haul out the heavy artillery, threats and/or ultimatums, Joe opted for a more subtle approach—a leak. Several days before he was due to meet with his boss, he made some copies of his resumé and strategically left one in the copier. He entrusted the rest to the office's reliable rumor mill.

Having planted the seed, he began watering it when he sat down with his boss, making vague but nonetheless directed remarks about "feeling stale" and "moving in new directions." Thanks to his leak, Joe's intimations had an added credibility to his boss who had to be thinking, "Gee, it's possible that I could lose this guy." Exactly how much the leak had to do with it is impossible to pinpoint, but Joe received $1,000 more than he ever had before. (A few words of caution: Joe happened to know that his position in the firm was extremely secure, so it was safe enough for him to spring such a leak. But if you're thinking about dashing over to the copying machine tomorrow morning, be careful; some companies and bosses don't react kindly to what they perceive as employee disloyalty and/or deception.)

Leaked information can be very valuable for your negotiation. By arranging for your selected nugget to filter back to your target indirectly, it becomes more credible than if you had divulged it yourself. There's something about the grapevine that seems to increase the import of what travels along it. I have an extremely adversarial relationship with one of my regular opponents. The nature of our respective jobs leaves us little choice but to confront each other. A while back, I was upset with the way he was handling a certain matter, so I called him up and told him so in no uncertain terms. No response—barely as much as a grunt. I decided that he was so accustomed to my fireworks that he'd fallen into the habit of tuning them out. This was a very important matter; I could ill afford to be tuned out. So I called a third party (one whom we both deal with regularly) and casually got around to mentioning how profound my dissatisfaction with my opponent was and how things could get nasty if we couldn't reach some kind of agreement on the issue. The third party dutifully passed along my comments to my opponent. Hearing it from someone other than me must've made him realize I wasn't just huffing and puffing because he called me—and we settled things—a few days later.

Sometimes, too, it pays to have your opponent "stumble" upon your leak himself. A student of mine, selling the contents of his home, was negotiating with a potential buyer for his antique oak drop-leaf table. It just so happened that my student left the business card of an antique dealer right on the table—a card which included the dealer's handwritten appraisal of $600. Allowing his opponent to come across it gave my student's Maximum Supportable Position a quantum leap in credibility.

Painting Yourself into a Corner

Think back to the case of the exasperated supervisor whose workers have been wreaking havoc with his work schedule by taking a vacation day here and there, rather than at a week or two at a time. You'll recall that he paid a visit to the personnel department and had a policy implemented prohibiting vacations of less than a week without prior approval from personnel. So the next time one of his workers bounded in and said, "Hey boss, I'd like to take off next Monday," he could say, "I'm afraid you can't do that. Haven't you seen the new vacation policy issued by personnel?"

What the boss did here was purposely paint himself into a corner. He imposed an artificial limit on his Settlement Range, thus creating a barrier as to how far he could be pushed and how much his opponents could hope to gain from negotiating with him. Painting yourself into a corner can be extremely helpful not only when you want to limit what your opponent stands to gain, but also when you want to avoid negotiating with him altogether.

When companies and businesses establish policies, the whole point is to paint themselves into a corner so as to restrict what they're *allowed* to give you, thereby limiting your negotiating room. I italicize the word "allowed" because that's precisely what they want you to think—that their hands are tied, that they're not allowed, as if by divine decree, to give you what you want. "I'm sorry, it's policy," they say and hope like hell you go away. The impression they assiduously cultivate is that you have no recourse. But often you do; often the policies are not so sacrosanct as they lead you to believe. If your opponent paints himself into a corner, make sure he really is in a corner and not just bluffing that he is. Policies, in many instances, are just bluffs. Take my negotiation with the pocket dictating machine salesman. After agreeing to exchange my defective machine the first time, the salesman painted himself into a corner: "I can't make another exchange for you. Our policy is only one per customer." Oh, well excuse me, I didn't know I was treading on one of your sacred policies. And how sacred was it? Not very, at least not so much that the salesman and his boss weren't willing to chuck it out the window so the company president wouldn't get a nasty letter from me.

Sure, there are times when you can't get around a policy. Say you're a twenty-two-year-old male with a couple of speeding tickets. You're looking for auto insurance, and the agent says, "You're an assigned risk. Our policy is not to give out policies to assigned risks." That's going to be a tough nut to crack. But the point is to test a policy if you have any doubts whatever about its supposed inviolability. Make sure your opponent genuinely has no options in the matter. Len had just purchased a new imported car. Fifty-three miles down the road, the rear axle seized, smoke billowed out the rear, and the shiny showpiece ground to an unceremonious halt. It turned out that the mechanic had failed to tighten the filler plug on the axle, which allowed the grease to escape. Len was told it would take several weeks to get a new axle, as it had to be ordered from Japan. "Can't you take one off another car in the lot?"

"No, yours is a brand-new model and we have no others like it," said the sales manager.

"Well, I have to have a car. Why don't you loan me one until mine's ready?"

"We can't. It's against policy." Len expressed his unhappiness and said he would write to the president of the company, if he had to, to get the matter resolved satisfactorily.

"Go ahead. Policy is policy." Along with the details of his complaint, Len, who had spoken with a lawyer friend, also let the president know he was seriously considering legal action, since the manufacturer's negligence could well have done him physical harm. Four days later Len got a call from the sales manager. "We've got a brand-new car for you. And, for no extra charge, we're giving you a four-door model and a rear defroster." Policies are not all that they're cracked up to be.

Be on the lookout for opportunities where you can paint yourself into a corner, seal off the bottom part of your Settlement Range, and place a limit on what your opponent can negotiate out of you. Deadlines, policies, laws or regulations—they all can work toward that end. But while the visibility of this tactic gives it high credibility ("I can't help you and here's why"), be aware that painting yourself into a corner also entails a high risk of deadlock in the event that the options you've left your opponent with are not within his Settlement Range. For instance, a while back I was party to a negotiation in which a state human services agency, seeking to curb its spending in certain programs for the elderly, arbitrarily passed a regulation declaring that locally run programs for the aged which did not provide services for at least one hundred people on a regular basis would not be eligible for state funds. This was totally unacceptable to the statewide network of organizations that provides such services. Rebuffed by the agency, they took their case directly to the legislature, which, under heavy pressure, put the heat on the agency to rescind the regulation.

A safer course of action than locking yourself into a position you can't get out of is pretending that you've painted yourself into a corner—such as by instituting a policy. That way, if your opponent is up in arms and threatens to fight you to the end, you can always allow for an exception to the policy.

Problem Solving

Negotiating for a new job, Shirley and her prospective employer have hit a snag. She wants very much to work there, and he wants very much to hire her. The problem, plain and simple, is dollars. What Shirley feels she's worth is more than the boss says he can pay. "I'm not disputing that you're worth every penny," he says, "but paying you that salary would send shock waves around here if the other workers found out. I can't afford an insurrection." Does this mean it's time to deadlock? Not at all—at least not yet. It means it's time for some problem-solving.

"What about a bonus at the end of the year?" suggests Shirley.

"That wouldn't work, I'm afraid. Everyone gets a bonus, and yours would be so much higher that I'd have the same problem as if I just hired you outright at the salary you're talking about." The boss does some more thinking. "Wait a minute. How would you feel about getting the extra income in a way other than up-front dollars? We could offer you a more comprehensive benefit package, an improved pension plan, and a company car. Taken together, these factors would move your income to an acceptable level, don't you think?"

"Of course I'll have to see the figures and details of what you're talking about, but yes, I think that arrangement sounds fine."

In negotiations where both you and your opponent *want* to settle but you can't agree on the specifics of *how*, problem-solving can be an indispensable tactic. It's a process by which you and your opponent join forces to try to find a way around a stumbling block so you can both get what you want—a settlement. In Shirley's case, for instance, she had a goal—a certain amount of money—that required an action on the part of the employer, namely, agreeing to that salary. But he could not do that. So they sat down and figured out a way her goal could be met by an alternative course of action. That's problem-solving in a nutshell.

A company wants to hire Roy to be the editor of its in-house publication. They agree on salary; the problem is that Roy is involved in a free-lance book research project and the company wants to hire him immediately. That requires an action—dropping the project forthwith—that Roy cannot accept. So the two sides put their heads together and decide that, for the month that Roy needs to complete his project, the retiring editor will stay on the job and Roy will work two days a week.

Another case of problem-solving to the rescue involves Ginny, who wants to have a bathroom installed in her basement. She has budgeted $3,500 for the job, but after checking around, the lowest estimate she got was for $4,000. She wants the bathroom and the contractor wants the job. "But I haven't got $4,000," she says, What to do? The contractor wants to meet her goal, the new bathroom, but he can't do it the way she wanted—tile floors and walls, a certain kind of sink and faucet, with design she had in mind—for $4,000. But thinking it over, he tells her he can meet her goal in a different way—a linoleum floor, waterproof wallpaper, a standard sink, and a few design alterations that will make the plumbing work easier. "The bathroom you'll get won't be different functionally," he says. "Just in frills. And I can do it for $3,500."

There is more than one way to skin a cat. When you and your opponent both stand to gain from a settlement, when you agree on a goal but can't quite agree on the action needed to meet the goal, tackle the problem jointly. Do some brainstorming; you'll be surprised how often the two of you can come up with an alternative plan that will circumvent the problem, fulfill the goal, and salvage the settlement.

Authority Limits

The salesman is practically drooling. His biggest commission in months is just a handshake away. Or so he thinks. "I've agreed to compromise and meet your $3,600 price. So we've got a deal, right?"

"As far as I'm concerned we do," says the buyer. "But first, of course, I have to check with my boss."

Sometimes it can be a big advantage in negotiation to have limited authority . . . or to say you have limited authority. Whether the buyer really did have to check with his boss, we don't know. But we do know that by invoking the tactic of authority limits, he gave himself some more time to mull the deal over.

This tactic assists you in other ways as well. For one thing, when you have an ongoing negotiating relationship with your opponent, it provides a good way of maintaining good relations when you have to say no. "Understand that I really wanted this deal to go through. But the board of directors put the kibash on it, and what can I do? They've got final say-so." The disappointment and/or anger your opponent may feel is tempered by the fact that he knows you're not responsible for it. Authority limits also give you a means to deflect the intimidation, anger, threats, etc., that your opponent may bring out in an effort to get you to settle. "This is ridiculous," your opponent rails. "You'd have to be a pretty shabby businessman to not recognize that you'll never get a better offer than this . . . anytime, anywhere. You haven't given me one good reason why you shouldn't accept it."

"I quite agree—it is ridiculous," you say. "I happen to think your offer is a very good one. It's the people upstairs who are dragging their feet, and they've got me under orders to drag mine."

By setting up an authority hierarchy for your negotiation, you also give yourself protection and the opponent a big incentive to deal squarely with you. A friend of mine recently was negotiating with a corporate legal department to change a clause in a contract. "I appreciate the way you're cooperating in this matter," he told them. "As soon as we're finished here, I'm going right over to my lawyer's and let him read it, so hopefully, if he has no objections, we can have this straightened out this afternoon." Knowing that Big Brother is watching, the legal department wasn't at liberty to try to pull any fast ones on an unsuspecting layman. The same thing went for the man who was negotiating with a teenager who was interested in buying his car. Any temptation on the man's part to conveniently forget telling the youngster about the car's liabilities were summarily dashed when the teenager announced, "My uncle who's a mechanic is coming over in a little while to look over the car and if he says okay, we can go ahead."

You also can use authority limits to apply a subtle pressure on your opponent to reach agreement with you, so you won't have to bring the authority into the matter. A student of mine recently told me of the time she was negotiating with a furniture salesman. She loved one particular sofa, which was marked $565. "Is this the one you want?" asked the salesman.

"Well—yes. But I'm afraid I'm going to have to check with my husband. He told me to check with him if I was thinking of buying anything over $500." Rather than risk losing the sale and dealing with her husband, who would probably try to talk her out of it anyway, the salesman quickly agreed to let her have the sofa for $500.

On the defensive side, always try to find out if your opponent has full authority. If he doesn't, demand to negotiate with whoever does. If you get resistance, which you often will ("Since the boss is tied up in a meeting now, he's instructed me to talk with you"), be careful not to give up too much of your negotiating room in bargaining with the subordinate. Because chances are, when the honcho enters the picture, he's going to be expecting you to give up even more. Also be on the lookout for the ratcheting ploy in which a series of opponents will try to extract every concession they can from you. This happens to salesmen all the time. They'll negotiate with one buyer, make a concession or two, and think they've reached a deal at $1,000 a widget. Then another buyer comes along, moves them down to $900, and bows out, clearing the way for still another cohort who will try to do likewise. Negotiate very grudgingly when you know you're not dealing with an opponent who isn't calling all the shots. Because no matter what you give away now, chances are you'll be put upon to give away still more later. Conversely, whatever concessions you get from your opponent are subject to approval by a higher authority. You may think you're close to nailing down a nice settlement, only to have the boss man come along and say, "I'm sorry, but Johnson here does not have the authority to grant such concessions. I'm afraid we're going to have to begin our discussions anew."

Often an effective way of dealing with an opponent of limited authority is to insist the agreements you reach be ratified piece by piece, thus protecting you from wrapping up the entire package only to have it unwrapped by the authority. Plus, this piecemeal approach tends to wear out your opponent and might be enough to induce him to put pressure on the person with clout to deal directly with you. Not many opponents will want to put up with continuously hearing you say, "Okay, check with your boss to make sure what we've just agreed on is acceptable, and then we can move on to the next issue. . . ."

Mind Tricks

The less willing you are to hold out and bargain hard, the more your opponent stands to gain from a settlement with you. With that in mind, many opponents will do everything they can to sap you of your negotiating drive, to manipulate you into caving in when they want you to cave in. The way they do it is with a far-ranging tactic that I call mind tricks, which is comprised of a host of specific tactics, all of which are designed to play on your mind—on your conditioning, your values, your fears, etc.—in a way that will induce you to negotiate with less resolve . . . or not at all.

This sampling of mind tricks is offered so that, should your opponent try to pull one or more of them on you, you'll be able to recognize them for what they are . . . and disregard them.

Fairness and Reasonableness. Beware of statements such as "Don't you think you're being unreasonable?"

"I think I'm being more than reasonable. Why can't you do the same?"

"Do you honestly feel that what you're asking for is fair?"

"What's wrong with a compromise? Don't you want to be fair?"

Remember, fairness is in the eye of the beholder. What you may think of as fair may be totally unacceptable to me, and vice versa. Your opponent is trying to get the best deal he can for himself, just as you are. Does that mean you're being unreasonable? Moreover, if he genuinely believes that you are being unreasonable, what's stopping him from walking out? Remember, he's appealing to you in this way to gain a tactical advantage—to move you toward your Least Acceptable Result. It's entirely possible, of course, that you *will* have to make concessions in order to reach a settlement. Just make sure you're backing off because you have to, and not because you've been mind-tricked into living up to your opponent's supposed standards of fairness and reasonableness.

Intimidation and Anger.

"Your offer is an insult!"

"Don't you know a great deal when you see one?!"

"You've been dragging this thing out for days now! Do you want a deal or not?"

"If you can't do any better than that, I'd just as soon call the whole thing off here and now."

"What do you think, I'm made of money?"

Keep calm. Withstand the torrent of abuse your opponent is heaping on you. Remember, if he gets the idea that you're susceptible to being bullied by anger and/or intimidation, he's going to keep it up. Conversely, if you show him you're not about to be dissuaded by his tactics, he'll likely abandon them and search for another way of getting you to settle where he wants.

Guilt-Peddling. You know your opponent is trying to work you over with this old favorite when you hear things like:

"I thought we understood each other better than that."

"I'm surprised at you."

"How can you do this to me after all I've done for you?"

"What do you think—that you're so much better than everyone else around here? Molloy, for example, he works just as hard as you, and you don't see him demanding the shirt off my back."

Hold on to your perspective. You're not doing anything you should feel guilty about. You're simply negotiating effectively to meet a particular goal. It's no doing of yours if your opponent chooses to take a dim view of your actions. You're not trying to take advantage of him; remember, you're merely trying to stand up for your own cause. What's there to feel guilty about?

Authority, Legitimacy, and Expertise. Often an opponent will employ rank, professional standing, and expertise to get you to back off by saying, in effect, "You shouldn't bargain with me because I am who I am." This is a particularly common ploy of doctors, lawyers, and other such folk who are accustomed to going unchallenged. Some for instances:

"I think I have a little more knowledge in this area than you, wouldn't you agree?"

"My bill is $500 because that's the accepted norm for this kind of work."

"You've got some nerve challenging me this way. Who do you think you're talking to, anyway?"

"You're asking for something that's just not done. Here, I'll show you where it's expressly prohibited in our manual of policies and procedures."

"I assure you, there's no need to read the fine print. It's a standard contract. I'm sure you've seen it a hundred times before."

When greeted with this mind trick, keep in mind—and tell your opponent—that you're not calling into question his professionalism or credibility. That's not the issue; the issue is your negotiating goal, which you have every right to pursue regardless of what your high-and-mighty opponent wants you to think. Don't let yourself be cowed just because he says this "isn't done" or because he behaves as though you've mortally wounded him merely by standing up for yourself. Remind yourself that he's pulling this stunt because he prefers not to negotiate with you, and not because he truly believes what you're asking for is out of line. Stick to your guns.

Flattery and Charm. Among the most insidious of mind tricks, this tactic is an attempt by your opponent to get you to swap your ego needs for his negotiating needs. He may talk about how wonderful your children are, how much he's heard about you and your splendid operation, how beautifully you've decorated the house, or how wonderful a job candidate you are and the fact that he can't pay you what you're asking should not be taken as a reflection of what he thinks of you, you impeccably qualified devil, you. Hearing nice things about yourself is fine and dandy. Just be careful that the stream of soft soap doesn't interfere with your negotiating with gusto for what you want.

Using an Agent

No matter how proficient a negotiator you are, there are situations in which you'll want a professional agent to handle the bargaining for you. Lawyers, real estate and insurance brokers, literary, dramatic, media, sports, and public relations agents—all of these people can be indispensable when you have to negotiate in their areas of specialization. Even apart from their superior knowledge of their fields, their contacts and their clout, agents are valuable to you in a number of other ways. They provide you with a screen behind which you can conceal your Settlement Range and the pressures on you to settle. A literary agent, for example, is attempting to sell a book proposal for a struggling young writer. At this point in his career, the writer would be willing to write the book for a paltry $2,000 advance. But by using an agent as a go-between, he pushes his acute need for the deal into the background. While the agent may in fact back down to $2,000, he's in a much better position to give himself extra negotiating room and push the book harder than the writer would be if he were to try to peddle it himself.

An agent also enables you to establish an authority hierarchy for your negotiation, the advantages of which we've already discussed. Your opponent is much less likely to try any funny business when he knows you have a pro on your side. The presence of an agent also leaves you the option of playing good guy/bad guy with your opponent. "I'd love to settle with you, Harry, but my client is really being a pain in the neck about this. He's not going to budge much, but let me try talking to him, and I'll see what I can do for you."

Be aware, however, that an agent's top priority is to his own business, not yours. While you don't want to meddle so much that you limit his effectiveness in representing you, neither do you want to give him carte blanche to do as he pleases in every situation. Your best interest and your agent's best interest do not always coincide. Recently I was negotiating with someone else's real estate agent, who, in her quest to wrap up the sale and get her commission, gave away her client's Settlement Range. "Oh sure, they'll come down $5,-000." Clearly, her self-interest superseded her clients'. You want the agent to handle the negotiation but stay close enough to it that you know what's going on and when your agent's needs and yours may be taking divergent paths.

Walkout

As the name suggests, walkout is a tactic that seemingly invites deadlock by your walking out of the bargaining. Indeed, deadlock *will* result if your opponent won't give up any more of his Settlement Range. But often, on seeing his potential settlement walking out the door, your opponent will give up something extra, and that's how walkout plays to your advantage. Many opponents, remember, won't make substantial concessions until the eleventh hour of the negotiation; by walking out, you're letting him know the eleventh hour is at hand and that if he's planning on improving his offer, he'd better do it or kiss the settlement goodbye. It's an effective way of putting added pressure on your opponent and of testing to see how much he needs the settlement. If he's close to reaching an agreement with you after all and his need is pressing, he's not going to let you get away so easily.

Walkout, of course, is not a tactic you want to use when *your* need for the deal is high. You don't want to run the risk of having him allow you to walk out and scuttle your chances of settlement altogether. But when deadlock is *not* an unthinkable prospect for you, you might consider giving walkout a whirl. If you've been bargained down to at or near your Least Acceptable Result, you don't have much to lose anyway. You're taking a greater risk, naturally, when your opponent's offer is comfortably above your L.A.R. and you're walking out in the hope of getting something even better. That's your prerogative; just make sure that you're walking out and rejecting an acceptable deal because your reading of your opponent and the situation tells you that the likelihood is that he can give you something more, and not because you simply feel like engaging him in a game of chicken. Put another way, don't let your ego talk you into rejecting a deal when there isn't a realistic chance of doing better.

Dirty Tricks

If your opponent has it in his mind to get the best of you, there are a host of underhanded options at his devious disposal—lying, cheating, distortion, blackmail, and fraud are but a few of them. But there *do* seem to be a few dirty tricks that are the most popular with unethical negotiators. I offer you brief descriptions of them here so that if you do run up against them, you'll recognize them for what they are and, if at all possible, avoid negotiating with that opponent any further. Agreeing to a deal with an untrustworthy opponent is like eating a bad apple; it may seem palatable enough at first, but sooner or later it's going to bite back.

Low-Ball. This is a tactic often used by unscrupulous car salesmen. What it involves is giving you a terrific price—so terrific, in fact, that it's lower than he can actually afford to give you. But that doesn't matter to the shifty salesman; he's just going to jack it up later anyway. What low-balling does is induce you to stop looking elsewhere (since you know you won't get such a deal anywhere else), and lure you into the salesman's clutches. Once he's got you, he tells you his boss has vetoed the price or some such tale of bull and tries to convince you that even though you'll have to pay more than you thought, the deal is still an extraordinary value for you. The salesman, of course, will be overbearingly apologetic about the "misunderstanding" and will do everything in his power to reinforce your decision to buy from him in spite of it. On the basis of the low-ball price, you've made up your mind to deal with him, and he doesn't want you having second thoughts.

If you suspect you're being low-balled, demand that the offer be made in writing. If your opponent resists—on whatever spurious ground—you'd be well-advised to take your negotiation elsewhere. But if you do decide to give him the benefit of the doubt and see if his offer is on the up and up, don't get your head locked into dealing with him. Once he abandons his offer, hit the road . . . and don't come back.

High-Ball. You're right; this is the opposite of the low-ball. High ball is an attempt by your opponent to buy something—goods, services, whatever—from you, with an inflated offer on which he has no intention of making good. When you've turned away the competitors and decided to accept his offer, he concocts some means of slipping out of his commitment. A student of mine was high-balled when she was looking for a job. A company made her what seemed to be an outstanding offer, which she accepted, only to be told later that, due to some murky personnel policy or salary scale, she would have to take $1,500 less. She told the company what to do with the offer, as well she should have; any company that would pull a high-ball stunt is not worth working five minutes for.

Here, too, if you think there may be something fishy about an offer, make sure to get the offer in writing. You've got every reason to think high-ball if your opponent will not cooperate.

Bait and Switch. An employment agency advertises a host of very attractive job openings. Sure you're interested, so you go in, only to be told that all the spots you want to pursue are filled. "But we've got many other attractive alternatives for you, so why don't you sign here and we'll find you something you'll be very happy with." That's bait and switch. This tactic is also popular with disreputable apartment referral services, which list apartments to arouse your interest—six rooms, river view, luxury building, $250—that do not exist. Having baited you, they'll tell you that the apartment has been taken, then make an impassioned plea for your $50 up-front money, so you can have the privilege of looking at their "extensive" listings in your price range and desired location. You're baited with A, then switched over to B; that's how this dastardly little devil of a trick works. If the bait seems to vanish before your eyes, best to take your nibble elsewhere.

Renegotiation. Renegotiation is an attempt by your opponent to reopen bargaining on a deal you have already closed. If your opponent is trying to get you to restructure the entire deal, you might as well walk away because if he tries it once, he's likely to try it again, each time angling to weasel something more out of you. On the other hand, if his desire to renegotiate focuses on a peripheral issue, it might be worth your while to hear him out. You can always scuttle the deal if you think he's trying to pull a fast one. If he's not and you do decide to reopen the bargaining, don't forget that renegotiation cuts both ways. If you make a change to accommodate him, he should be willing to make an extra concession somewhere for you. In any case, exercise great care when an opponent seeks to renegotiate. Make him show you that he's dealing in good faith before you accede to his wishes.

As in every other facet of negotiation, it's best to trust your instincts when it comes to dirty tricks. If you smell smoke, there's probably a fire smoldering there somewhere, and if you allow it to ignite, you stand a good chance of getting burned. Be very wary of deals that seem too good to be true; they probably are too good to be true. Don't yield to the temptation of get-rich-quick schemes, of deals that promise something for nothing. In sum, no settlement, no matter how good, is worth pursuing if you suspect the guy on the other side of the table is dealing in bad faith because, in spite of all his avowals to the contrary, the deal probably isn't worth the paper it's written on. Your opponent's promises and a token will get you on the subway and nothing more.

Don't allow greed to get the better of you. Be content to get something for something. Because, fortified with everything you've learned in this book, the somethings you get . . . through ethical, legitimate negotiating skill . . . will compare very favorably with the somethings you give.

CHAPTER 11

Research and Planning: A Little Digging Goes a Long Way

THE ROAD OF negotiation is littered with question marks. Much as I would like summarily to sweep them away for you, it simply can't be done. Uncertainty is inbred in the negotiating process. No matter how accomplished a negotiator you are, there will always be variables you cannot control. And as long as there is another human being on the other side of the table, there will always be a large element of guesswork to contend with. To wit:

All people negotiate.

All people can be unpredictable.

All people who negotiate can be unpredictable.

Q.E.D.

Because so much of negotiation revolves around trying to read someone else's mind and because reading minds is a problematical enterprise at best, negotiation can't help but be problematical too. What is your opponent's Settlement Range? What are his fears? pressures? needs? How good a bluffer is he? How trustworthy is he? What is his negotiating style? Is he likely to be a mouse or a lion, a softie or hardliner? What will he think about you and your demands? What will his reaction be? Guesswork abounds. Is there a mind reader in the house?

Still, your inability to read minds notwithstanding, you *can* take steps to minimize the guesswork. These steps are subsumed in a single, wide-ranging process: planning. When you enter a negotiation, you want to have as few question marks as possible swimming around your head, and that's what

138

planning is all about. Planning assists you in two critical ways: it enables you to make at least an educated guess about the things you can't know (i.e., your opponent's needs, fears, reactions, etc.) and to gather as much information as you can about the things you can know (i.e., the germane facts surrounding the negotiation and your own needs and goals). While you can't crawl into your opponent's head, with careful planning, you can get pretty damn close. And while you can't know *all* the facts, you usually can uncover enough information about an assortment of factors (How's your opponent's financial picture? Did a new used-car dealer just open up across the street? How's his standing in the company? Is he in his boss's doghouse, and can you help him get out? What's the demand for what he's offering? Are people knocking down his door to deal with him? etc.) to provide you with valuable insight into how to approach the negotiation.

Planning has an unjustifiably bad reputation. Many people I've encountered seem to think of it as a thankless, painstaking process, which, if done properly, must result in a veritable encyclopedia of information. That simply isn't so. The amount of planning you do for a negotiation should be proportional to the importance of the negotiation to you. You have to do a little cost-benefit analysis of the situation. If you just want an extra hour for lunch because you're meeting an old friend, are you really going to go to great lengths to plan your negotiation with your boss? Of course not. For one thing, you see no reason why he won't agree, so the likelihood is that you won't have to negotiate with him at all. Besides, it's not all that important to you to warrant going to a lot of time and trouble. So maybe the extent of your planning will be to make sure, when you go in to talk to him, that you have the report—the one he's been asking for—in your hands. Not long ago I was walking past a discount appliance store when I remembered that I had been wanting to get a new clock radio. Was I going to put a lot into the planning of the negotiation? No. It would've been silly. I knew the store had good prices, and I decided it wasn't worth $10 or even $20 to run all over town, trying to find a better price so I might be able to talk the storeowner down. My planning began and ended with the idea of offering to pay cash instead of using a credit card in exchange for a ten percent discount.

Now if I had been shopping for a new living room set, that would've been a different story. Just as it would have been a different story if you had wanted to ask your boss, not for an extra hour for lunch, but for an extra two weeks vacation for the year. You want the amount of effort you put into planning to be commensurate with the importance of the negotiation. Get in the habit of asking yourself, "How much is this negotiation worth to me? How much planning does it warrant?"

Whether you decide it's worth two minutes or two weeks of planning, the important thing is that you plan. Always plan. You'll be happily surprised how many question marks it will sweep away.

Setting Goals and Your Settlement Range

The first question marks you want to dispense with are your own. The first step toward accomplishing this is to ask yourself, "What exactly are my goals in this negotiation?" You have to know *what* you want to get it. Particularly in simple buy-sell negotiations, what you want could hardly be more obvious. In our ongoing negotiation, for instance, your goal is to buy a typewriter and mine is to sell one. But there *are* times when your goal is not so readily apparent, and that's when you have to take care to really zero in on what you want. Remember the case of the woman negotiating to do a series on cooking for a public television station? Initially, she was thinking of the negotiation strictly in terms of dollars; it was only after further probing that she focused in on her true goal—getting exposure for herself and, thus, increased sales of the cookbook she had written. This is not to say that locating your true goal in even a complex negotiation is anything terribly elusive or difficult; rather, to point out that it will do you well, just as a precautionary measure, to think carefully through what you want to pursue once the bargaining begins.

After establishing your goal, the next step is to define how your opponent can help you achieve it. Again, in the simpler negotiations where your goal is completely tangible, it's obvious what actions your opponent can take to help you. I can sell you the typewriter. No mystery there. But in complex negotiations, where there are often goals that are not distinctly quantifiable, the actions your opponent can take are not so obvious.

For example, let's say you're about to negotiate with a prospective employer for a new job. There are a number of different factors of importance to you, so you establish a number of different goals—salary, pension, other benefits, success on the job. For your first three goals, the way your opponent can help you is clear. All he has to do is agree to them, and that's that. But what about your goal of success on the job? He can't just say, "Okay, you'll succeed on the job," this goal is not so cut and dried. For you to succeed on the job, your prospective employer must provide you with the requisite tools such as a budget, manpower, and scope of authority. You can't meet your goal without these tools, so those are the demands you must make to achieve it.

Your next step is to establish a Settlement Range for your various goals. You need a Settlement Range for each separate action you want your opponent to take to enable you to meet your goals. Thus, if different goals require the same action on the part of your opponent, they will require a single Settlement Range. In your job negotiation, for example, your first three goals—salary, pension, and other benefits—all call for the same action, which can be reduced to something very tangible—money. As a result, these goals can be subsumed under one Settlement Range. Since your other, less quantifiable goals require different actions by your opponent, you need a separate Settlement Range for each action. So you set up Settlement Ranges for budget, manpower, and scope of authority.

Once you've lined up the Settlement Ranges that you'll need for the negotiation, you calculate precisely what their parameters will be—that is, you calculate for each one a Least Acceptable Result and a Maximum Supportable Position. The sum of your M.S.P.'s for all your Settlement Ranges constitutes your opening demand in the negotiation. Maybe you've decided that the most you can justifiably ask for salary/pension/benefits is a combined total of $50,000; for your non-personnel budget, $100,000; for manpower, ten workers; for scope of authority, the right to report directly to the vice-president for marketing. Taken together, those M.S.P.'s form your collective M.S.P. for the negotiation. However, it's a different story at the other end of your Settlement Ranges. The sum of your Least Acceptable Results may or may not equal your Least Acceptable Result for the entire negotiation. Perhaps you've determined that the job would not be worth your while if you are pushed to your L.A.R.'s across the board.

If that is the case, how can you locate the settlement that is at least minimally acceptable to you? And with so many Settlement Ranges to keep track of, how do you know which mix of proposed settlements from your opponent is the best for you? The answer is that you must try to rank each proposal by determining the relative priority of each demand and deciding what trade-offs you would be willing to make between them. For instance, let's say that you've determined that, for this negotiation, the dollar package is your top priority. To secure a deal that would give you as close to your $50,000 M.S.P. as possible, you've decided that you would be willing to back down to your L.A.R. on all the other demands. Now, what if your prospective employer offers you only a $35,000 salary/pension/benefits package, but gives you tremendous scope of authority. "You'll report directly to me," he says. "And you might be interested to know that the last three persons who've had your position have all moved up to top management positions." Now what? Well, you've got to get into a juggling act with your trade-offs. Does your broad authority and the excellent opportunity for promotion mean enough to you to accept the lower dollar figure? Salary is your top priority, remember, but it's nonetheless conceivable that these factors might be attractive enough to make that a trade-off you would be willing to make. Or what if the financial offer totals only $30,000, but the employer agrees to meet your M.S.P. for every other demand? Is that a trade-off to your liking? Is it worth it to you to come down that far in dollars in exchange for having an outstanding chance to do a bang-up job and getting a handsome raise in the near future?

These are the kinds of questions you must contend with in multiple-goal negotiations such as this. It all comes down to your priorities. When you have so many alternatives to grapple with, ranking the settlements is not an exact science. Your only recourse is to judge each proposal by weighing the trade-offs you have to make and determining how well it meets your top priorities of the negotiation.

Fortunately, most of the negotiations you'll be involved in will not be anywhere near this complicated. Usually, you'll have a single goal and won't have to worry about sorting through priorities, making trade-offs, or ranking settlements. But while multiple-goal negotiations are a special and often confusing case, the basic steps you take to plan them are the same ones you take in simpler negotiations. First, you set your goals. Second, you translate the goals into actions the opponent can take to help you achieve them (whether it's directly, such as with money or simply selling you a car; or indirectly, such as by providing you with the means to succeed on the job). And third, you set up your Settlement Ranges for each action you desire your opponent to take. Once you know what *you* want and you have your own house in order, you can turn your planning efforts toward your opponent and the facts surrounding the negotiation.

Information Gathering

Say you're stranded in a dark, cavernous mansion. You grope around in the utter blackness, uncertain of where each little step might lead you. Stumbling into a wall, you happen upon a light switch. Flick—what a difference. Less tentative now, you move into another room and find another light, then another. Glimmers of light lace the once uninterrupted darkness. You can't see everything—you probably never will—but you have a much sharper sense of where you're going.

So it is with researching the facts of your negotiation. A little bit of fact can cast an awful lot of light on the subject. The more you know, the better you'll be able to see where you're going. Why negotiate in the dark when you can do it in the light?

Say you're shopping for a used car. You spot an advertisement in the paper for the right model in the right price range. Before you go see it, you do a little research. You consult back issues of *Consumer Reports*, checking the car's maintenance record and how it fared in the safety and handling tests. Looks pretty good. You call your friend Hank, the auto mechanic. "A solid, reliable car," he reports. "But one thing to be aware of is that they tend to be very hard on transmissions. If the car has more than fifty thousand miles on the original transmission, you might want to think twice about it." Investing a mere hour in research has yielded a good amount of valuable information. Not only do you now have much keener insight into the worth of the car and a basis for altering your Settlement Range accordingly; you have also provided yourself with increased credibility for the upcoming negotiation. "I know these things have a history of going through transmissions," you say. "Is this the original?" How is your opponent going to respond? Apart from being impressed with your knowledge, he's probably going to start thinking, "This guy sounds like he really knows cars. He's probably going to be a tough customer to bargain with." Bravo for you—that's just what you want him to think. When you come across as an expert, or at least as someone with more than passing knowledge of a subject, you send your opponent a powerful message: "Don't try to snow me. I know what I'm talking about." It gives you the upper hand, which frequently translates into a better settlement for you.

Your display of information also instills in your opponent an uncertainty as to how good a deal he can get from you. People tend to lose much of their resolve when they're face-to-face with a well-informed opponent. They clam up, not wanting to run the risk of saying something that sounds foolish or is wrong. "I notice there is uneven tire wear on your car," you comment. "Has the front end been checked out lately? That right upper ball joint concerns me too. It's quite loose. Does she shimmy a lot on the highway?" With each such tidbit you throw out, your opponent's willingness to hold out is shaken.

Go back to the typewriter negotiation. You've done a little digging before coming to see me. You've leafed through *Consumer Reports* and learned some things about the performance rating, durability, and service record of my machine. You've stopped in to see a local dealer and happened to find out that, in his opinion, my machine is the best one that manufacturer has ever put on the market. "Practically indestructible," he said. You've even unearthed a writer's magazine outlining four simple tests you can use to judge the typewriter's condition.

You've changed the tenor of the whole negotiation. You're in the driver's seat. You're telling me things about my machine that I don't even know. "What's this stuff about problems with the carriage on this model?" I'm wondering. I'm positively wowed when you start running through your battery of tests. You have me thinking that you know more about the worth of my machine that I do. I have to take you seriously. More importantly, I have to take your M.S.P. seriously. Your research has bolstered its credibility, while at the same time eroding the credibility of *my* asking price. The result is that you stand a much better chance of talking me down.

Preparedness also breeds respect. Take a new job negotiation, for instance. Think how much more favorable an impression you'll convey if you have some basic facts about the company at your command. "I'm aware that distribution has presented some problems for you in the past. Have these difficulties been rectified or would that be part of my responsibility?" Just like that, you have significantly enhanced your attractiveness as a candidate. You've demonstrated to your prospective employer not only that you are knowledgeable, but also that you had the interest and resourcefulness to explore the firm's situation. That says a lot for you. You're not just another hopeful who's telling them how much it would mean to you to work for their company.

For virtually every negotiation, there's a wealth of information to be had; all you have to do is find it. I've found the best place to start the hunt, and often end it, is at the library. Between books, magazines, almanacs, digests, and directories, you're bound to come up with information that will be very useful for your negotiation. If you get stuck, talk to your librarian. He should be able to tell you what's available on the subject you're pursuing.

Another enormously helpful means of gathering information is networking. Ask ten friends if they know anything about the subject of your negotiation. If that inquiry turns up dry, ask your ten friends to ask ten friends of theirs. In no time you've tapped a network of a hundred people, and the odds are excellent that someone in that group is going to be able to provide you with some valuable information. Networking has a place near to my heart because that's how I started on the road to getting this book published. Having researched and conducted seminars on negotiation for several years, I was ready to take a crack at writing a book on the subject. The only problem was that I didn't know the first thing about book publishing. So I asked some friends if they could give me any leads and/or information, and they asked some friends, and before long I got the name and number of a woman with several contacts in the industry. I called her, and she gave me the name of an agent/packager who was on the lookout for new projects. I sent him a chunk of material outlining my proposal, and he said words that were music to my ears: "I think you've really got something here." He hooked me up with a writer, Wayne Coffey, and several months later, we had ourselves a book contract.

An important thing to keep in mind when you set about researching your negotiation is that there will never be *enough* information. You simply can't find out everything you would like to know. Unless the negotiation is of overriding importance, don't let yourself get bogged down in the information hunt. Just find out as much as you can and move on to the bargaining table. As long as you have *some* basic facts to illuminate the negotiation, you'll be out of the darkness . . . and into an enviable negotiating position.

Researching Your Opponent

Paula, an experienced public relations consultant, schedules an interview with a prospective client, a mid-sized company we'll call C.L.C., Inc. Several days beforehand, Paula decides to see what she can find out about the company, so she contacts a friend who works there and gave her the lead in the first place. "I don't know how busy you are with other clients," Paula's friend tells her, "but I think this could be a great opportunity for you—and I mean a full-time opportunity. The P.R. department here consists of one person, an elderly man. He was recently hospitalized, and I've heard that since he's close to retirement age anyway, there's a good chance he won't be coming back. Word around here is that the honchos are itching to find someone to take over the department full-time."

Paula has picked up some invaluable information about her opponent. She now knows not only that C.L.C. is looking to hire someone full-time, but also that they want to find someone in a hurry. It puts her in a fantastic bargaining position. Assuming they are impressed with her and her work, of course, Paula knows she can use to her advantage the company's pressing need to install a new P.R. director as soon as possible. While she doesn't know precisely how high a salary she can get from C.L.C., she *does* know that their high degree of need is likely to make them quite flexible in their bargaining.

Researching your opponent, as Paula has, is a vital part of planning your negotiation. Of course, you won't always get hold of the kind of bombshell that Paula did, but usually you can come up with something that provides some insight into what your opponent is thinking. Try to step inside your opponent's shoes. What might be his degree of need for the deal? He'll try not to let on, but is he tipping his hand in any way? Is he tense or fidgety? Does he seem in a hurry to get it over with? Bluffing is a big part of negotiation, but all of us, at one time or another, can be awfully transparent. Sometimes there will be no bluff to see through, and your opponent will mistakenly offer a valuable tidbit right in the course of the bargaining. Wayne told me of a negotiation he had for a car he was selling. After a short test drive, his opponent inquired, "Is the car available right away? I'm going back to school on Saturday." For some inexplicable reason, the student felt obliged to reveal his deadline—his pressing need to find a car before Saturday. No surprise that Wayne got exactly what he had asked for.

What pressures might be impacting on your opponent? Is it 110 degrees in the shade, and is your opponent, looking like he has just run the Boston Marathon, interested in buying the air-conditioner you advertised? If so, I would say you have no sweat. Has his arch-rival, the guy who moved into the sparkling new showroom last week, just put up his "Grand Opening—Discounts Galore" sign? What about your opponent's negotiating style? Is he especially aggressive in his salesmanship or defending his position? Often, such fireworks are a smokescreen for a latent pressure. A friend who was shopping for a house told me of a negotiation he had with a real estate agent. She was so strident in her sales pitch, he said, that she may as well have screamed in his ear, "I really need to sell this house—now!" He wound up getting an extraordinary deal on it. Or what if you encounter an opponent who seems especially timid? Does he offer no counterarguments to bolster the credibility of his position? Does he seem uncomfortable bargaining with you? Having the negotiation over with is probably his top priority. Propose to conclude it with a concrete offer at the top of your Settlement Range.

Also, don't forget to be on the lookout for any unstated needs of your opponents' that may be lurking in the background. Not infrequently in negotiation, the main event can be clinched by your ability to latch on to—and fulfill—such latent needs. Remember the example of Tom, the executive in the truck-leasing company. During discussions with a potential customer, Tom learned that the customer was having problems finding a place where his drivers could park their trucks. With extra parking space at his disposal, Tom met that need and signed on a new customer. Another example: A literary agent is negotiating a book contract with an editor. It comes out amid the bargaining that the editor needs two rewrites done by next month. With a couple of starving writers at his beck and call, the agent says he has just the people for the task. The agent is a hero all the way around; he gets work for needy clients, he meets the editor's peripheral need, and he secures a good deal on the contract to boot.

It also never hurts to see if you can find someone who has negotiated with your opponent before. Learn about his style. Does it follow a pattern? Does he always come on with lots of bravado but turn into a lamb if you don't buckle under right away? What about his track record on following through? Is he as good as his word? If he isn't, is there any way you can possibly avoid negotiating with him? What about his ego? Would it fill the Rose Bowl? I've been in more than one negotiation where I was able to parlay an opponent's considerable ego need into a bargaining success. There's really nothing to it; give him enough of the old soft soap, and he's going to have such overwhelming respect for your judgment in people that he'll likely agree to anything . . . and probably ask you to come back real soon.

The whole idea in researching your opponent in a negotiation is to turn yourself into a sponge. Soak up every morsel of information you can. Be attentive. Look for clues as to what his needs and pressures might be. Study his mannerisms and style. What you're able to absorb, taken together with what you already have learned from your research of the facts relating to the negotiation, will be enormously helpful in getting an idea of where his Least Acceptable Result might be. And that, after all, is what you're trying to get a handle on. You want to say to yourself, "Given the circumstances and given what I've learned about my opponent, how would I be thinking about things if I were him? How willing would I be to hold out for something better, to risk deadlock? How much would I be willing to concede to get a deal?" If you can come up with reasonable estimates of the answers to those questions, you will have done a splendid job of research and given yourself a great shot at getting the best settlement you can.

Anticipating Your Opponent's Reaction

Another question mark you want to obliterate in planning your negotiation involves how your opponent will react to you. To find out, you have to ask yourself, "If I get what I want out of this deal, what shape will that leave my opponent in?" Will he come out ahead? behind? or is it uncertain at this juncture how he will come out?

Anticipating your opponent's reaction is vital to successful planning because your planning, to a large extent, will be dictated by his reaction. For instance, what if you expect that you will have to convince your opponent that it's in his best interest to negotiate with you? For your opponent, then, it's a Show-Me Negotiation; you have to show him what he stands to gain from talking to you. If you hadn't bargained on that reaction, you might well be up the creek. True, you might be able to come up with a compelling reason for him to negotiate with you on the spot, but that's an iffy proposition at best. You have to do enough thinking on your feet in negotiation as it is; the more you do before you even get to the table, the better prepared . . . and better off . . . you'll be.

Remember the case of the secretary who wanted a new typewriter from her boss? She knew she was involved in what probably would be a Show-Me Negotiation, and she planned accordingly. She came up with an incentive for her boss to negotiate with her—namely, that the machine she wanted would more than pay for itself by saving her time and freeing her to attend to other duties around the office. Correctly anticipating her boss's reaction enabled her to devise a sound negotiating plan.

What if it's a one hundred percent Oh-No Negotiation to your opponent, and you're going to have to drag him to the table? Being prepared for that reaction is even more important than being prepared for a Show-Me Negotiation. Because, as we've seen, the way to bring an unwilling opponent around is by creating a Backhanded Need for him; that is, threatening him with something he very much wishes to avoid and, thus, making it in his self-interest to negotiate with you, rather than see the threat carried out. A credible threat (and remember, it must be credible, or it's not going to have any impact at all on your opponent) usually isn't the sort of thing you can come up with on the spur of the moment. It requires some forethought to devise a threat that you're not only capable and willing to follow through on, but also strikes a nerve in your opponent. Sometimes even a carefully thought-out threat—one that you're certain will bring your opponent running to the table—will fail to strike a nerve. You have to come up with another one, no easy task if you haven't given it any consideration beforehand.

Go back to the negotiation I had with the pocket dictating

machine salesman. I had a good idea that, after he had already made one exchange for me, he wouldn't be too keen on doing so again. Not surprised by his "I-can't-help-you-this-time-goodbye" response, I was ready and armed with what I felt would be an effective threat—writing a letter to several of his big customers, explaining my dissatisfaction with the company. You'll recall that that threat got me a big nothing. I failed to hit a nerve. Not to worry. I went back and planned another threat—to contact the president of the company—and, lo and behold, that one did hit home.

What you want to avoid at all costs is getting caught flat-footed by your opponent's reaction. If you approach him to negotiate, and he says "Oh no" and starts fleeing for the hills, and you have no threat on hand to induce him to bargain with you, your negotiation may be over before it even begins. Sometimes you can grab hold of a threat after the fact and come back and approach him again. But since he has slipped away from you once, he may think he'll be able to do it again. The best time to lay the threat on him is the moment you see that "oh no" expression flash across his face. And to have the threat ready at that moment, you will have had to have done some prior thinking about his reaction.

If, after giving it some thought, you decide that your opponent will come out ahead in the negotiation (an Oh-Boy Negotiation), then you don't have anything to worry about. Because he stands to gain from the deal as well, there's no need to convince him that he should negotiate with you or threaten him with certain consequences if he doesn't.

Anticipating your opponent's reaction helps you in another way too, quite apart from aiding in the planning of your negotiation. By giving you an inkling as to what to expect, it siphons off some excess tension and psychologically braces you for what's to come. Being confronted with an unwilling and, perhaps, even hostile opponent is not a pleasant experience. But it's a lot less pleasant still, when that reaction comes as a surprise. Try not to let yourself be caught off guard. Think about how your opponent is likely to react. In the event of a negative reaction, it will enable you to cope much more effectively with the tension. And in the event of any reaction, it will enable you to plan much more effectively.

Looking into the Future

If you know you probably won't be negotiating with your opponent in the future, you have the luxury of being concerned only with the negotiation before you. You can negotiate for the moment without worry of what may happen down the road. Of course, this doesn't give you carte blanche to pull out every dirty trick in the book to get your way; you still have to square your negotiating behavior with your own sense of ethics. But it does give you more room to move. When there's no future with your opponent, you need not be overly concerned about the impression you make, about whether he thinks you are unreasonable, about his reaction to your negotiating style, or, more generally, about projecting a certain image that might help you in negotiations to come. It would be nice if your one-time opponent thought you were reasonable and if he took a liking to you, but sometimes things don't work out that way. I'm sure the guy who works in the dry-cleaning store that lost my shirt doesn't think the world of me. Hell, I threatened to subpoena him to small claims court because he would not cooperate. He probably thinks I'm a real bastard. It's too bad that I had to do that, but the way I see it, he left me no choice. *C'est la vie.* To me, it was more important to be compensated for my loss than to be in the good graces of someone whom I'll never see again.

I may not be especially fond of you either if you take a hard line in our typewriter negotiation. I may think you're unreasonable, perhaps even that you're taking advantage of me. And if I do, of course, I always have the option of not dealing with you. If it distresses you that I feel that way, you can soften your stance and find ways to show me you're not such a cutthroat after all. If it doesn't distress you, well, then, you'll probably forge ahead, trying to secure the best deal you can, my estimation of your character notwithstanding.

The point is that you have that latitude in one-time negotiations, and you don't have it when you expect to be negotiating with your opponent in the future. An ongoing negotiating relationship complicates the situation. It gives you a lot more to keep track of. First off, you want to avoid, if possible, the little cracks that conceivably could grow into a big rift and seriously impair your future relationship. You don't want your opponent to dislike or distrust you or have a distaste for the way you operate. Nor do you want to engage in ego games with him, where each of you, continually is looking for revenge. The idea is to build a mutual trust and respect, attitudes that will provide a solid basis for productive negotiation. Without them, a successful negotiating climate will be impossible because every move will be suspect and nothing will be accepted at face value. You'll wind up spending more time trying to catch each other with a hand in the cookie jar than in finding ways to apportion the cookies to meet your mutual needs.

On the positive side, you want to establish your credibility from square one. You also want to serve notice early on that you are to be taken seriously, trusted, respected, and that you are not the sort to cower in the face of confrontation or intimidation. First impressions die hard. Make yours a good one in the eyes of those you will be negotiating with in the future. A student of mine failed to do that, and he paid the price for two years. His first mistake was accepting a salary offer that was nowhere near commensurate with his responsibilities. From there, he was so eager to perform well for the company—and to avoid confrontation with his superiors—that he agreed to take on extra projects, acceded to outrageous demands, and generally shouldered much more than his share of the work load. It would've been one thing if he had been fairly compensated or given a bonus or something. But the fact was that he was shamelessly manipulated by people who knew he would not stand up for himself. He'd been branded a pushover, and it was an awfully hard tag to shake. When he finally began to try—after a year or so of shabby treatment—he was always put back down in his place. It wasn't hard for his bosses to do; a little guilt-peddling, a hint of confrontation, and he backed off. He finally left the company, and I'm happy to report that his efforts there have served him well in subsequent jobs. But it was a helluva tough way for him to learn a lesson.

To take the other extreme, look at Marvin Miller, the executive director of the Major League Baseball Players Association. In a series of collective bargaining agreements with the owners, Miller has successfully negotiated the players into a position of unprecedented power and earning potential. He was the main architect of the free-agent system, which allows (with a few restrictions) a player to play out his option, leave his team after his contract has expired, and sell himself on the open market. From what we already know about the value of competition, it's hardly surprising that the bidding wars the owners wage for the free agents have resulted in astronomical salaries for the players.

Miller has solidified his negotiating style and reputation impeccably. While many owners (if one can believe the media accounts) despise him, they all have to have a grudging respect for him. Time and again, he has demonstrated that he must be taken seriously, that he'll hold out, take risks, and deadlock, if necessary, and that he cannot be intimidated—not even by twenty-six angry owners—into accepting a settlement that's not in the best interests of the players. Miller has set up his future negotiations beautifully.

When you're going to be negotiating with an opponent in the future, you have to approach your match like a chess player. Plan ahead. If possible, avoid engendering ill-feeling that might harm the future relationship. Work to build mutual good faith, trust, and respect with your opponent. Assert yourself early. Put your best foot forward, cementing your reputation as someone who must be taken seriously; who will listen, but who also must be listened to; who will give, but who also will take; who can be cooperative as well as competitive; and who, while not interested in playing a game of chicken, is not afraid to hold out and risk confrontation, if that's what is necessary to meet your needs.

If you're able to establish yourself in this manner, I can assure you're future negotiating relationship with your opponent will be a fruitful one.

Lining Up Your Ducks

As you get more and more into the planning of your negotiation and get more of a feel for what kind of negotiation it likely will be, you'll get a much sharper idea of what actions should be taken before the bargaining begins. Maybe you're expecting an Oh-No Negotiation, and you'll need a threat to get your opponent to bargain with you. Maybe it's a Show-Me Negotiation you're expecting, and you'll need a way to convince your opponent he'll benefit from the bargaining too. Or maybe, in your planning, you've decided on some goodies you might want to sweeten the pot with, an ally who might be of particular value to you, or perhaps even a way to change the circumstances of the negotiation in your favor.

Once you decide what actions you want to take, take them.

Line up the ducks for your negotiation. Planning doesn't end
with conceiving of ideas to abet your negotiating cause; you
have to implement your ideas for them to have an impact on
the bargaining. Start the wheels in motion. If you determine
that you have to make a threat, sometimes it might be
enough to tell your opponent, "If you won't bargain with me,
I'm going to be forced to do x, y, and z." But sometimes
voicing your threat won't be enough, and in any event, your
threat will carry a good deal more clout if you can show your
opponent that you have already begun to implement it. Recall the case of the employee who was promised a bonus
from his boss but, after leaving the company, had a helluva
time collecting it. Knowing the boss was not in the good
graces of the company's stockholders, the employee elected
to threaten his former boss with a letter to them. But his
planning didn't stop there. He actually wrote the letter and
showed it to the boss when he went in to confront him. The
threat had much more credibility because the employee
flashed concrete evidence that he was indeed prepared to
carry it out.

A group of tenants in an apartment building were upset by
the landlord's poor standard of services. Repeated complaints
got them nowhere, so they decided to threaten him with a
rent strike if the situation did not improve forthwith. And to
show they weren't just talking, they sent him a copy of a peti-
tion, authorizing the strike and bearing the signatures of
ninety percent of the tenants. They devised a threat and then
gave it some muscle. The particular method doesn't much
matter, so long as you get across the message that your threat
is not just a plan, but a well-thought-out course of action that
has already been set in motion.

If your plan calls for enlisting an ally, go ahead and line
up that ally before the bargaining begins. Perhaps you're
preparing to approach your employer for a raise, and you
want all the ammunition you can muster. You start thinking
that maybe that longtime customer of yours, the one who
does such a large volume business with the company and
with whom you enjoy such a cordial relationship would be a
terrific ally. Make sure you get him to write a letter to your
employer saying what a pleasure it is dealing with such an ef-
ficient and professional salesman as you before you sit down
with your boss. Go back to the example about the self-em-

ployed person having difficulty convincing a landlord to rent him an apartment. He came up with a potential ally—a wealthy friend to co-sign the lease—and went ahead and lined him up.

We're not talking about anything terribly abstruse here. All I'm saying is that often mere planning is not enough and that you have to take steps to implement the plan before the negotiation begins. If you plan to change the circumstances, go ahead and change them, the way Arthur, the newspaper editor, did in surreptitiously hiring the accounts manager and then confronting his boss with the success of the maneuver after the fact. If you want a way to generate competition for your impending raise negotiation with your boss, get that offer from the other company in writing. If I want other options for our typewriter deal, I'll go out and try to get an offer for it from a used-typewriter dealer. If you're running the garage sale and you want a nice goody to throw in for the larger items, get hold of your neighbor with the pick-up truck so you're sure the goody is in fact available.

Common sense will tell you when planning *is* enough by itself. With many goodies, for instance, all you have to do is line them up in your head. Apart from coming up with them, I didn't have to take any action to offer you the goodies of the ribbons and service contract with the typewriter. But just be aware of when the situation warrants putting your plan into action beforehand, and do it. Sowing the seeds of your plan, rather than just holding them in your head, can make a big difference in what you will eventually reap from the negotiation.

Defensive Planning

Thus far, our discussion of planning has focused on offensive planning, that is, gathering information about your opponent and the facts of the situation that will enable you to formulate a course of action to help you get what you want. But negotiation is a two-way street, and you can't lose sight of the fact that your opponent will be trying to find out the same things, so that he can plot a way to get what he wants. He'll be trying to find chinks in *your* armor—a high degree of need you might have, pressure points and/or fears he might be able to exploit, and weaknesses in your case for your Maximum Supportable Position.

You don't want him to find those chinks, and that's what *defensive* planning is all about. The key step in coming up with an effective defensive plan is to take a thorough, honest inventory of your position in the impending negotiation. How badly do you need the deal? Is there anything you can do to reduce it? What pressure and fears are you especially vulnerable to? Can they be eliminated or reduced? What weaknesses will your opponent probably try to exploit?

By thinking through your own negotiating nerves, you stand a much better chance of blunting your opponent's attempts to take advantage of them. Sometimes you can find a way to eliminate a nerve altogether. A while back I had an air-conditioner that was on the blink. Sometimes it worked, sometimes it didn't, but in the midst of a scorching summer, I wasn't eager to live and sweat by its whims. When it refused to cooperate and keep me cool one sweltering afternoon, I resisted the urge to get right on the phone with a repairman. I figured, with my need being what it was, that I would be much more likely to agree to even a wildly exorbitant repair bill than I would if I summoned the repairman when my need was less pressing. I knew I would be negotiating from a position of weakness, and I didn't want to do that. (It's entirely possible, of course, that the repairman's price would not vary, regardless of how much I needed his services. In practice, however, I've found that to be a dangerous assumption to make. There is an ample supply of business people in the world whose sense of ethics is overpowered by their sense of greed when they know they've got you over a barrel.) So I opened the machine, fiddled around for a while, and, much to my amazement, I was able to perform a makeshift repair. With the machine back in commission—and my nerve eliminated—I went ahead and contacted a repairman, comfortable in the knowledge that if the price wasn't right or I didn't care for his terms or service guarantee that I could exercise other options without fear of spending sleepless nights in a pool of perspiration.

In our discussion of timing, we talked about the value of trying to time your negotiation so it coincides with a relatively low degree of need, e.g., don't wait until you have a kitchen-ful of perishables turning funny colors to go looking for a new refrigerator. But we all get caught in a bind sometimes, and we can't always negotiate at optimum times. When you can't, try to find a way to reduce the need or pressure impacting on you. A couple of years ago, a friend of mine had his car racked up in an accident. He needed transportation desperately, but he also realized, after we discussed it, that, being in such a weak negotiating position, he wouldn't be able to shop for a car—in terms of either quality or price—the way he would like. "Why don't you rent a car for a week or two?" I suggested. "My feeling is that you'll get back what you lay out and probably more by being able to look and negotiate without that pressure hanging over your head." So he rented a car and wound up getting a reliable used car at a quite reasonable price. Reducing the pressure made all the difference.

When you cannot come up with a way to circumvent your negotiating weaknesses, often an effective defensive plan is to beat your opponent to the punch by addressing yourself to your weaknesses. By taking the initiative in this fashion, you deflect your opponent's offensive sally and prohibit him from generating negotiating momentum that would put you on the run. Say, for instance, that you're interested in buying a car from me. Rather than wait for you to tally up the car's deficiencies and use them to gain the upper hand, I might say something like, "The only money you should have to put in the car is for a couple of tires in the rear. They're not bad, but you'll probably want to replace them within a couple of months. Or perhaps, "I know the passenger side of the front seat is not in the greatest shape. I've been meaning to get it redone. In fact, I've checked with Joey's Auto Upholstery, and they said with $60 dollars of work, it'll be as good as new." The benefits I accrue from doing this are two-fold: First, by volunteering information on the car's liabilities, I'm demonstrating to you that I'm negotiating in good faith; and second, I'm denying you the opportunity of exploiting its liabilities and using them to undermine the credibility of my asking price. Sometimes acknowledging a weakness can even turn it into a strength. Suppose for some reason I feel I have to unload the car by next week. You show up and I say, "I'm going to be straight with you. I'd really like to have the car sold in a hurry. That's why I've priced it to sell." In a backhanded way, I've bolstered the strength of my asking price and sent you a subtle message that I'm not going to back off too far from it.

The point is that by knowing your weaknesses and anticipating your opponent's probable line of attack, you can plan a much better defense. As another example, say you're being interviewed for a job for which, at least on paper, you are underqualified. Don't sit there hoping that the interviewer will overlook your lack of qualifications or not bring the subject up; you can be sure he's aware of your underqualification and will use it for his negotiating advantage in due time. If he is impressed with you, maybe he'll wait until the end of the interview, then say, "Well, to be frank, you are a strong candidate, but of course we would not be able to match the salary given in the advertisement in view of your lack of experience." From your standpoint, it would be much better to broach the issue yourself early in the discussion. "I'm aware, Mr. Waldman, that I do not completely meet all of the stated prerequisites for the position. However, I'm confident that the broad scope and intensive nature of my experience more than compensate for whatever I may lack in terms of years." In coming out with this, not only do you deflate one of his negotiating assets, you also project a forthrightness and self-confidence that will be taken, not as arrogance, but as a sign of your willingness to stand up for yourself.

No matter how well you preempt your opponents' main offensive thrust, it's an exceedingly rare opponent who will simply fold up and accede to your demands. If he does, more power to you. But you have to figure that, one way or another, he's going to try to find a way to undermine the credibility of your position. For that reason, another key element in your defensive planning is having your justifications and rationales for your position lined up and ready to go. The moment your opponent begins assailing the tenability of your Maximum Supportable Position, you want to riposte with all the reasons that make your position *supportable*. Don't forget, if your credibility is eroded early, you're going to be in for a long negotiation. So if your prospective employer wants to know why you're asking for such a high salary, you might want to whip out the reprint from a business magazine, showing your demand to be commensurate with the average salary of a graphic designer with your experience. (Aren't you glad you did your research?) Or when the potential car buyer starts making noises about your lofty asking price, it's time to pull out the repair records, remind him of the low mileage, and point out that this model traditionally has one of the highest resale values in the used car market.

Even if your opponent succeeds in bargaining you down

from your opening position, it's still important to have your comebacks on hand. You want to be able to buttress your position by having ready answers to questions that often come up: Why isn't my offer acceptable to you? Why did you propose that settlement? Why aren't you willing to be more flexible? Your opponent may not word his queries this directly, but these questions reflect what he will be driving at. By coming up with sound replies to them, you at once enhance the credibility of your stance and increase his doubts as to whether to hold out for something better. Try not to let any of these "why" questions go unanswered. Be prepared with a comeback, even if it's simply restating in different words a point you made earlier. "I think I've shown that I'm more than willing to compromise," you might say. "But I've also shown that what I am offering is worth every bit of the price we're talking about." Just the fact that you say *something* is often enough to get your opponent, if not to settle then and there, to think that he has pushed you about as far as he is going to.

It's often said in the world of sports that the best offense is a good defense. The same can be said of the world of negotiation.

Summing Up

The idea behind planning your negotiation, as we stated at the outset of the chapter, is to eliminate as much of the guesswork as possible. But no matter how thorough you are, there will still be unanswered questions when the bargaining actually begins. There's a limit to what you can know beforehand. Planning provides you with an invaluable orientation for your negotiation, but be careful not to get *locked in* to that orientation. For better or for worse, things may not pan out the way you expected. Don't be fazed if things don't go exactly according to plan. They rarely do. The dynamics of a negotiation are constantly changing. New facts, needs, pressures, fears, all these things and more may pop up during the course of bargaining. The best thing you can do is simply go with the flow. Trust your instincts. Think on your feet. Most important of all, continue to search for factors that may enhance your bargaining position. Play the part of the sponge. Just by studying and listening carefully to your opponent, you may be able to soak up valuable tidbits about his needs, fears, style, and resolve. Fifteen minutes of feeling out your opponent may tell you more about the negotiation than fifteen hours of research.

The important thing to remember is the planning and information-gathering processes are not ends in themselves. They don't stop once the negotiation begins. Their purpose is to minimize the guesswork and give you some insights into what to expect. And even if, as the negotiation begins, new variables come up which change your expectations, you're planning will still serve you in good stead because it will provide you with a solid base of knowledge that will enable you to put the new factors in proper perspective.

PART IV

Face to Face

CHAPTER 12

A Matter of Style

NANCY IS BEING interviewed by two executives of a mid-sized company for a position as publicity director. She feels good about the way the interview is proceeding. Her interviewers seem impressed with her credentials and her ambitious, innovative ideas to improve the department.

"Before we go any further," interjects one of the honchos, whom we'll call Mr. Beers, "I think we should discuss what you were looking for in terms of salary."

Nancy pauses. She knows the least she would accept for the job is $18,000, but she wants to avoid getting locked into a Maximum Supportable Position just yet. She's thinking along the lines of $22,000, but who knows, they may be willing to pay her more. "Well, it's difficult for me to gauge my salary demand without knowing more specifically what my responsibilities would be"—a deft job of skirting the question. She adds, "If I may inquire, what are your thoughts on what the position is worth?"

Beers leans back in his chair and puffs on his pipe. "I think my associate, Ms. Young here, might disagree, but I was thinking of about $18,000. What do you think, Ms. Young?"

"Realistically, John," she says to her comrade, "I think we have to expect to go substantially higher to attract someone of Nancy's caliber. [This really happened—honest.] I was thinking more in terms of $25,000." Beers puffs away, seemingly unfazed by the figure. Nancy can hardly believe her ears. Here are her two opponents negotiating—and in the right direction—her salary in her presence. Despite her happy surprise at this development, she's careful to maintain her equanimity on the outside.

The interview ends several minutes later. Nancy is told she'll be hearing from them. Two weeks later, she gets a call from Mr. Beers who offers her the position for $25,000. She gladly accepts.

What did Nancy do so well in this negotiation? She was the consummate actress. She did not tip her hand. She held off from divulging her Maximum Supportable Position. And later, when her opponents tossed out a figure that exceeded her wildest dreams, she sat there impassively, registering no outward reaction when in reality she was ready to fall off her chair. Had she not done such an effective acting job, had she jumped at the mention of $25,000 and said something like, "That figure seems very agreeable to me," even those opponents—woeful negotiators that they were—might have been able to talk her down from there. But by keeping a poker face and hiding her true reaction ("Praise the Lord and a thousand hallelujahs"), she turned the tide in her favor.

Her opponents, conversely, hid practically nothing. They didn't hide their lack of planning (if they had, they wouldn't have aired their differences as to the job's salary). They didn't hide their keen interest in her (which greatly enhanced her bargaining leverage), and they certainly didn't hide their need for the deal—a fact manifested by their astonishing leap from $18,000 to $25,000. For all their foxiness, they might as well have handed her a check and said, "We want you. Fill in the blanks."

Negotiation is about keeping secrets. If you're unable to keep secrets—about your fears, weaknesses, pressures, your need for the deal, your doubts, the location of your Least Acceptable Result—the settlements you want are going to slip away from you in a hurry. Remember, your opponent will hold out if he has the slightest reason to suspect he can do better. And often, all it takes for him to suspect that he can is even a small lowering of your guard—a worried look, a hasty concession, a blatant eagerness to settle on the spot, even a barely perceptible weakening of your resolve. A student of mine purchased a used camera, which, several months later, required a $75 repair. Although the camera was under no warranty, my student decided to try to get compensation from the owner of the store where he had bought the camera. He called the owner who, after some initial hemming and hawing, seemed to come around and offered him $50. That was acceptable to my student. The only problem was that between the time of the call and the time my student went to pick up the $50, the owner changed his thinking. "Twenty-five is all I can give you. Take it or leave it," he said. My student was understandably incensed at this breach of ethics. But he took it.

I suspect what the storeowner was thinking was, "Hell, if this guy agreed so readily to come down to $50 from $75, I'll bet I can save myself some more bucks and get him to take $25. His shabby ethics notwithstanding, the owner was correct in his appraisal. He detected a weakness in his opponent's resolve and shamelessly exploited it. Had my student pushed hard for $75 and only grudgingly acceded to $50, I would wager that the owner would not have pulled that stunt. He likely would've been thinking, "This guy came on strong from the start. If I try to weasel him down now, who knows, he may start up with letters to the Better Business Bureau or the department of consumer affairs. I would be better off just giving him the $50." But my student failed to keep a secret. With no warranty and with considerable doubts about the strength of his case, he went into the negotiation with a marked lack of firmness, a weakness which he obviously betrayed to the storeowner.

It doesn't take much to give yourself away. An opponent can detect a weakness not only in what you say but in what you don't say. Take Nancy's negotiation, for instance. If her opponents had not been so foolish as to escalate the salary to $25,000 and had stuck with $18,000, what kind of negotiating position would she have been in if she had not raised some objection to that figure? Not very good, since her opponents would then deduce that $18,000 must be at least close to what she would be willing to take the job for. Often in negotiation, an opponent will do just that—throw out an offer that he doesn't really expect, but hopes, you will accept, just to measure your reaction. If you don't show much resistance, or fail to make it clear that the offer is entirely inadequate, your opponent will then zero in on that offer as the focus of the bargaining.

Be mindful, too, of your tone of voice, your body language, your eye contact, for nonverbal behavior can divulge your secrets as well. If you're nervous or uncertain—shifting around a lot, avoiding his eyes, speaking haltingly—an alert opponent will pick up on it. Sometimes even an overreaction can give you away. I used to negotiate frequently with a fellow who made very effective and calculated use of anger to get what he wanted. Eventually, however, I got wise to him. By studying, probing, and feeling him out, I came to realize that he only resorted to anger when he was most insecure about the strength of his position. The tirades never worked for him again.

I'm *not* saying that you should misrepresent yourself when you negotiate or that you should sit stonelike through the entire course of the bargaining. If your opponent thinks you're not being straight with him or thinks that talking to you is like talking to a wall, he's probably going to avoid dealing with you if he possibly can. You can convey a sense of enthusiasm and responsiveness without mortally wounding your negotiation. If you get a knockout offer, as Nancy did, you can say, "I feel confident we'll be able to work something out," (as opposed to saying, "Where do I sign?") and not worry about compromising a secret.

Of course, once the negotiation is well along, you sometimes can't help but let on about a weakness or pressure, or run the risk of losing the deal. Say I'm selling a used riding lawn mower, and I've concealed all along that I need the money to pay a whopping bill that's due next week. You've offered me $400, which is near the bottom of my Settlement Range. If you say, "Well, I've got other mowers to look at, I'll check back next week," I can't very well let you walk away. So I might say, "I was hoping to wrap this up before then. If you'll give me $500 its yours." Maybe you'll accept, maybe not. If you don't, I'll back down to $400 and be happy. That's in my Settlement Range, and I can forestall my creditors.

Nonetheless, particularly in the early stages of negotiation, it's paramount to play the bargaining close to your vest. You have secrets you want to keep, and so does your opponent. The one who does the best job of it stands the much better chance of generating positive momentum and winding up with what he wants.

Master Mouth: The Effective Communicator

You're overworked and understaffed. You want two more people for your department. You take the matter to your boss.

"We just can't continue doing what we're doing," you state. "Everyone in the department feels as though they're working their tails off just to stay in the same place. Having a couple extra sets of hands would really make our lives easier."

"I understand the situation," the boss says sympathetically. "And I'll tell you what. I'll bring it up in the executive council meeting next month. But I can't promise you anything. You know as well as I this last year hasn't been anything to write home about."

Let's take it from the top. You're still in the same bind, but this time you approach your boss like this: "I've given it a lot of thought, and I think I've got a sound plan to increase our profit margin. You know my department has been undermanned for a year and a half now, ever since Herman left and Caputo switched over to sales. We're doing our best, but there's a limit to what we can do in our current situation. I would like to hire two more people. Here's a cost-benefit analysis I came up with. You can see what the extra help would mean in terms of our output. The more we produce, the more the company stands to gain. And that can't make us look anything but good."

"Looks like it makes a lot of sense," the boss says as he glances at your analysis before adding with a laugh, "I'm all for anything that makes me look good. I'll see if I can't push it through at the next council meeting."

See what you've done? With your second approach to the negotiation, you've changed the whole tenor of the bargaining. It's like the old line about the half glass of water—Is it half full or half empty? Your first approach took the half-empty road; the second, the half-full. It's no coincidence that the half-full road proved smoother.

Communication is at the heart of the negotiating process. The better you're able to communicate your point of view, the better your chances of walking away with what you're after. The way you present the things you want to say can make all the difference. Strive for that half-full glass of water; try to shade what you say in the most positive light possible, in a way that will do the most good for your negotiating cause. The reason you met with better success in our hypothetical example the second go-round is because you emphasized the positive, not the negative. You didn't badger your boss with a tale of woe about how overworked everyone in your department is. You demonstrated to him how the hiring of two more people could be not only to your benefit but to the company's and *his* as well. And did his ears ever perk up when he heard that. By taking a positive tack, you converted what probably would have been an Oh-No Negotiation ("I really would like two more workers. Will you give them to me?"), from which the boss had little or nothing to gain, into an Oh-Boy Negotiation ("With improved output in my department, together we can do great things for the company"), from which he stood to gain a good deal.

As another example, suppose you're selling a car, a sturdily constructed mid-sized model. In talking with your opponent, you learn that he's a traveling salesman who does a lot of highway driving. Angle this fact to your advantage. "This is the best highway car I've ever driven," you might say. "It holds the road beautifully, rides smoothly. And it handles so easily, it's like it's driving itself. Other cars might do better for you on gas, but this one does pretty well, and personally, I think the security you get from driving a solid car like this more than makes up for the difference." Don't be hesitant to play up your strong points or to show your opponent the advantages he'll get from reaching a settlement with you. Many negotiations involve salesmanship. Often just stating your case won't be enough. You may have to hype your wares and convince your opponent of their worth by showing him how they'll fulfill his needs. Find a need of your opponent's and meet it—that's what salesmanship is all about. You don't have to give him the hard sell; in fact, as we've noted, coming on too hard often betrays a weakness in your own position. All that's necessary is to shade your case positively in a way that makes clear to your opponent how much he'll benefit, i.e., how many of his needs will be met, by dealing with you. That's precisely what you did in your car negotiation. You found out your opponent had a need for a highway car, so you angled your argument in the most favorable way you could. You were able to meet a need of his, and you played it up. If he didn't give two hoots about highway performance and had some other need, you would have tried to play up to that. Suppose he was buying the car for his grandmother and was especially concerned that the car handle easily and be reliable. You then might talk about the power steering and power brakes and about how, in five years, the car has never failed to get you where you were going.

We're not talking about deception here, just creativity. I'm not suggesting you sell your opponent on the car's reliability if the thing breaks down every other week or that you concoct bogus reasons for your opponent to settle with you. All I'm saying is that you have to try to be creative—quick and creative—to search for the best ways to shade your case so as to meet your opponent's needs and to put your most positive foot forward. When you're able to communicate your points in ways most beneficial to your cause, your glass will begin to runneth over with delightful regularity.

Involving Your Opponent

You walk into a thrift shop, a desirous eye fixed on the brass-trimmed mirror in the window. You approach the owner and come out with both guns blazing. "Can you do any better than $50 on that mirror over there in the window?"

Perhaps he can do better, but that's not the way to find out—not unless you're the first person he's seen in months or he's right up there with the world's worst negotiators.

Talk is the stuff of negotiation. Rarely will you get anywhere simply barging into the bargaining that way. Talk is much more than a way to lay out your case to your opponent. It's a way to get your opponent involved in the negotiation. It creates the necessary chemistry and ambience of interaction. People respond to other people. They do not respond to supercharged negotiating machines. Come on as a person first, a negotiator second. Talk to your opponent. Get him involved with you, even if it's by way of meaningless banter at first. As the conversation turns to the subject of the negotiation, don't be reluctant to convey your interest. While you don't want to overdo it ("I've been looking for that exact mirror all my life") and undercut your bargaining position, it never hurts to let your opponent know you're genuinely interested in what he has to offer.

Apart from giving you the chance to feel him out and perhaps discover some of his needs, what this negotiating foreplay, if you will, accomplishes is to gently break the ice and ease you both into the bargaining. It establishes you as someone your opponent can take seriously and, as the talk continues, fosters an investment of his time and energy and whets his appetite to achieve a settlement with you. If he has shown you the various merits of every mirror in the store—and he *know*s you're interested—he's not very well going to want all his trouble to be for nought. You're nibbling, and after making the investment of setting up his line and dangling his bait, he wants to do all he can to reel you in.

Several years back I was shopping for a comforter in New York's Lower East Side, the negotiating capital of the Western world. I saw several things I liked, but nothing at a price I liked. The storeowner must've pulled out twenty-five comforters, and as we went on, I sensed that his appetite for settlement was becoming increasingly voracious. He'd put so much into it that I knew he couldn't bear the prospect of this "sure sale" walking out the door. So when that's what I started to do, he jumped out from behind the counter and bodily prevented me from going any farther. Then, just as I had hoped, he steered me back to a comforter I had shown particular interest in. "You liked this red one, yes? Beautiful, beautiful. Superior quality. Is marked $50. Costs twice as much uptown. But I want you for *my* customer, I let you have it right now for $40." I resisted settling there, even though $40 was within my Settlement Range, figuring he could come down more and still realize a reasonable profit on the sale. I offered him $25, and after a small amount of haggling, we settled on $33. He was happy and I was happy. There's no way I could've gotten it for that price if I hadn't taken my time, talked with the guy, and aroused his interest sufficiently to have him make a substantial investment of his time and energy into the sale.

Involving your opponent has another value as well, and that is that it engenders a mutual momentum toward settlement. If your opponent doesn't think you can or will give him what he's looking for, he's going to stop negotiating with you. The same goes for you. But if the talking continues, it indicates that both sides feel there's at least a fairly good chance of reaching a settlement. And many times, the longer the talking goes on and the more involved each side gets, the better is the prospect for a settlement. Not just because of the investment, but also because, as time passes, you and your opponent naturally become accustomed to each other—to each other's negotiating style, needs, demands, etc., thus making the negotiating environment less foreign and threatening for all concerned. This is particularly important in more complex negotiations where there's a lot at stake and a lot of items on the agenda. You want to build a rapport with your opponent. You want to have your opponent get used to you, and you to him. Gradually, whatever skepticism your opponent may have harbored toward you abates, and his resistance to settlement often follows. Sometimes it just takes a good deal of time and talk for your opponent to fully grasp where you're coming from.

Several years ago I was part of a negotiation between two social service organizations which were basically duplicating each other's service. The issue at hand was to negotiate a merger. The major stumbling block was that one group had a much larger endowment than the other, and the well-endowed group was concerned that the other was just trying to gain access to extra money. I was negotiating on behalf of the less well-endowed group, and my feeling was that the longer I could keep the talks going, the better were our chances for settlement. Time was an indispensable ally in this negotiation; I knew I needed it to show the other group that we were dealing in good faith, that we weren't just after their money, and that we, like they, were only interested in improving the quality of service to the community. I tried to steer clear of any issue that might snap the discussions. I made concessions aplenty; if they wanted to safeguard their funds by reserving the right to handle them, that was fine. If they wanted to put a ceiling on the amount of money available for the operating budget of the merged organization, that was okay too. My aim was to prove we were trustworthy, reasonable, and cooperative and, most important of all, to keep the ball rolling. In time, I hoped our credibility in their eyes would grow enough that they would come around. It did take time—two months of it—but they did come around, and the merger was successfully negotiated. Keeping the channels of communication open generated just the momentum we needed to reach a settlement.

Keeping It Pleasant

In a world that sometimes seems to grow more hostile and impersonal by the day, I think all of us feel good when we can punctuate our everyday life with little pleasantries: bidding a bouncy good morning to Vic, the nice young man who works at Sathrum's Stationery where I picked up my morning paper on the way to work; talking sports with Norm when I go to his deli to eat the B.L.T. on a hard roll he has waiting for me every day at 12:30; catching up on the latest town gossip from Ellen and Thomas, who run the mom-and-pop dry cleaners. I could go to one of the other barber shops in town and save myself a couple of bucks, but I like Vinny and I like the way he cuts my hair, so what's the point? Just the way he tells his stories makes going to his shop worthwhile. There's no putting a price tag on a smile.

The simple fact is that people like to do business with

people they like. It's the same for negotiation. If your opponent takes a liking to you, he's going to be much more inclined to negotiate with you. A woman comes over to look at the dinette set you're selling. You get to talking and one thing leads to another and you find out that her daughter goes to the same college—even lives in the same dormitory—as your daughter. You share a good chuckle about the coincidence over a cup of coffee. A bond has been formed. It gives you both an extra incentive to negotiate. This is precisely what a good salesman will try to do—form a bond with you so you'll want to buy from him. He knows only too well that you could go to the other guy down the street. But if it's pleasant dealing with him, you'll be less disposed to exercise that option.

Do your best to set a friendly tone in your encounter. Don't be bashful about letting your true, charming self shine forth. Warm up to your opponent. Establish a good rapport. This doesn't mean you have to hand out a questionnaire to determine what you have in common or to go to any great length to ingratiate your opponent. The idea isn't to get your opponent eating out of your hand so much as to create a pleasant atmosphere that will be conducive to a successful negotiation.

When it comes time to begin the actual bargaining, you should be careful not to allow the nice, pleasant vibes to deter you from zealously pursuing your negotiating goals. But you can do that and still keep the atmosphere cordial. Remember, the person on the other side of the table is an opponent, not an enemy. You're not looking to swindle him, and you don't have to turn into an instant ogre the moment the talk turns to the topic of who gets what. You're looking out for your interests, and your opponent is looking out for his. It's not always a matter of trying to win and making your opponent lose. In many, many negotiations both sides can win. If your goal is to buy a typewriter and mine is to sell it and we agree on a deal, we've both won. I'm still a winner, even if you did a masterful job of negotiating and convinced me that I couldn't do better than my Least Acceptable Result of $500. Because, by definition, settling at my L.A.R. is still better than not settling at all.

There's no inherent reason why any antipathy should be engendered between you and your opponent just because each of you is protecting his own interests. Don't feel as though your opponent is assaulting your character or violating the friendly tone you've established because he bargains in earnest. Keep your ego and your feelings off the table. De-emotionalize the negotiation by viewing it in the context of business. Just as you sought to engender friendliness to foster a positive tone for the bargaining, try to depersonalize whatever discord may arise. If you had made me an impossibly low offer for the typewriter, I wouldn't have felt insulted or mortally wounded. I would only think that you were doing just what I was trying to do—get the best deal possible for yourself.

De-emotionalizing negotiation can be difficult. If this attempt to reassure you that you can bargain hard without carrying a headful of guilt has been unavailing, why not go back and flip through the chapter on fears. Even the best of negotiators need a refresher on this score now and then.

In some negotiations, of course (notably those of the Oh-No ilk), cultivating a friendly tone is more difficult, and occasionally impossible. There are times when you just have to accept the fact that pounding the table and making threats is the only way you're going to get anywhere. But just make an effort to distinguish between those times when your only recourse is to behave that way and when you're allowing your ego and feelings to run amuck in the bargaining. When anger is not necessary and calculated, it can bring on the undoing of a negotiation faster than you can say your favorite expletive. It hardens your opponent's resolve, foments discord, and whisks the negotiation out of the business context and into a personal one. If you feel yourself getting hot under the collar for whatever reason—because things aren't going your way or your opponent makes light of your offer or he refuses to budge from his position, no matter what you say—take a step back from the situation. Think things through. Ask yourself if you stand to gain anything from blowing your cool. Even if you feel your outrage is justified, try to throttle it. If you shriek, "You're a cheap jerk who doesn't know a good deal when he sees one!" you can kiss the negotiation—and quite possibly your physical well-being—goodbye. Much better to calm yourself and say coolly, "If that's the best you can do, I'm afraid there's no sense in discussing it further." By responding this way, you're at least leaving the door open for him to come back with an improved offer. Maybe he'll stage a walkout, then call you tomorrow. Maybe he was being stubborn just to test your mettle. Maybe not. The deal may be dying, but at least you've left it breathing, however fitfully. It's as good as gone once you resort to abuse.

When You're on the Receiving End

What about when the abuse is being heaped on you? What then should be your negotiating style? Suppose you're involved in an Oh-No Negotiation. You're confronting your landlord about the dilapidated state of the front porch, the one he has promised to fix for seven months. The whole thing shakes even when you tiptoe on it, the boards are rotting out, and one of these days you're going to fall right through. The moment you finish airing your complaint, he hits the roof. "That's what I like—gratitude!" he bellows. "I try to keep costs down. I haven't raised your rent in a year and a half, and you come in here with this sob story about the damn porch. It's not like you're going to break a leg, for Chrissakes. You can walk around the weak part, can't you? Or is that too much of an inconvenience?"

Clearly, building a friendly tone for this negotiation is going to be tough. So what to do? First of all, de-emotionalize. Realize his tirade is a calculated ploy to make you go away. Focus on your goal. Don't allow yourself to be intimidated, which, of course, is what he wants. Often, an effective response to such venom is to waltz right through it, behaving as though he had just said, "Good morning. Nice day, isn't it?" With some opponents, that's all it takes to demonstrate to them that you're not to be dissuaded and that the abusive approach won't work with you. Or you might want to reaffirm your stance with a simple, direct statement. "I'm not asking that you overhaul the house. But that porch is a definite health hazard, and it has to be fixed." Responding in any fashion— except, of course, to say, "You're right. I'm sorry. I should've been more understanding"—will probably be enough to convince him you're not going to back down. And that's what must be made clear to him. Because if he senses that you're knuckling under, that his guilt-peddling tirade has cut into your resolve, then he's going to keep it up.

You might even try appealing to his self-interest. "I would've thought you would be glad I reminded you about this. Repairing it would be a lot less of a hassle than dealing with a lawsuit after someone has been injured, don't you think?" Chances are, nothing you come back at him with is going to induce him to pull out a chair and offer you a cigar. He still wants to avoid negotiating with you if at all possible. But by withstanding his reaction, you keep your cause alive. If he won't cooperate, so be it. But at least you're still there to let him know that you have no choice but to go the county housing department with your complaint.

The key is to detach yourself sufficiently so you can maintain a negotiating style that will help you meet your goal. Don't get unnerved and stifle the urge to respond with an abusive torrent of your own. That just might make him angry enough—and rouse his ego enough—to fight you till the end, your threat notwithstanding.

But as with just about everything else in negotiation, there are exceptions to the rule. On occasion it *does* pay to fight fire with fire. I once confronted a co-worker who I strongly felt was not fulfilling his responsibility and who, consequently, was making my job more difficult. Understand that this particular co-worker was extremely large—on the order of six foot five and two hundred and forty pounds. Suffice it to say he was not used to people getting angry at him. But when he greeted my grievance with a loud and angry outburst, I responded in kind. His initial reaction was part "How dare you," and part "Who do you think you're talking to that way?" Moments later, though, he began to chuckle at his own response. That broke the ice, and we wound up having a very productive talk about our working relationship.

However you react, be sure that it's not out of momentary fury, but a product of a thought-out negotiating style that you feel will advance your cause.

Taking Risks

Ted is a contractor negotiating a deal with a builder. After studying what the job will entail, Ted decides the least he can accept for it and still make it worth his while would be $25,-000. He also decides to peg his opening position at $45,000. The builder initially offers Ted $20,000, and even after several lengthy bargaining sessions, the best Ted can get out of him is $27,000.

The question is, should he accept that offer, even though it's pretty far down his Settlement Range? Ted's gut feeling is that he can do better, probably get the builder up to $30,000 or $32,000. The extra bucks would be most welcome, but in realistically assessing the situation, Ted decides he can't afford to risk losing the deal for an extra couple of G's. Business hasn't exactly been booming; in fact, it's been downright rotten. Ted opts for the safe road, agreeing to $27,000.

Let's take it again. Ted's involved in the same negotiation, but this time the circumstances are different. With negotiations pending on three other contracts, he doesn't feel the pressure to settle at $27,000. He decides to go for broke, hold out as long as he can and see if he can't tug the builder much closer to his M.S.P. If the deal happens to fall through in the process, well, that's a risk he can afford to take. "It's worth shooting for the sky on this one," Ted thinks. "I've always got the other deals to fall back on."

There's no right answer to the question of how much you should risk in a negotiation. The longer you hold out for a better deal, the better you will do—*but* the chance you will deadlock is higher. What you have to measure is whether the chance for a better settlement is worth the risk of deadlock. It all depends on the circumstances. What, if any, options do you have? How much do you need the deal? What pressures are working on you? Is time running against you? Do you need a settlement, even a marginally acceptable one, right now, not next week, so you can have it on your boss's desk when he begins your salary review tomorrow?

Sometimes you can afford risk, sometimes you can't. But the important thing is to base your decision on the circumstances, on a calculated analysis of the strength of your bargaining position, not on a predetermined attitude. Some of us are high rollers and some of us aren't, but when it comes to negotiation, you have to try to de-emotionalize your attitude toward risk, detach yourself from your natural predilection, and choose the course of action the circumstances warrant. Put another way, don't enter a negotiation predisposed toward taking risks or not taking them. Size up the situation before making your choice. It would be the height of folly to let an acceptable deal slip away just because you like to go for broke, even though there isn't another opponent in sight and you know you need the money to pay for your kid's appointment with the orthodontist next week. And it would be every bit as shortsighted to cave in near your Least Acceptable Result when there are two other stamp collectors who've been badgering you to call them if you want to sell your collection.

Let your risk-taking stance flow with the variables of the

given negotiation. Base your decision on an examination of the potential gain versus the potential loss—on how valuable the gain might be and how damaging the loss might be. The result will be most salutary for your negotiation; you'll hold out when you *should* hold out and settle when you *should* settle.

Catering to Your Opponent's Ego and Emotional Needs

Cliff and Stan run a youth soccer program. It's grown enormously over the last several years, and that growth has created problems. They can never seem to get the town to schedule them enough field time, and that has forced them to cut back their number of games, which stinks for the kids. Sure, there's a townwide field shortage, but the other soccer leagues seem to do all right. They have expanded schedules and play at the better times and dates to boot. Cliff and Stan are tired of nine o'clock games on Sunday mornings.

To right the situation, they have to deal with old T.J. Herman, the town director of recreation. For twenty-five years, T.J. has been the man behind the scenes for anything and everything having to do with sports. Need the lights turned on? Talk to T.J. The field isn't lined? Talk to T.J. A scheduling conflict? T.J. is the one to see. Sometimes people make fun of him because he treats his job as though he's second only to the mayor in scope of responsibility, but T.J. does his job well.

Cliff and Stan are planning their preseason fund-raising banquet when Cliff stumbles on a masterstroke. "Why don't we invite T.J. to be our main speaker and guest of honor? His stories about the old days would be good for some laughs, it would mean a lot to him, and who knows, it wouldn't do us any harm as far as our scheduling problem goes." T.J. accepts the invitation with relish. He is deeply flattered that they would think to select him as guest of honor when they could've gotten some college coach or one of the local semipro stars. And wouldn't you know it, when it came time for the season, Cliff and Stan had more field time than ever before—none of it on Sunday mornings.

We all have our individual ego and emotional needs. They vary widely from person to person, but we've all got them—

you, me, and your opponent. Many times when you negotiate, you can discover one or more of those needs in your opponent, cater to it, and wind up doing your negotiating needs a world of good. Precisely as Cliff and Stan did. T.J. Herman, they knew, got a particular rise out of feeling like a big wheel; and who wouldn't, after laboring in anonymity for all those years? They addressed his need, and when it came time to negotiate with him, it was a big boost to their cause.

I'll give you another example. John is a plant manager for a manufacturing company. A half-dozen or so times a summer, John and a bunch of the guys from the plant go out to the ball park to take in a game. They sit in the bleachers, take off their shirts, drink beer, and grouse about how every player on the field makes more in one game than they do in a week. It's a good time. Well, John has gotten into the habit of making sure to ask his boss, Walt, if he wants to join them whenever they're heading to the park. Walt's a white-collar type now, but John knows he has fond memories of the years he spent working in the plant with the other guys. Walt likes the sense of belonging, of still being one of the guys, even though he's "management" now. He can't always make the outings, but to him it's the invitation that really matters. By cementing his relationship with Walt and by catering to one of his needs, John is able to do his own job much better. He has made it very easy for himself to negotiate with his boss. He doesn't have to worry about pulling teeth to get what he needs. Whatever it is—an extra forklift, extra workers to load the trucks, temporary help for the inventory—all John has to do is make a reasonable case, and the need is as good as filled.

When you're face to face with your opponent, often you'll detect another sort of emotional need—a need to avoid the anxiety that negotiation engenders. His unsettled demeanor is screaming to you, "Wouldn't it be great if we could just stop right here and reach an agreement?" Fine. If he's so uncomfortable bargaining, you're more than happy to defer to his need and call it a deal . . . and walk away with your negotiating needs fulfilled. His discomfort will probably be a big help to you in the long run, too, if you have an ongoing negotiating relationship with him. After all, he would much rather deal with you—someone who is reasonable, doesn't push him too far, and doesn't force his anxiety to reach panic proportions—than someone who might push him to the wall.

There are all sorts of such ego and emotional needs that

you can pick up on before and during a negotiation. Maybe your opponent wants to feel appreciated, to feel right, or to be lauded for his expertise in a particular field. Maybe his need takes the form of self-preservation, and you can assure him that his job is secure or he's not going to meet any terrible fate. Or perhaps he merely wants to be consulted; I've negotiated with many an opponent who creates all kinds of havoc when he's not consulted but who invariably rubber-stamps my needs when he is. Some people have a need to avoid confrontation at all costs, while others savor it. If your opponent gets off on knocking heads with you, knock heads. (These sorts *do* exist.) Use the negotiation to meet that need; he'll feel good about having a good go at it, and you'll feel good getting what you want.

This is not to say, of course, that the moment you push the button to meet one of these needs, your opponent will immediately be satisfied and abandon his *real* needs forthwith. But by catering to him on an ego and emotional level, you make him feel better about things, more fulfilled. He'll gain a sense of having accomplished something, and often that sense will predispose him to settle where you want . . . or at least to not push so hard for what he wants. What you're doing, in essence, is swapping his ego and emotional needs for your negotiating needs. A good deal, any way you cut it.

By the same token, try to take stock of your own ego and emotional needs when you enter a negotiation. Once you recognize them, you'll be aware of when your opponent is appealing to them, and you won't allow yourself to be sidetracked from the reasons you're negotiating. In short, don't permit psychology to work on you. It may feel good to have those needs catered to, but it's not worth the price you may have to pay in the process.

Saving Face

Another need people have is to feel they've negotiated well. Nobody likes to admit that they were taken or that they could've secured a better deal if they had negotiated more skillfully. It's not very often that you'll hear someone come back from a negotiation and say, "Wow, did I ever get my clock cleaned in that one!" In small part, that's because none of us is particularly wild about baring our deficiencies to the world, but mostly it's because we wouldn't have agreed to the settlement in the first place if we genuinely felt we'd had our clocks cleaned.

No matter how good a deal you feel you've gotten, never let on to your opponent. Wait until you get home to do your crowing. But be careful; the world is smaller than you think, and if you crow too loudly or to the wrong people and it filters back to your opponent, you may get yourself in trouble. If he's angry enough, he may try to renege on the deal. And if you'll be negotiating with him in the future, you can bet you're going to have a revenge-minded opponent on your hands. Moral: If you feel the need to crow, do it discreetly.

Try to help your opponent save face. Look for ways to enable him to justify the deal not only to himself, but to others as well. As the bargaining draws to a close, you might want to say, "You know, you really drive a hard bargain." A last-minute concession also works nicely. Often you'll be involved in negotiations where you'll sense that you're very close to settling on a good deal and all that's needed to wrap it up is to give your opponent some eleventh-hour reassurance that he's done his job well. "All right, you win, I'll take off another fifty bucks, but that's it." Even if you're still near the top of your Settlement Range, a last-minute concession like this often gives your opponent an exhilarating sense of triumph.

Another effective way to help your opponent save face is by throwing in some goodies. Suppose you're running a garage sale and you and your opponent are dancing around a price of $100 for your lawnmower. You notice he's also been checking out some of your gardening tools. "Tell you what," you say. "I would just as soon start clearing some of this stuff outta here. I'll throw in the trowels, rake, and hoe with the lawnmower." You've got your opponent thinking he's getting all this other stuff for nothing. And you've also given him a great way to justify the agreement; he's going to return home and tell his wife, "Look at these tools—I got the guy to throw 'em in for nothing. All this stuff—and a lawnmower—for $100." Of course, he didn't really get them for nothing. He got them in exchange for settling at a price that you were very pleased with. By tossing in some goodies that were worth maybe $10 on the garage-sale market, you reduced his inclination to hold out and provided him with a very palpable way of showing the world how well he'd done in the negotiation.

One more point about helping your opponent save face:

Never let on to him that he could've done better. Mask your L.A.R. to the end and after the end. Make him believe he got the best settlement out of you that he possibly could. This is especially important when you'll be negotiating with him in the future. If he finds out you were bluffing this time, he'll be much more inclined to hold out next time. It's just like when you're playing poker and your bluff induces the other players to fold. You don't want to turn over your cards because once they see they were suckered by your $10 bet on a measly pair of twos, they're going to start calling your bluff in the future. When your opponent agrees to settle, encourage him to think that he bargained effectively and it's the best he could've done. It'll be your little secret that he had the cards to do better.

Overwinning

It doesn't happen very often, but every once in a while it's possible to win too big in a negotiation. Unreasonable deals have a way of breaking down. If you feel your opponent really has gotten a raw deal, the best thing to do for all concerned is to reopen the bargaining and make the necessary amends. It's not only an ethical course to follow, it's practical. The recriminations, resentments, and hostilities that inevitably spring from an extremely one-sided settlement are hardly a worthwhile price to pay for whatever unexpected extras you would initially walk away with. A miserable and irate opponent who feels like he has been manipulated or strong-armed into accepting a bad deal will come back to haunt you.

Overwinning is particularly dangerous if you'll be negotiating with the person again or if you're involved in a joint venture with him. On the job, for instance, the last thing you want to do is incite the ill will of a boss, subordinate, or coworker by getting them over the barrel in a negotiation. Not only will it prove injurious to your working relationship, it also will probably make him hellbent on revenge the next time he negotiates with you. Neither consequence is worth risking. You need his best efforts and cooperation to do your own job effectively, and you *don't* need him trying to bring you to your knees the next go-round at the bargaining table. The same holds true for partnerships. They tend to be delicately constructed relationships, and all it takes is one party feeling like he's being taken advantage of to dissolve the whole relationship in a hurry. It's in your best interests to keep your partner happy; the long-term benefit you'll derive from a solid relationship vastly outweighs the short-term benefit of getting too much of your way.

In negotiation, remember, your goal is to get what you want, not deny your opponent what he wants. The two do not have to be mutually exclusive. But if you feel they are in a given negotiation and your opponent's groveling for crumbs while you're feasting on a bounteous repast, go back and share some of the wealth. Just make sure you do it after the bargaining, never during it. Everyone will feel better, and you won't have to live in fear of an anger-oozing opponent showing up at your door.

Also remember that overwinning is a *very rare occurrence*—a bridge crossed infrequently by even the best of negotiators.

CHAPTER 13

At the Bargaining Table: Putting It All Together

YOU'VE HAD A lot of information come your way. I would be immensely surprised if, at this point, everything seemed to fit neatly together into a cohesive whole. We've touched base with all the fundamentals of negotiation, but some loose ends are inevitable. In this chapter we're going to tie them up. We're going to pick up all the pieces of what we've talked about and put them all together in a way that will make clear to you exactly what you have to do when the moment of truth arrives—when you're face-to-face with your opponent at the bargaining table.

Pushing and Probing

While a new muffler was being affixed to my car, I sat in a dingy customer waiting room, leafing idly through an old, coffee-stained magazine. It was nearly as uninteresting as the placards of platitudes they had posted on the walls—things like, "If we please you, tell a friend. If not, tell us," and "Someone else may say he'll do it for *less,* but it'll wind up costing you *more.*" Abruptly, my boredom was interrupted.

"Hey mister," grated the mechanic, "I was just under your car, and those shocks you got are shot. I can give you new ones all around for only ninety-nine bucks." I hadn't given new shocks an iota of thought. Nor had I ever done business at this place before, so I didn't know if I could take the guy at his word.

"Give me a minute and I'll come and take a look at them,"

I said. I ducked into the bathroom with no tactical intent other than to empty my bladder. I saw this sign on the wall:

NOTICE TO EMPLOYEES: A FIVE-PERCENT COMMISSION IS AWARDED FOR EVERY ON-THE-FLOOR SALE YOU MAKE.

Well, what do you know. I didn't know whether I needed new shocks, and I probably wouldn't have had any better idea even after looking at them. But now I *did* know that he had an ax to grind, a fact which I felt, with all due cynicism, could conceivably have influenced his judgment of my shocks. I decided to get a second opinion and subsequently learned that the shocks were fine.

But the condition of my shock absorbers is not the nub here. The nub is that useful information for your negotiation can turn up everywhere. Don't rule out any possibility in your search for information. Keep on probing. Be a sponge. Be observant. Take maximum advantage of the time you spend face-to-face with your opponent by finding out as much as you can about both him and the facts surrounding the deal. You never know when you'll discover a valuable tidbit. Years ago I was negotiating to buy a used car. I ran down a list of questions I had about the car, one of them being, "How is it on oil?"

"No problem, no problem," my opponent said hurriedly. "And check this out. You should see the trunk space in this thing." His response seemed a bit strange . . . and strained, almost as if he didn't want to talk about it. I tucked my reaction away, but the next day when I went over to his house to make him an offer, something brought it back out again. "I wonder if he's being straight with me?" I decided to find out. Before ringing the bell, I slipped into the garage (at which point it also dawned on me that he'd always had the car in the driveway when I was around) and checked out the condition of the cement in the spot under where the engine would be. Suspicion confirmed. It was black and crumbling, sure sign of an oil leak. He must've seen my car because he came out while I was in the garage.

"What's the trouble?"

"Well, I see there seems to be an oil leak. I was under the impression there was no problem with the oil."

"Oh, yeah, uh, it's just a matter of tightening the gasket. It'll take two minutes to fix. Nothin' to worry about."

I wasn't having any of that. Who knows, maybe he was telling the truth *that* time, but his credibility in my eyes had already suffered irreparable harm. I never did make an offer. By being alert and continuing to search for information, I spared myself from buying a potential lemon . . . from a lemon.

It's vital to know if your opponent is being honest with you. Because if you can't rely on his word, where the hell is your negotiation? Nowhere. You never know what you're getting is fact or fiction. One effective way of gauging your opponent's honesty is by playing the dummy. Do your research, get your facts straight, then go and ask him questions about what you've learned. You'll know immediately if he's a shady character.

Recently I was looking into buying a stereo system. I checked out *Consumer Reports*, and picked up some basic knowledge about the various makes and models in my price range. While *Consumer Reports* is not the Bible and it is possible for an honest salesman to have a different opinion about a particular component, the magazine nonetheless is very useful in providing a background of information you can use for comparison. In one store, the salesman seemed to be at odds with what I'd learned on just about every subject I brought up. I asked him about the turntable of one system—a turntable that was thoroughly panned by *C.R.*—and he responded with an unconvincing "It's solid" and deftly steered the discussion to all the wonderful things about the system. His persistence in pushing it on me led me to believe that, for some reason—perhaps a deal with the wholesaler or manufacturer—it was in his self-interest to sell that one to me. My suspicions sufficiently aroused, I went elsewhere, where, happily, I seemed to get uncommonly straight answers to my questions.

When your information search is focusing less on your opponent and more on the facts, it's often to your advantage to take the opposite tack—playing the expert. Act as though you know the whole story, even if you only know half. It's the old police ploy. You've probably seen a movie or read a book in which a cop, interrogating a suspect, says, "Look, don't try any double talk. We know you were in Huntington the night of the fifth, and we know you were prowling around the Beighlie house."

"Yeah, but I swear, I didn't do nothin' to the girl. She took off when she saw me. All I did was chuck the silver stuff in a bag and get the hell outta there." Oh, really? You may not get your opponent to spill his guts—this isn't Hollywood we're talking about here—but you may very well pick up some meaningful morsels of information. Say you're being interviewed for a high-level administrative position for a company that you understand has had recurring problems with executive turnover. You begin, "I'm well aware of the rather chaotic personnel situation that has beset the company. What I would like to know is—"

"I can assure you," the interviewer interrupts, "that those problems are a thing of the past. Kelly and Crawford, the two troublemakers, have been dismissed. They were good when they stuck to their jobs, but they were obsessed with proving their ridiculous and unfounded notion that Goldson was diverting funds for his personal use. . . ." Quickly, you have some interesting questions to pursue—questions the answers to which may well determine if you want to work for that company.

Don't forget, too, that leading your opponent to believe you're on top of the situation tends to make him much less inclined to snow you. You're an expert in his eyes, and he would look like a fool if he tried to slip something past you. He's also likely to feel that he won't be able to push you very far when it comes time to bargain. Expertise awes people. It breeds an aura of command and respect, an aura that tells your opponent, "I know what I'm talking about and I know what I want." Only the most hale and hardy of negotiators are going to try to forge their way through that kind of aura.

The best way of all to gather information for your negotiation is simply to ask questions, lots of questions. Listen and observe carefully as your opponent responds. Does he seem anxious? Is there anything in particular he seems reluctant to discuss? Did he seem like he was undergoing rigor mortis before your very eyes when you inquired about the reason for the no-liability clause in the contract? Does he seem to be pushing or steering you in a certain direction? Is he giving you the hard sell? Does that indicate an urgency for settlement that he's trying to conceal? Let your opponent talk as long as he's willing to. Practice the fine art of silence. Those five minutes of inane babbling may conclude with just the clue you were looking for. Don't race through your questions like you're trying to beat the buzzer. Negotiation isn't a game show. Take your time. Let the discussion flow as it will. Whether it amounts to seconds or weeks, your time at the bargaining table with your opponent is precious. For the alert negotiator, it can provide just the missing pieces you were searching for to solve the puzzle of when to persist and when to settle.

Beyond the Wish Point

A big advantage you'll have over the vast majority of the people you'll be negotiating with is you'll have a carefully calculated Settlement Range. You'll have a Least Acceptable Result, one that's the product of a thorough analysis of the need and pressure you have to reach an agreement. And on the basis of that analysis, you'll know when you've reached rock bottom and would be better off walking away. At the other end, you'll have a truly Maximum Supportable Position, one that whisks you as far as possible in the direction of meeting all of your goals, while still keeping you in the bounds of crediblity.

Most of your opponents, on the other hand, will assemble a crude Settlement Range. They'll ask for a little more than they expect to get so as to leave themselves room for concession before settling. But the chances are slim that they'll shoot as high as you because they'll be afraid to come out with an opening position that may be regarded as excessive and unreasonable. And it's a good bet that they'll have no real Least Acceptable Result at all. Instead, the bottom of their Settlement Range will likely be a wish point, a rough idea of where they'll settle if they can't do better. "I would like to get this pool table for $500, but I suppose I'll go as high as $600 if I have to"—that's usually the extent of the thought that goes into a wish point. It's fuzzy, hardly the result of the rigorous process you've undergone to arrive at your L.A.R. The fuzziness plays right into your hands because, with persuasive bargaining, you can often move an opponent beyond his wish point and back him down to his true Least Acceptable Result. Let's return to our typewriter affair. Suppose I'm the one with the severe case of bottom-line fuzziness; I'm thinking that $500 would be an okay settlement for my machine, even though I don't have any notion why I'm not drawing the line at $525 or $475 or anyplace else. I'm just thinking that $500 is as far down as I should go. You come out with both barrels blazing, laying an array of compelling arguments on me to bolster the strength of your opening stance of $250. Eventually you come up to $450 (still a ways from your L.A.R. of $600), and I get to thinking,

"Well, maybe $450 wouldn't be so bad. It's not too far from $500, and he seems pretty adamant, so I think I'll go ahead and settle there." Just like that, you've obliterated my wish point and convinced me to agree to a deal that's less than what I was hoping for.

Of course, there's no way of knowing whether your opponent has a true L.A.R. or merely a wish point. Nor will you know whether you've gotten him to settle at a lower point than he wanted to. But the point is to keep pushing and prodding his bottom line because if he hasn't a firm idea of where it is (and the betting line is that he hasn't), you give yourself a chance for an even better settlement. Putting it another way, be aware that your opponent probably doesn't have the commitment to his bottom line that you have to yours. Know that he hasn't thought about things the way you have, that he has only a vague sense of what deals would or would not be acceptable to him and that you can slip between the cracks in his nebulous thinking and move him in the direction you want.

Who Should Make the First Offer?

Jeannette works for a consumer protection agency. She was negotiating on behalf of an elderly woman who paid $125 to a dishwasher repairman only to have the dishwasher continue to malfunction. When Jeannette first contacted him, the repairman offered to give the woman $25. "She wouldn't accept that," replied Jeannette. "What would she accept?" he asked, but Jeannette deftly ducked the question. "It'll take a lot more than that."

A week later, she called him again. This time he offered $40. She declined once more. When she contacted him a third time, he said pointedly, "I'll give the lady $60 and that's that, not a penny more." Knowing the woman was not eager to carry out the implied threat in this negotiation—small claims court—Jeannette accepted. The woman was ecstatic with the settlement. And Jeannette's boss was astounded. His feeling had been that since they didn't have much of a case (and, in fact, they didn't; the repairman did install a number of new parts and put in several hours of labor), Jeannette should've asked for $45 in the hope of nudging the guy from his original $25 offer.

But Jeannette was shrewd. She didn't want to commit herself to a specific figure because she didn't know how high he would be willing to go. Even though she didn't really expect to get much of an improvement over $25, she kept him in the dark, and the result, in effect, was that she had him negotiating against himself.

Go back to the negotiation we discussed earlier in which Nancy was being interviewed for a position as publicity director. She did the same thing; she held off announcing her opening demand (which was in the vicinity of $22,000), hoping to feel out her oponents to see if they might be willing to give her more. And sure enough, the next thing she knew they were talking about $25,000.

As a general rule, when you're completely in the dark about your opponent's Settlement Range, try to keep your opening position under wraps. Get him to make the first offer. Who knows, he might throw out a proposal that's better than what you were planning on asking for. Even if he doesn't, it does you a lot of good knowing where he stands. For one thing, you'll find out right off if he's within your Settlement Range. If he is, it eliminates a major source of tension because you already know a deal is possible. For another, it reveals some things about his position. If he doesn't seem to be shooting very high, for instance, you have good reason to believe he needs a settlement badly. Or perhaps he will aim high, but then make a big concession or two, another indication that he wants to settle in the worst way.

Holding back your own M.S.P. also gives you some precious extra time to gather more information and probe your opponent's pressures and needs. In Nancy's negotiation, for example, she found out how impressed they were with her and how much they wanted her for the job, insights which greatly enhanced her bargaining position. Vic, a student of mine, was negotiating to buy a car from an opponent who was asking $1,500. Going in, Vic had pegged his M.S.P. at $1,300, but he didn't divulge it. Instead, he checked out the car thoroughly, taking careful stock of its liabilities. Poor alignment, two balding tires, lots of miles, an aging battery—the information he collected provided him with extra negotiating ammunition, prompting him to move his M.S.P. to $1,100. Unable to dispute the things that were wrong with the car, the opponent was induced to come down from his asking price much more quickly than if Vic had simply come out with his $1,300 offer from the start. Vic wound up paying $1,250—$50 better than what was going to be his original M.S.P.

There are negotiations, however, where you have no choice but to make the initial offer. For instance, when you're proposing to sell certain goods or services, there's simply no way around it. A friend of mine is a free-lance business consultant, and he can't very well go into a company, lay down a brochure, outline of his services, and then say, "Make me an offer." If he did, his professional credibility would be nil. He has to assert himself as an established, trustworthy businessman, so he has to say, "This is what my services include, and this is my fee for same." In fact, this is a case where coming out early with a firmly entrenched M.S.P. plays to his advantage. Because if the company subsequently attempts to bargain him down, he can reply, "You must not understand. This is *the* fee for these services," and then show them where it's listed right in the brochure. The company may persist, and he may even come down a little, but by initially treating his price as a nonnegotiable issue, he bolsters his bargaining position.

Making the initial demand can work to your advantage in other ways as well. Suppose you're negotiating with your boss about next year's budget for your department. One month before the budget request is actually due, you march into his office and lay on him the basic bottom line figures you expect to be asking for. After he picks himself up off the floor, he says incredulously, "This is a one hundred percent increase over last year! Where do you think we're going to get $50,-000 from—the tooth fairy?" Keeping your cool, you state your case firmly, citing the special projects you'll be undertaking, the increased manpower they'll require, the ways in which last year's paltry budget dramatically limited your output, and, finally, your admirable track record in managing money in the past. By approaching him this way in advance of the actual negotiation, not only have you made a compelling case in support of your position, you've also given him some lead time to digest it. You don't expect an immediate answer; budget negotiations are still a month off. But during that month, he's going to have time to get used to your request and, assuming you *have* indeed made a strong case for it, it will gradually seem less unreasonable to him.

I'll give you an analogy. A couple of years back, when the price of coffee went through the roof, I could barely bring myself to look at it, much less buy it. It was partly principle, partly pragmatics, but I couldn't handle paying $4.00 for the same coffee I was buying a month earlier for $1.50. But given a couple of months' time, I gradually got accustomed to that scandalous price, and after a while, it just didn't seem so scandalous. I came to accept the fact that that's what coffee cost. And damned if I didn't start buying it again.

Knowing when and when not to put forth the opening demand is a matter of feel. But as a general guideline, the more you know about the facts of the situation and the more you know about your opponent and the forces impacting on him, the safer it is to go ahead and lay out your M.S.P. Take your budget negotiation with your boss. That's not a situation where you want to say, "Make me an offer." You've dealt with him before, you both know the basic facts that are germane to your proposal, and as a result, you're much better off setting out your demand early and building the best case you can for it. Conversely, when your opponent and the facts are more elusive, when you don't really know what he's shooting for, then it's best to hold off, just as Jeannette did. At the least, you give yourself the opportunity to find out more about your opponent and how he's feeling about the deal; and at best, you leave yourself open to getting an offer that's better than what you were going to shoot for in the first place.

Be aware, too, that sometimes you'll encounter an opponent who will demand that you start your opening position. He may say, "I have to know if we're going to be able to do business," or "You've got to show you're serious about negotiating with me." While there are ripostes to those statements ("That's what I'm trying to determine, sir—if we're going to be able to do business," or "I assure you, if we can reach a satisfactory agreement, I'm most serious about negotiating with you"), if the opponent is adamant, you may have to either make an offer or look for another opponent. If you choose to deal with him, don't think it's the end of the world that you're making the first offer. Just make it count for all it's worth. State your Maximum Supportable Position and bolster it with everything you've got. Don't be afraid of how he may react. Stand firm. You have plenty of time to back down from it if need be. But if you throw out your M.S.P. without conviction or if you retreat too hastily from it, he's going to sense it immediately and know you have plenty of room to move in his direction. Don't let it happen.

Unleashing Strategic Force No. 1

Okay. The offers are on the table. Both you and your opponent have laid out your opening positions. The bargaining is set to begin; it will now be determined who gets what. Now is the time to trot out your first Strategic Force, which, you'll recall, will help you to get your opponent to settle at his Least Acceptable Result—in other words, to get the best deal you possibly can out of this negotiation.

The success of your first Strategic Force hinges on your ability to convince your opponent that he's not going to do much better than a settlement at your Maximum Supportable Position. By infusing him with doubts about how far he can move you down, you sap his willingness to hold out. So when you announce your M.S.P., back it up with all you've got. Throw out every justification you can think of, every little fact that will convey to him that this is no snow job, that this is really where you have to settle . . . for all the reasons you've given him. It forces your opponent to take your position seriously. Your hypothetical budget negotiation is a perfect example. Even though your boss initially was floored by what you asked for, he was not at liberty to dismiss it outright. You didn't let him. No sooner had you asserted your position than you launched into all of the justifications for it. You didn't pick $50,000 out of thin air, and now that you've shown him and proved to him that you indeed have a strong case behind you, he has no choice but to take your M.S.P. seriously. The fastest way I know to bring about the undoing of your negotiation is to give your opponent an inkling that your opening position is a hollow one. If you leave your M.S.P. dangling, unprotected by a shell of justification, your opponent's going to reach up and pluck it right away from you, and he'll keep at it until he has plucked all the way to the bottom of your Settlement Range.

Building the credibility of your Maximum Supportable Position does double duty for your negotiation. Not only does it display to your opponent the resolve behind your offer, it also gets him to thinking that your bottom line can't be very far away. After I've staunchly defended my opening stance of $900 in our typewriter deal, what are the chances that you'll come anywhere near figuring that my least Acceptable Result is $500? Likely none. Instead, you'll be thinking, "If he's really as intent as he seems on getting $900, he'll probably only come down as far as $850 or maybe $800." By riveting your attention on the top end of my Settlement Range, I've kept you away from the bottom, and that's absolutely essential if I'm going to get the best deal I can from you. Because if you detect—whether by my lack of rationale for my M.S.P., by my apparent lack of conviction in it, or by your sense that I need this deal very badly, whatever—that my L.A.R. is a good distance from my M.S.P., my prospects for that best deal are about as good as the prospects for the return of the penny postcard.

The Fine Art of Making Concessions

Not long ago, I was looking for a typist. One woman I called told me, "My rate is $1.50 per page." Before I could utter so much as a word, she added, "But if the job is substantial and the material isn't too technical, I can probably do it for $1.25 per page." Introducing the star pupil of the How-Not-To-Make-Concessions Class.

She never gave her M.S.P. a chance of working. Instead of standing firmly behind it, she ran rapidly away from it. And what was I left to think? First, that she probably had a pressing need for the job (why else would she have retreated so hastily?); second, that her Least Acceptable Result was probably a good ways down from a $1.25. By making too big a concession too early, she pulled the rug out from under her M.S.P., gave the unmistakable impression that she could easily be talked down further, and, in the process, completely undermined her negotiating position.

Knowing how and when to make concessions is critical to the success of your negotiation. A single, well-timed concession often can insure landing the settlement you're hoping for, just as a poorly timed one can insure losing it. Concessions must be handled with great care. Start small; give grudgingly, and give with pain. If you're too generous with early concessions, you reveal things about your bargaining position that you definitely don't want your opponent to know.

Say you're negotiating for a new job, and you've asked for $20,000. Extensive experience, solid references, impressive track record—you toss out all these things to buttress your position. "I don't doubt that you're eminently qualified for the job," your opponent says, "or that you'd be a valuable addition to our company. But the fact is I'm between a rock and a hard place. Look at this budget I'm working with. There's just not that kind of money available for this position."

"I like the way you operate here," you reply. "I think I would fit in well, that I could contribute to the company, and also further my own long-range career goals. In view of that, I'm willing to be flexible. If I have to, I will come down to $18,000 if that's what is necessary in order for us to work something out."

What have you done? For starters, by coming down so far so soon, you've eroded the credibility of your M.S.P. Your opponent no longer has to take it seriously, because, by retreating this quickly, you've told him, in effect, that you were bluffing, that you weren't very committed at all to your opening stance. You've also let him know you have room to move. After all, already you've backed down $2,000; what's to stop him from thinking he can move you still more? For a good negotiator, receiving concessions is like eating candy; he gets a taste, and he wants more. Don't expect that because you make a sizable concession—as you've done here—your opponent is going to say, "That was damn charitable of him. Let's settle right here." It doesn't work that way. More likely he'll think, "That was a big chunk of candy he gave me. I wonder how much more he has?" No negotiator in his right mind is going to agree to a deal if he thinks you still have more to give—and that's precisely what too big a concession will make him think.

Not only should concessions be small, they should also be justifiable. The last thing you want your opponent to think is that you're backtracking of your own volition because you don't think you can get a settlement at your M.S.P. You want him to think you're doing so, not out of internal pressure, but from external reason—because you understand his situation, because you're a reasonable person, because you know that negotiation involves giving as well as taking. Putting it another way, avoid making your concession seem like a unilateral caving-in; make it seem like a reasoned response to some factor that came up in the bargaining. Take your hypothetical job negotiation. Rather than simply conceding because you don't think you'll get the $20,000, wait for your opponent to give you a way to justify your concession. Say your prospective boss tells you about all the room for advancement in the firm and how all the vice-presidents worked their way up through the ranks. Even if that isn't particularly important to you, you can make it seem like the rationale for your backing down. "While I firmly believe that my demand is reasonable, I can see there are other considerations to weigh here. Being rewarded for my efforts is important to me, and since we see eye to eye on that and since I can understand your budgetary problems, I'm willing to be somewhat flexible. Assuming, of course, that the other benefits are as we discussed, I could live with $19,000." Rather than retreating out of self-doubt, you've made a concession born of a credible reason—your future advancement—for you to be more flexible. You've also sent your opponent a very clear message: "I'm serious about my opening position and am moderating only after careful thought and with good reason, so don't get any wild ideas about pushing me around." I know a consultant who recently negotiated a contract with a company. He asked for $20,000, but could only get their top offer up to $15,000. That was comfortably within his Settlement Range, but rather than agree to the deal outright, he told the company that to do the job for the lower price, he would have to make some cuts in the work he was proposing to undertake. In fact, the change was of minuscule importance, but he made it nonetheless so as to justify his concession. He was afraid that if he had jumped at $15,000, the company might have thought he could be moved some more and withdrawn the offer.

You want your concessions to be small, but at the same time, you don't want your opponent thinking of them that way. You want him to think you're making a substantial sacrifice. You want to show him how reasonable you are, how far you're willing to bend in the interests of reaching a deal, thus building up in him a sort of "concession debt." What you're saying to him, in effect, is, "Okay, I've given up some things that are near and dear to me. [After all, if you were so reluctant to make concessions, mustn't they be worth quite a bit?] Now it's your turn." The more you concede in negotiation, the more "justice" in your demand that your opponent make concessions in return.

Suppose you're selling a used stereo system. Throughout the bargaining you've made it abundantly clear that your offer does not include your brand-new head phones. The price you're bargaining over is well up in your Settlement Range. You'd be happy to settle there, but you get the sense that he's going to try hard to move you down. "Tell you what," you say. "I think we're close. I'd like to settle this business. If we can agree to the price we've discussed, then I'll throw in the head phones." Maybe they are worth $30, but it's a good bet your opponent is attaching added value to them because you've been so insistent in your desire to hold on to them. Your aim in making concessions is to trade your small ones for his large ones, your low priorities for his high priorities. Your opponent, of course, is not going to have any part of it if he thinks what you're giving him is peanuts. Like so much in negotiation, it all comes down to your ability to play the actor. Even if something is of but minor value to you, give it up as if you're giving up your left arm. Make it seem like you really don't want to concede it, but you will in the interest of settlement, provided, naturally, that your opponent is willing to make a concession of equal magnitude.

When you're involved in a multiple-goal negotiation, your concession strategy can work wonders if you set up your straw men tactic. That is, along with your real goals in the negotiation, throw in some bogus ones, things that you're pretending are important to you when in fact they are not. Then, when you want to propose a trade-off in concessions with your opponent, simply drop one of your straw men in exchange for something you really do want. Some years back, a student of mine was negotiating for a new job with a prospective employer. She had come to terms on the salary issue, and was grappling with several nonmonetary concerns. From the start, she had been pushing strongly for a lofty job title, something like "executive director of . . . ," while her opponent was maintaining that the position had always been called "division manager of . . ." In reality, the title was near the bottom of her negotiating priorities. But she didn't let him know that; she treated it as if it were of surpassing importance. Consequently, when she finally—and grudgingly—yielded on that issue, she was able to exact from him a concession—the right to report directly to the head man instead of one of his henchmen—that truly was of surpassing importance to her.

One warning about concession-making: While you do want to make what are truly small concessions seem to your opponent to be substantial, be aware of staying within the bounds of credibility. No matter how ardently I try to convince you otherwise, you're simply not going to buy the fact that the giving up of my goal to keep my pet parakeet in my office qualifies as a major concession. What you're billing as a sacrifice must be at least somewhat credible as such; if it's not, your opponent is going to see right through it, completely discount it, and thus be unwilling to match it with any concession of his own.

To sum up: Start small. Give up relatively unimportant things, give up straw men, but whatever you do, give them up grudgingly. Imbue them with added significance by leading your opponent to believe they're more important to you than they really are. Build up his concession debt and be sure to justify your actions, so that your opponent doesn't get the notion that you're succumbing to your own internal pressure. As the negotiation goes on, it may become apparent that only major concessions on both sides will salvage the deal from deadlock. Proceed with caution. Make sure that, in return for *your* major concession, you're getting a settlement that's still to your advantage to accept. Finally, don't get so preoccupied with your own concession-making that you fail to study your opponent's. Watch him carefully. You can learn an awful lot about his bargaining position by what and when he concedes.

Playing on Your Opponent's Need for the Deal

As you'll recall from our discussion of Strategic Force No. 2, the greater your opponent's need for the deal, the less likely he'll be to risk anything to lose it. If the I.R.S. has notified you that they're going to come a-knocking at your door next week to collect the $1,500 in back taxes you owe, are you really in a position to diddle around when you sell your motorcycle to get the money to pay Uncle Sam? No way. The bike's book value is $1,900, and that's what you'll ask for, but the first soul who offers you $1,500 or more is going to walk away with a two-wheeler.

Sometimes when you negotiate, you'll be dealing with an opponent who wants to settle so badly that he'll be extending his hand the moment your offer slips into his Settlement Range. Other times, however, your opponent's need will not be so acute, and he'll need some coaxing to settle where you want. Despite your best efforts to convince him that a better deal is not forthcoming, he'll seem intent on holding out.

When you're face-to-face with an opponent such as this, keep in mind that there are ways to heighten his need for settlement and thus sap him of some of his persistence. I'm talking about goodies and threats, the two components of your second Strategic Force. You'll recall that goodies and threats both work toward the same end—increasing the opponent's need—but do it in opposite ways; goodies work by throwing some extra sweetener into the pot, a sweetener which is worth something to your opponent and thus makes it harder for him to turn his back on the deal; and threats work by bringing to light a negative consequence—one your opponent wants to avoid if he possibly can—that will come about if a settlement isn't achieved. Take the case of Jeannette, the consumer advocate who negotiated with the dishwasher repairman. She might've said to him, "You know, we do a lot of referrals in the home-repair area, and I'd be happy to include you on our list of reliable and trustworthy businessmen. Provided, of course, that we can reach a satisfactory agreement." A top-notch goody, Jeannette. Now the repairman has an extra incentive to settle; she has him thinking that merely by coming up with enough cash to appease the elderly woman, he might be able to do his business a lot of long-term good.

On the other side, Jeannette might've said, "We keep an active file of all our outstanding complaints—all the cases that were not resolved to our client's satisfaction. Naturally, when people call us looking for a particular service, we're obliged to advise them of those businesses with which we've experienced difficulty in the past." Here she has injected a threat into the picture. Now the repairman has to ask himself, "Is saving twenty-five or so bucks worth enough to me to run the risk of losing potential customers because of the agency's complaint file? Odds are his answer will be no. Jeannette's threat effectively gave him a backhanded need for the deal. She completely changed his priorities. Instead of trying to get off with paying the woman as little as possible, he suddenly felt pressure to agree to a deal that would satisfy her and enable him to avoid the consequences of deadlock.

When you're involved in a more complex negotiation, building momentum for a settlement is another effective way to increase your opponent's need. Suppose you and your opponent are negotiating five separate issues. One of them is a biggie, the potential stumbling block, which you've suggested—and your opponent has agreed—to put aside until later. By resolving the four ancillary matters, not only do you infuse a positive atmosphere into the bargaining, you also exert a positive pressure on your opponent to settle. After all, now he has more to lose if the deal falls through. Everybody hates to undo progress; by getting the ball steamrolling toward settlement, you get your opponent thinking, "Gee, we've already come so far, it would be a shame to lose it all now."

Be aware, however, that building momentum also puts pressure on you, so this approach must be used judiciously. A rule of thumb to follow is that if you sense you need the deal more than your opponent, if you feel that reaching agreements on the side events puts more pressure on you than him, then by all means do not build momentum for a settlement. Say you operate a small T-shirt business. Most of your orders come from local clubs and organizations and fall in the three to four dozen range. Somehow, a corporate giant finds out about you, loves your work, and wants to place an order for two hundred dozen shirts. You can live off this deal alone for months; clearly, your need for it to go through is paramount. When you sit down with the firm's vice-president of promotions, there is an array of issues on the table. He seems extremely eager to get the more peripheral matters settled. He agrees to assume responsibility for pick-up and delivery of the shirts. He hints that he'll be able to give you a very sizable chunk of cash up front and assures you that he doesn't expect you to finish the order in an unreasonably short time. But knowing that reaching firm agreement on these issues would only heighten your already acute need for the deal, you talk your way around it. (You also get the distinct impression that, by being so agreeable on these matters, he's attempting to build up your concession debt, in the hope that you'll make substantial concessions in your price.) "So as not to waste your time or my time," you assert, "I think the first question we have to approach is the price per shirt. Because obviously if we can't agree on that score, all of the other concerns will be moot." Good show! He can't argue with your logic, and you've spared yourself from being put in a position of feeling pressure to accept a lower price than you want, simply because so many of the other issues have been agreed on.

Building momentum for a deal is a good way to induce your opponent to come to terms. Just be sure to use momentum only in situations where the bulk of the pressure from the steamrolling negotiation falls on your opponent, not you.

Altering Your Opponent's
Settlement Range

Valerie, an author of a cookbook, has been approached by a
public television station to appear on one of its programs. You
might recall that when we last left Valerie, she'd determined
that her Least Acceptable Result for the negotiation would be
nothing, reasoning that the additional sales of her book she
could expect from the exposure would by themselves make
the appearances worth her while. Well, Valerie's lot has
changed quite a bit over these last couple of hundred pages.
She has crisscrossed the country on an author tour, and the
book has been selling like Alka-Seltzer on New Year's day.
In light of her newfound celebrity, she has decided that her
L.A.R. for the program negotiation will be $500.

But when she sits down to bargain with the station manager, he informs, "The series has really taken off since we
had our preliminary discussion. By our calculations it now
reaches some forty percent more households than we had orig-
inally projected." Valerie is happily surprised; more households means more potential book sales. Digesting the new
information, she thinks back to her Settlement Range and
tells herself, "With the expanded market, it's more in my interest than ever to be on the program. I'm going to lower my
Least Acceptable Result to $250. (Her asking price remains
the same; but she now knows if she is pushed back, she can
afford to accept less.)

It was a sound decision by Valerie; after all, the increased
visibility made the program significantly more valuable to her
and, that being the case, it made perfect sense that she would
be willing to accept less money to appear on it if push comes
to shove. It also was a sound negotiating move by her opponent, who knew that the disclosure would increase the
pressure on her to settle and, in all likelihood, induce her to
accept a lower fee to do so. Try to do likewise when you're
at the bargaining table. Make your research count for all it's
worth. Bring to light any reasons, arguments, or bits of information you've found that may step up the pressures on
your opponent to reach agreement and prompt him to alter
his Settlement Range accordingly.

In our continuing saga of the typewriter (this sure is one
long negotiation we're hooked up in, isn't it?), suppose, after

hearing you out, I came back at you like this: "This machine is only three years old, and the average life of this model is fifteen years. And that's not all, it has the highest resale value of any typewriter on the market." Naturally, I've got the figures on hand, just in case you're skeptical. The information I've thrown out can do nothing but enhance its value to you; hell, you'll probably have use of the thing for the next twelve years, and if you ever decide to unload it, you have the comfort of knowing it'll be in high demand. Whether you actually change the location of your L.A.R. in response to my arguments I'll never know, since, like any good negotiator, you've kept your bottom line under wraps. But I do know that I've increased your incentive to settle. All of this presupposes, of course, that I'm disclosing information you did not already know. If you did, then it already would've been processed into your Settlement Range and thus would be worth a big fat goose egg as far as my aim to put additional pressure on you to settle is concerned.

It bears repeating that you can never be one hundred percent certain that the new information you've injected into the bargaining has, in fact, prompted your opponent to alter his Settlement Range. It would be nice to know, if only for the gratification of knowing that you had negotiated well and got the best deal you possibly could. But it really doesn't matter. What does matter is that by introducing one or more new factors into the bargaining—factors which augment the worth of what you've brought to the table—you've exerted additional pressure on your opponent to reach an agreement. It's the same as when you change the circumstances surrounding the negotiation. Rarely do you know if the change actually has made your opponent recalculate his Settlement Range.

Go back to the case of Arthur, the newspaper editor who went ahead and hired an advertising manager for the paper, collected evidence that the move was profitable, and then presented the publisher with a fait accompli. True, the publisher in the past had shown great reluctance to hire any other employees—to do anything, really, that would enable the paper to grow. Nonetheless, Arthur had no way of knowing with absolute certainty that the publisher's Settlement Range did not include hiring an advertising manager. There is *no* doubt, however, that by changing the circumstances, Arthur brought more pressure to bear on the publisher to agree to what Arthur wanted.

Don't be fazed by the fact that you don't have tangible evidence that your changing the circumstances or disclosing new information has expanded your negotiating possibilities by altering your opponent's Settlement Range. Because what's important is that you've put new pressure on your opponent to settle, and that, ultimately, is what's going to enable you to walk away from the table with what you want.

Pace, Patience, and Persistence

It happens to the best. Despite all your efforts to steer it in the opposite direction, the negotiation seems to be slipping away from you. Momentum is staunchly situated in the other guy's corner. Your anxiety glands are working overtime, and you're certain you're showing it. Your resolve is teetering, and you sense you're being backed into a place you don't want to be. What to do?

Stop it! Like a basketball coach watching his team unravel in a close game, call time out. Go to the bathroom. Take a lunch break. Tell him you have to go feed your dog, tell him you hear your mother calling in the distance, tell him anything, but whatever you do, recess! Give yourself a chance to think things through, to regroup, to reassess the situation. Don't allow yourself to be thrown off balance. Negotiation can be confusing enough by itself; if you're feeling confused on top of it, your chances for bargaining with any coherence and effectiveness are nil. Suggest an adjournment until tomorrow. "Holy mackerel! Did I ever lose track of time! I'm late for a doctor's appointment. Can we continue our discussion tomorrow?" The deal will still be there. If you think it won't be there tomorrow, take a long enough break for you to gather your wits. Refresh your memory. Have you thrown out all the arguments you have to support your position? Is there any new information you've forgotten to bring up? What about your goodies? threats? Have you overlooked anything that might put pressure on your opponent?

Being able to control the pace of negotiation is very important. You want things to proceed at a comfortable and productive clip. If they're not, it's up to you to do something about it. Maybe your opponent has proposed a settlement with a new twist; he wants to pay you half in cash, half by designing custom draperies for your living room, and you need time to decide if that's acceptable. Maybe the two of you are knocking heads, and you feel it's counterproductive to continue with tempers getting ever shorter. Fine. Arrange a time when you might resume with cooler heads. Maybe, if you're part of a negotiating team, one member of your side is unaccountably divulging too much about the deep, dark secrets of your Settlement Range. "We'd like to talk things over," you tell your opponents. "Can we resume our discussions in a half hour or so?" Pull your team out and find out what the hell your loose-lipped compatriot is trying to do. Or maybe your opponent seems especially itchy to settle, making you suspect that there's a potent pressure working on him. You decide to go slow ("Why don't we talk again next Thursday?") to see if you can put the pressure to work for your negotiating advantage. Whatever the situation, strive to keep on top of the bargaining pace. Trust your instincts; when things don't feel right, you can wager that they aren't right. And when they do feel right, by all means keep the momentum going. Just take care to do it in a way that doesn't betray to your opponent what you're thinking, "I can't believe I'm going to get everything I wanted out of this deal." Because if your opponent detects your elation, then *he* is going to be the one pushing for recess—precisely what you don't want when things are going swimmingly for you.

Showing patience and persistence at the bargaining table is also critical to the success of your negotiation. Realize that in most cases the settlement you want isn't going to be achieved forthwith. It's going to take time—time to build the credibility of your position, to feel out your opponent, to find ways to exert additional pressure on him to settle, to know when to make what concession, and to convince him that he shouldn't hold out because there's simply not a better offer forthcoming from you in this negotiation. You know that some degree of tension is inevitable (Can I make a deal? How good a deal can I make?), so do your best to live with it and not let it interfere with your bargaining. Hang on to your position, stand by it, and show your opponent your resolve in spite of what you're feeling inside. Remember, if you cave in too quickly, you're going to be in a peck of trouble. Reassure yourself with the knowledge that the settlement you want—the big breakthrough, the concession your opponent's been resisting making—may not come until the eleventh hour. Negotiation isn't only a test of wits, it's a test of nerves. The better you're able to stifle yours and show your opponent how determined you are, the more uncertain he'll be, and the more likely he'll be to settle where you want. Don't underestimate how damaging it can be to show any sign of impatience, haste, or anxiety. If your opponent picks up on any of them, he's going to start thinking that there's more pressure on you than you're letting on. And once he starts thinking that, he's going to get ideas about holding out for something better, which is precisely what you don't want to happen.

Be patient, be persistent, and sit on those butterflies flitting around in your stomach. You'll put a stop to your opponent's ideas of holding out before they even start.

Dealing with Deadlock

The Shuffleboard Club of Greater Secaucus (SCOGS) is in a quandary. It seems like all eighteen members have a different opinion about where the club's annual Labor Day outing should be held. Charlie's pushing for a beach by the ocean. "It'll be wall-to-wall people," says Margie, who wants to have it in a park upstate. Marilyn thinks chartering a sailboat for a ride up the Hudson River is a dandy idea. But Spiro thinks that would be prohibitively expensive and suggests either a New York Yankee game or a nearby mountain lake as an alternative. "Who wants to spend a holiday at the ball park!" jabs Amy. Personally, she thinks they should chuck all these ideas and have the outing in someone's backyard. It seems like a hopeless deadlock. The more the discussion goes on, the further apart everyone seems to get.

Frank, SCOGS's outing chairman, has heard quite enough. "This shouldn't be that hard," he says. "First of all, I think we all agree that we should not have the outing at that bug-infested swamp under the freeway again. Let's go back through the basics. Let's sort out our priorities. Do we want to have a barbecue and maybe do some swimming? Or would we prefer a fishing trip or maybe a boat ride? Some people have expressed an interest in hiking. Do we want a place that has trails? And how far are we willing to travel? As the members respond to the questions Frank has posed, a consensus gradually begins to emerge. Most everyone agrees a barbecue is a nice idea. There's agreement, too, on finding a place within an hour-and-a-half drive. Hiking trails would be nice, but swimming seems a higher priority. Everyone gets a lot less edgy and a little more excited as the focus of alternatives gets sharper.

Suddenly, a brainstorm descends on Frank. "Hey, I think I

got a place we can go, and I think it has a lot of the things we're looking for. Last year, they just opened up this big place—I think it's called Thomas L. Biracree State Park—about sixty miles west of here. I haven't been there, but I've seen one of those brochures, and it says they have a lake and picnic benches and a couple of different trails through the woods. Plus it's far enough away and new enough that it probably wouldn't be crowded. And if my memory serves me right, Marilyn, I believe you can even rent those little sailboats there." The response is overwhelming. Frank gets a wholehearted go-ahead to check the place out, and if it's all the brochure said it was, everyone agrees it would be an ideal place for the SCOGS annual outing. Even Spiro goes along with it. "I guess I can listen to the Yanks on the radio," he says cheerfully.

When you're confronted with a deadlock, don't despair. It's not necessarily unresolvable. Don't just say, "Well, we've reached a deadlock. That's it," and let it go at that. Look for ways to get around it. Try going back to the basics, as Frank did, and reestablish the common ground you and your opponent share. Emphasize the narrowness of the gap between you and the number of issues already resolved, rather than the outstanding differences. Sometimes, just in the rehashing, you can break through an impasse.

Keep searching for your opponent's hidden needs. Who knows, if you can meet one or more of them, it might be just the impetus you need to push a settlement through. It worked for Tom, the executive with the truck-leasing firm. You'll recall that he was negotiating the terms of a leasing agreement with a prospective customer. They were going round and round in their dollar discussions until Tom learned about the problem his opponent was having with truck parking. With acres of extra parking space at his disposal, Tom was able to meet his opponent's need and reach agreement on the leasing contract.

Or take the case of your T-shirt negotiation with the large company. You've tried to get around it, but the deadlock comes down to dollars and cents. You've calculated that you have to get $7,200 to make the deal worth your while. The corporate official says the absolute top figure he's authorized to spend on the shirts if $6,000. "I'd really like you to have the business," he says, "but my boss would have my head if I spent anything more." The two of you have been bargaining over several weeks now. The deadlock notwithstanding, the negotiation has been conducted with mutual respect and good faith. You keep the dialogue going, exploring each other's needs and goals. "You're a small, independent businessman," he says. "Would it be presumptuous of me to say that you have some cash-flow problems from time to time?"

"Not at all."

"Well, what if we restructured the financial arrangement? How 'bout if I give you, say, five grand up front instead of the thirty-five hundred we discussed earlier?" That would help quite a bit, you're thinking. You have your quarterly taxes coming up, after all.

"That gets us closer," you reply. "But to be honest, after all my time and expenses, that still doesn't leave me with enough profit to take on a deal of this size." Running out of time, you decide to adjourn for the day. Things still look pretty dim.

The next day you get a call. "I think I've got it!" he exclaims. "You were telling me once about the hassles and expense you've got to go through to deliver your various orders.

"Yeah, it's a pain in the neck. The guy I use is expensive as hell, and he isn't even reliable."

"Listen, the guy who runs our distribution department owes me a couple. I talked it over with him, and I can get use of a twelve-foot carry-all on Saturdays and Sundays for, say, the next three months. Whaddya think?" It sounds promising. You tell him you'll get back to him later on. You sit down and figure how much the van would save you and if, taken together with the extra up front money, the package would be enough to compensate for the lower price. You call him.

"We've got a deal."

Persistence and creativity are essential when you're trying to work your way around a deadlock. When you're stalled over a specific issue—whether it's money or mules—often imaginative problem-solving can result in a new element that just may get things going again. A client of mine sells advertising space in one of those weekly shoppers. He was negotiating with the proprietor of a hair-styling salon, but they couldn't get any closer than $50 apart. Finally, the proprietor said, "I'll give you and your publisher one free hair styling apiece. If I get a good response from the ad and decide to keep running it, I'll give you each a fifty percent discount every time you come in." Unusual? You bet. Did it work? Well, the shopper is run by two of the most neatly coiffed men in town.

There are times, of course, when all the persistence and creativity in the world won't be enough to navigate you around a deadlock. Don't mourn over it, and don't consider the deadlock a failure. Some deals were just not meant to be. As long as you feel you've tried every angle you could think of to slip past it, forget it and move on to the next one. One of the few things negotiation cannot accomplish is turning lead to gold.

Closing the Deal

Once you and your opponent shake hands on a deal, make sure you know what you're shaking hands about. It may sound silly, but I've seen more than one settlement dissolve out of misunderstanding somewhere between the bargaining table and the actual exchange. Nail it down. Erase all trace of doubt. Particularly in more involved negotiations, it's a good idea to repeat the various points you've agreed on, just to make sure there's no discrepancy. "I'm going to make two hundred dozen red-on-beige T-shirts for you, to be ready by June 1. You'll arrange for pickup and delivery. The price for the shirts is $5,500, five thousand of which is payable on the formal signing of the deal. And, not to forget, I will have access to a twelve-foot carry-all van on weekends for the next three months. Have I got it all?" Once you've agreed verbally, get it in writing whenever possible. Some negotiations, of course, don't lend themselves to getting it in writing. If you've just negotiated with your child's dance teacher to allow him to stay in her class even though he's already had four "last chances" to clean up his act, you're not very well going to ask the teacher for a written deposition. Let your instincts be your guide. If the deal is at all delicate, intricate, or valuable to you or if you feel it's especially important to spell out what each side has agreed to do, then by all means get it on paper.

On occasion, however, (remember, *every* rule has its exceptions), it may be in your interest to *not* make things so explicit, to leave some aspects of the negotiation open-ended. This is especially true when you're beginning what will be an ongoing relationship with your opponent, and you need time to build a bridge of trust and good faith between you. A good example is the negotiation I talked about earlier in which I played a part in the merger of two social service organizations. There wasn't overtly bad blood between the two groups, but it wasn't all that good either. I guess you could say there was a degree of mutual suspicion. For that reason, it would've been foolhardy to attempt to reach firm agreement early on about several symbolic, potentially explosive issues such as who would hold on to what title ("We want our director to be the new director."——"No, our director should assume that position." That kind of bickering was what we wanted to avoid) and who should report to whom and what the name of the new organization would be. If we had pressed our case too ardently, we would've possibly heightened their suspicions and led them to believe we were orchestrating some sort of power play. By allowing time to pass before tackling these matters, we were able to dampen the doubts on each side and solidify a working relationship and minimize the potential for a serious rift emerging. Remember, though, that it's only in special cases of negotiation—when it'll simply take some time to foster the necessary credibility between you and your opponent for your future dealings—that purposely leaving some issues vague is a good idea. In all other instances, nail the deal down. After expending all that energy negotiating, the last thing you need is a mistaken impression or misunderstanding blowing your efforts sky high.

PART V

The Negotiator's Workshop

CHAPTER 14

Twelve Common Negotiations: How to Handle Them and Get What You Want

Negotiating with Insurance Companies

Problems with insurance companies generally arise in two areas.

Rate Disputes and the Insurance Company Dropping Your Coverage. The key in these negotiations is using allies. If you can't straighten out the problem with the company itself, and you've purchased the coverage through a broker, he's the first ally you want to call on. If your broker cannot or will not assist you or if you've bought the policy directly from the company, switch your sights to the state department of insurance. All fifty states have such departments, which are responsible for regulating insurance rates as well as the conditions upon which insurance premiums can be charged.

The state department of insurance came to my rescue once. After trying to find out for months what my new premium would be on an automobile insurance policy, the company finally dropped the bombshell on me; although I'd had no tickets and no accidents, they had reclassified me into a high-risk category and jacked up my premium from $300 to $500. Upon hearing that, I immediately changed companies. I was willing to pay the company for those months . . . but at the old rate. The insurance company, naturally, wanted me to pay at the new rate. I called the department of insurance, got the name of the appropriate official, and wrote him a letter detailing the problem. Within two weeks, the company contacted me, agreeing to my demand that I pay them at the old premium rate.

Making Claims. Bear in mind that every time an insurance company pays a claim, that payment represents a drain on its profits. Some companies are prompt, courteous, and reasonable in their claim settlement policies, others are notoriously bad, and most fall somewhere in between. (*Consumer Reports* rates auto insurance firms on the basis of claim settlement; it's a good idea to research a company before you sign on with them.)

In making your insurance claim, it's essential that it represent your absolute Maximum Supportable Position. Remember, you only get one trip to the well; you might get less money from the company, but you're certainly not going to get more. Don't hesitate to file your claim with every conceivable reparation you're entitled to. As I mentioned in our discussion of allies, my wife Jeanne and I once had some steam damage in our apartment, and an antique table, which had not been in showroom shape beforehand, was further damaged. Nonetheless, I requested the cost of having it refinished along with some other relatively minor items. Be creative in making your claim. Don't invent things just to pad it, but don't overlook anything either. Odds are the company will offer you less anyway, so make them start their bargaining from a dollar figure that is as high as you can credibly make it.

Should the company refuse to offer a settlement that is above your Least Acceptable Result, your next step would again be to appeal to your state department of insurance. If the department is unable to resolve it to your satisfaction, consult with your lawyer if you haven't already done so. If you don't have a lawyer, get one. Insurance companies are under a special legal obligation to pay you when a legitimate claim arises, and besides, the presence of a lawyer on your side enhances your credibility and serves notice to the insurance company that you are not to be fooled with. If the company continues to deal in bad faith, if they try to intimidate you, harass you, or otherwise attempt to skirt their obligation, they may be liable to pay what they already owe you and substantial punitive damages as well.

Negotiating Salary and Benefits for a New Job

The biggest problem most people have in conducting new job negotiations is they sell themselves short. This tendency— often reinforced by the prospective employer—betrays an attitude which says, in effect, "Oh please, Almighty Employer and Holder of My Future, please be so kind to let little old me toil for your noble enterprise."

Take stock of your assets and of what you can mean to the company. One student of mine went so far as to write down his special strengths and qualifications for a job and consulted it from time to time during the interview to bolster his bargaining case. Many people feel that when they've been selected for a job and are negotiating salary, they're in a weak position because if they can't reach agreement, the company will simply move on to the next candidate in line. While that can happen, it usually doesn't because it's not in the best interests of the firm to let its most highly regarded candidate slip away over a relatively minor difference (the differences usually *are* minor) in salary. Having conducted a number of searches and hired many people myself, I know that seldom, if ever, are there two candidates so closely matched that a company will hastily abandon its first choice and move happily on to the second. Almost inevitably, one is substantially better than the next, which is why he or she is the first choice. Sometimes the employer may even be in the situation of having only one genuinely qualified candidate. Also keep in mind that the search process is both time-consuming and costly, and the last thing the company wants to do is start going down the ladder, or worse, beginning the ordeal all over again.

Remember, too, that your leverage at this point is greater than it will ever be again. Once you're hired, it's much more difficult to walk away. By shooting high, you also convey a sense of self-worth and self-confidence and set yourself up well for future raise negotiations.

Money is important, but it's not everything. Ask for as much as you can possibly justify, but at the same time don't lose sight of valuable nonmonetary benefits and a host of other important issues such as what your title may be, whom you are going to report to, what kind of budget you'll have at your disposal, where your office is going to be, and so forth. Now is the best time to straighten out these matters; indeed, there will never be a better time. Stand up for yourself; the most important impression is the first one.

Finally, be creative in your bargaining. Just because you may not be able to agree on the major issues doesn't mean a deadlock is in the offing. Use the problem-solving tactic to see if differences can be worked out. I know someone who was offered a job at a salary he simply could not accept. The problem was that he wanted the position and knew that the salary offered was all that he could hope to get out of this particular employer, not because the employer didn't want to give him more, but because of the ripple effect it would have on other employees in the organization. Instead of deadlocking, he sat down and did some problem-solving with his boss, and together they worked out a package of nonmonetary benefits—travel allowances, education benefits, expense account allowances, etc.—that translated into a package worth some $3,000. On that basis, he decided to take the job.

Negotiating Price on Big-Ticket Items

Washers, dryers, dishwashers, refrigerators, freezers, stereos, TV sets, furniture—many of the big-ticket goods we buy, and even some of the smaller ones, can be had for substantial discounts. Advertised specials often exceed reductions of thirty percent, with the retailer still making a profit.

Keep in mind that this is an Oh-Boy Negotiation; your opponent wants very much to deal with you. The key to these negotiations is setting your Maximum Supportable Position and Least Acceptable Result, and the key to that is information. The more you know about pricing structure, the market, and the competition, the better you'll be able to negotiate a good price for yourself. Two of the best ways to gather pertinent information are consulting *Consumer Reports*, which publishes articles on numerous items you might want to purchase, and simply shopping around, not just for price comparisons but also to learn more about the product. My experience has been that every time I've talked with a salesman, I not only learn his prices but also more about the product, which is a big help in determining what my final selection will be. Armed with solid information, you can then start with the lowest offered price and negotiate an even better price from there.

Remember to get your opponent to invest some time and energy in the deal. Don't walk in and tell him you want $50 off the food processor. Take your time. Establish yourself as a serious customer, someone who, if the terms are right, is going to earn the salesman a nice, healthy commission. Once he has spent time discussing the pros and cons of various models, exploring your needs, talking price, etc., he has an increased stake in reaching a settlement with you; after all, he doesn't want his efforts to go for nought.

In many stores, the salesman will do everything in his power to convince you that the price is not negotiable. He may be telling the truth, but more often than not, he's simply doing his job as a negotiator and bolstering the credibility of his opening position. Test him; you have nothing to lose and dollars to gain. I strongly suggest, after spending some time with your opponent, that you walk out at least once before buying. No need to storm out or act churlishly; simply say, "Well, I need some more time to think it over." In many cases, the depressing sight of you headed toward the door will elicit a better offer from him. And even if it doesn't, you can always go back and bargain with him some more. But again, the key here is testing and probing. Don't accept the salesman's claim at face value when he says he can't make any price concessions. By holding out, by letting him know that his price is not within your Settlement Range, and, eventually, by walking out, you'll find out soon enough if he means what he says. If he does, so be it; you've lost nothing for trying.

Negotiating a Raise

The toughest thing about negotiating a raise is that unless you're planning to quit if you don't get what you want, it's a bit difficult to define exactly what a deadlock is, which in turn makes the establishment of your Least Acceptable Result very difficult. If you ask for $5,000, set your L.A.R. at $3,-000, and your boss only gives you $2,000, what's going on? Assuming you don't quit, from your boss's point of view, you have a deal; you keep on working and he's giving you $2,000 more. But what about from your point of view? Does the fact that you're accepting $2,000 mean that your L.A.R. wasn't a true bottom line but a wish point?

Your first step, therefore, is to define what the consequences of deadlock are. Essentially they are two; one, that you quit, and two, that you continue working, but that you are now an unhappy employee who feels he has been mistreated.

A few observations about quitting. Don't threaten to do it unless you mean it. Don't actually quit unless you have another job lined up (unless you're one of those lucky few who is so outstanding and well-known in your field that the offers will come streaming in once word is out that you're available). And be aware that threatening to quit, at least overtly and directly, is clumsy, not very subtle, and, at best, leaves a bad taste if you get your raise, and, at worst, leaves your loyalty to the company forever in question. The one advantage to quitting if you don't get what you want, of course, is that it leaves no doubt about the consequences of deadlock: You're gone.

But if you don't plan to quit and the offer you receive is outside your Settlement Range, then you have to make it clear to your boss that you have in fact reached a deadlock. When the boss refuses to budge on his $2,000 offer, you should tell him, in effect, "You are deciding this by fiat, and you should understand that we have reached no agreement as to what my salary should be." The implication is razor sharp; he knows that, to one degree or another, he now has a disgruntled employee on his hands.

Setting your M.S.P. is critical. Make sure it's high—don't be timid—but on the other hand, make sure you have ways to back it up. Remember that you have to do the sales job because no one else is going to. Also remember that this likely is an Oh-No Negotiation for your boss; he would rather that you hadn't broached the matter at all. It's a rare boss indeed who looks forward to a tough raise negotiation with an employee.

Make sure you have a true and uncolored understanding of your worth to your employer. If your employer doesn't care whether you quit or whether you're unhappy, your leverage is going to be zilch. But if he does care, and you know he does because of all the wonderful things you've done for the company, your leverage is going to be dramatically increased. If he has a great stake in holding on to you, you have much more freedom to hold out.

Keep in mind that money isn't the be-all and end-all and that, particularly in large bureaucracies, substantial raises may be very difficult for your boss to obtain, even if he wants to. Remember there are a whole range of other handsome forms of compensation you can negotiate for: going to a particular convention that you've always wanted to attend, a new title, a new office location, flexible hours, permission to do consulting on the side, assignment to a working group with high visibility to the higher-ups, agreement to take on that project you've been pushing for, etc.

There are two "best times" to ask for a raise. The first is when you have a better offer. Don't barge in and say, "Meet it, or I'm gone." Be subtle. "To my surprise, I seem to be somewhat in demand. I'm really not interested in working for that outfit—I'd much rather stay here—but I can't deny that the offer is very attractive. It's awfully hard to turn your back on an offer of *xxx* dollars. Can we discuss an arrangement which would make it possible for me to stay?"

The other best time to ask for a raise is when you're really needed. It's good timing to ask when you have just done a bang-up job on an important project. It's better timing when you ask for it when the company desperately needs a big project done in the coming months, and you're the only one trained to do it. Your timing could never be better than when you've just earned high praise for your performance on that big project, *and* they want you to start on another right away —the one that's so critical to the firm's future that they can entrust it only to you.

As with every other kind of negotiation, timing is essential when you're asking for a raise. The more they need you, the more negotiating leverage you're going to have to get the bucks you're looking for.

Buying and Selling a House

Whether you are buying or selling a house, the first person you're likely to deal with is a broker. Since the seller pays the broker's fee, in theory at least, the broker works for and represents the interests of the seller. Despite this, the broker will give the buyer the impression that he is really on *his* side. Both assumptions are false; the broker works only for the broker. The broker's bottom line is getting the sale closed so he can collect his commission. The broker isn't even all that interested in what price the house goes for. On a $100,000 sale, the broker gets $6,000. Five thousand more or less means a difference of only $300 in the commission.

Often, the broker will want to act as an intermediary in negotiating the price between buyer and seller. Sometimes you may want to accept this arrangement, and other times you may prefer negotiating directly. Whatever you decide, don't be fully open in sharing your Settlement Range with the broker! If the broker thinks he can close a sale by revealing your Settlement Range (he'll come down $5,000) to the other party, rest assured it will be done. Indeed, when I bought my current home, the broker revealed the seller's Settlement Range to me before we'd even begun negotiating the price.

Keep in mind that the price of the house is not the only factor to consider. In a time of high interest rates, financing may be more critical than the actual cost of the house. For the seller, it can be to great advantage to use the washer, dryer, refrigerator, et al., as goodies so as to avoid coming down in price. But if you're the buyer, beware. You're trading hard cash in exchange for appliances that may or may not work too well too long. If you are interested in the appliances, consider making a separate offer based on their market value. What you want to avoid is paying $5,000 more for the house, just because the deal has been sweetened with $1,000 worth of "free" appliances.

Frequently, the broker will try to prevent you from talking directly to the owner, especially without the broker being present. Make every effort to do so anyway. Learn as much as you can about the owner. You may find out some interesting tidbits, such as how many offers he has actually gotten, how long the house has been on the market, when he has to sell by, etc. If you're having an especially hard time getting around the broker, you can always "forget" something, like whether the basement was finished or how the closet space sized up or the dimensions of the living room (And where was the fireplace? After all, you've been looking at *so* many houses), and go back to the owner yourself to refresh your memory.

Whatever else you do, *don't ever sign anything without your lawyer's approval*. No matter what the broker says, no matter what anybody says, don't sign. Not even an autograph. The broker will try to push in front of you an innocuous-looking statement which he will call a binder, say is nonbinding, and otherwise try to induce you to put something on paper. Resist. Once you've signed, you may be committed, no matter what the broker says.

Some other points: Don't buy a house without having it inspected by an engineer. Inspection will cost you a little money, but it's well worth it. If the roof needs to be replaced, if the furnace is going, if the foundation is buckling, you had better know it before you sign on the dotted line. Also, line up your engineer before you find your dream house. When you're trying to close a deal in a competitive situation, it's no time to start looking for a reputable housing inspector.

Check the house the day of the closing and tell the owner in advance that you intend to. A friend of mine recently bought a house, did go and check it out on the day of closing, but neglected to look in the garage. Later she discovered that the previous owners had taken with them the automatic garage door opener, although she had expected it to be included with the house.

If there is a problem—any problem—in your final inspection, don't hesitate to bring it up at the closing. When Jeanne and I inspected our house before signing, we discovered that one of the air-conditioners no longer worked. The seller's attorney agreed at the closing to give us $50 for the repair.

Buying and Selling Automobiles

Automobile negotiations have a certain ritualistic quality about them. They are expected, everybody does it, and it's almost always done pro forma. By using the precepts in this book, however, and with a little preparation, you can do a lot better.

Buying a New Car. The key to a car purchase is knowing the dealer's cost, and that couldn't be easier to find out. There's a book called *Edmund's New Car Prices* that you can buy in any bookstore or get at the library, that gives you the list price and the dealer's cost for every car, every model, and every option. It's a simple matter to calculate the dealer's cost of the car and the options you desire. Another useful approach is to use the fixed percentages given in *Consumer Reports*, which you should consult anyway before buying a car. The dealer's cost for the base car is a fixed percentage of the list; the dealer's cost for the options is a different, lower fixed percentage. The dealer makes more money on the options than on the base car.

The best you can probably do is to buy a car at $100 over list by using a buying service. Actually, the dealer gets $100 over list and the buying service gets a commission of $50 to $100, so you wind up paying around $150 or $200 over list. The dealer is willing to do this because it steers additional business to him that he wouldn't ordinarily get and because no salesman's commission is involved. When a salesman *is* involved, probably the best you can do is around $200 over list, but it is not unreasonable to set your opening demand at $100 over list and work your way up.

While buying services may be able to get the best price for you, keep in mind that there may not be one nearby and besides, with seemingly more and more cars coming off the line with defects these days, it may be very valuable indeed to negotiate directly with a reputable local dealer who will honor the car's warranty and be there when you need him.

Buying a Used Car. Your bank loan officer and most libraries have a book that's updated monthly called the *N.A.D.A. Official Used Car Guide.* This lists the retail and wholesale price for every car, with options, mileage deductions, etc. This gives you a starting point, although the figures given are by no means ironclad.

A few words of caution: Never buy a car without having it checked out by a mechanic of your choice. Also make sure the owner has all the requisite papers—title, registration, etc. (The requirements vary from state to state). Stolen used cars are on the market, occasionally unknown even to the seller. If you buy a stolen car and it is repossessed, it becomes your responsibility to collect from the person who sold it to you—not always an easy task, even if the seller happened to be a dealer.

Selling a Car. Again, use the *N.A.D.A. Official Used Car Guide* to get the price range. But remember, the price the car is worth is what somebody is willing to give you for it, not what the book says it's worth. I once sold a car that the book said was worth $1,000 and that I thought was worth about $300. I nonetheless advertised it at $1,000 in the paper, at a cost of $3 per week. Each week, I lowered the price until I got to $650 when I got some strong nibbles and knew I'd hit the market for it. I ended up selling it for $600. A lot less than the $1,000 it was listed at in the book, but also a lot more than $300 I thought I'd get.

Negotiating Contracts

Now and then you'll be in a situation where you're asked to sign a long, hopelessly legalistic contract, whether it's to get an auto loan, to rent an apartment, to join a health club, or whatever. Be very careful with these contracts. They are written to cover every possible contingency in favor of the person who handed it to you. I once wanted to rent some office space and took the proposed lease to my organization's lawyer. She glanced at it briefly and said, in essence, "If I had to review this as a lawyer, I could never advise you to sign it. But in all likelihood, if you sign and go ahead and rent the property, everything will be fine and don't worry."

No matter what your opponent says to convince you otherwise, don't for a moment think that because the contract is printed and official looking, that it cannot be changed. It can be changed, and if you insist on it, often your opponent will go along with you. Know, too, that there is no such thing as standard language. Everything is negotiable. Take the contract home, and make what sense of it you can. If an outfit refuses to let you take an unsigned contract home, there's every chance you're dealing with a shifty operator. Be careful.

Contracts also often have blatantly illegal and unenforceable clauses in them whose sole purpose is to intimidate you from exercising your rights in the event of a problem. If a contract is for anything other than a trivial matter, always have it reviewed by a lawyer. We bought our house from a corporate relocation firm, and when I looked at the contract, I saw nothing terribly offensive. However, when my lawyer reviewed it, he reported that it was the worst contract he had ever seen—not for what it said, but for what it didn't say. The moral is that only lawyers are truly capable of protecting you adequately. When it comes to an important contract negotiation, or when you have a problem with an existing contract (remember, some of those clauses may be illegal), don't try to handle it on your own.

Complaints

Almost invariably, complaint negotiation are of the Oh-No variety. Whatever the nature of your gripe—whether your opponent has sold you defective goods, made a faulty repair, failed to live up to his word, refused to refund a deposit, overcharged you for a service, and on and on—his stance can likely be summed up in two words: Go away. Perfectly content with the status quo, he knows negotiating with you means he is going to lose something, probably money. So your first step is to give him an incentive to deal with you, and that means coming up with a backhanded need. Find a threat that will change his thinking, that will convince him that negotiating with you is a preferable alternative to not negotiating with you in view of the consequences of your threat. Remember, too, to let him know in no uncertain terms that you can and will carry out your threat if he doesn't cooperate; the threat won't hit a nerve if it's not credible. Legal action, a letter to his boss or company president, contacting a governmental agency or industry watchdog council, forever losing your business—these sorts of threats will often be the inducement your opponent needs to bite the bullet and negotiate with you.

If such threats don't seem to move him, it's time to line up allies for your cause—people and/or agencies that may be able to exert some pressure on him. Here's a sampling of allies that can effectively come to your rescue:

Better Business Bureaus. While they are industry-controlled, B.B.B.'s will often intervene on your behalf to resolve a problem. It's in their interest, after all, to keep the peace between consumers and businesses. Let them know how unhappy you are, and see what they can do. Just be aware that the helpfulness and clout of B.B.B.'s varies from area to area.

Local and state offices of consumer affairs. If you're fortunate enough to have an efficiently operated consumer affairs agency in your region, you may have to look no further for an ally. They can make a huge difference. They also can be slow, understaffed, and marginally effective. Don't expect miracles, but let them hear from you anyway. The more lines you have in the water, the better are your chances of landing the ally that will see you through to satisfaction.

Industry-sponsored organizations. Manuals are available in libraries and bookstores that describe various organizations that industry councils have established to resolve consumer complaints. With automobiles, for instance, there are organizations called AUTOCAP in some twenty states, which often can be of assistance. For major appliances, there is the Major Appliance Consumer Action Panel (MACAP), and so forth. While they are industry-sponsored, it's still in their interest to give you a sympathetic ear. They don't want their industry getting a bad name.

Lawyers. Your lawyer can be a terrific ally . . . and without costing you an arm and a leg. A legal letter on your attorney's station will often elicit a response where your letter has failed. Also, simply involving your lawyer, even to a minimal extent, tells your opponent you're very serious about the matter, and that can do nothing but good for your cause.

Small Claims Court. Small claims courts deal with cases up to a certin dollar ceiling (it varies from state to state), usually $1,000. You don't need a lawyer, and for a few dollars in court fees, you can take your opponent to the halls of justice. Small claims courts are usually staffed by volunteer lawyers, who will frequently try to negotiate a settlement before they actually render a decision. Sometimes just threatening court action—without actually filing papers—will resolve the matter, particularly if your opponent is clearly in the wrong. In any event, initiating a small claims action, much like involving your lawyer, will send an unequivocal message to your opponent that you are not taking this lying down . . . and that he best not either.

Be imaginative in searching for allies. There are others out there, lots of them. Remember the story about my father who was having an awful time getting a manufacturer to repair his defective TV set. Finally, one phone call to the Japanese consulate in New York City apparently lit a fire under the company, which quickly acceded to his demands.

Utility Companies

In dealing with utility complaints, you really have only one ally, your state public utilities commission, but that ally has a lot of clout. P.U.C.'s, which are responsible for regulating most aspects of the utility's activities, can be enormously helpful because of their considerable ability to create a ripple effect. A command is issued high in the chain of authority, and by the time it gets down to the appropriate official in your local utility company, it tends to carry the weight of a presidential order. And speaking of presidents, a story surfaced recently about Amy Carter, who, while doing her history homework, wanted an answer to a question on the Industrial Revolution. Rosalyn asked one of the White House staffers to call the labor department for the answer (isn't research a snap when you're a presidential offspring?), and by the time the message drifted through the department, it had become a top-priority presidential request, and a whole staff of people worked an entire weekend putting together a briefing paper on the Industrial Revolution for Jimmy! What you want is the P.U.C. to generate ripples on your behalf in like manner, so that when your complaint filters down to the installer or meter reader or whoever you need to help you, it has become a matter of pressing concern.

This has worked for me in getting a phone installed properly and avoiding having my water service cut off due to a billing mixup. When you contact the public utility commission, make sure you get the name of the person you talk to and solidify the contact—perhaps with a follow-up note rehashing your problem and thanking him for his cooperation—so you can keep close tabs on the situation by staying in touch with your ally. The personal touch goes a long way in large bureaucracies.

Negotiating with Landlords

The first thing to remember is that you have a lot more rights than you think you do . . . or than your lease would lead you to believe. In fact, many provisions in your lease are probably unenforceable or illegal and are included for the express purpose of deterring you from exercising your rights.

Your first step is to find out just what your rights are in your jurisdiction; a lawyer or a tenants' group are two excellent sources for the answers. You may have the right to pay for repairs and deduct it from your rent. You may have the right to establish a rent strike and put your rent money in escrow until the complaint has been remedied. In cases where there are serious health and safety hazards, you may want to call the local building inspector or health department. It's also a good idea to send your landlord a registered letter, informing him of the exact nature of the problem and making it clear that you will hold him fully responsible for any damages that may result from his negligence in not correcting the situation. Better yet, have a lawyer write the letter, since he knows the current laws which bear on the case.

If you don't have a tenants' association and have had recurring problems with your landlord, give some thought to forming such a coalition. There is indeed strength in numbers. By banding together with fellow tenants, you will have much more clout in dealing with the landlord and make it much more difficult for him to harass or intimidate you, since he's up against a buildingful of disgruntled folks, not just one person.

Negotiating with Government and Other Bureaucracies

Government is supposed to exist to serve you, right? Think again. When you negotiate with a governmental agency, usually they don't want to talk to you. Why? Because you make waves, because you want exceptions and special attention, and because, in any case, what you want will require more work for them, which is the last thing they want to do.

Some tricks to keep in mind: Often an agency will tell you there's a policy against what you want. Force them to give you the policy and read it carefully; many times it's not what they said it was or there are loopholes or ways to get around it. Use their own policies against them. And remember, no matter what they say, virtually no policy is so sacred that it can't be waived or adjusted to meet your needs.

Go to the top, rather than the middle, and start your friend, the ripple effect, in motion, so that by the time your problem reaches the agency or bureaucrat you really want to negotiate with, they're at least going to have to give you a hearing, rather than refusing to deal with you. Also, see if you can find a friend in court, somebody who works in the agency. If you don't know anyone, ask your friends. Look for an in, and if you can't find one, do your utmost to create an in for yourself by establishing a personal relationship with the person you've chosen to deal with. Let them know you're a real live person, not just another faceless problem.

Pump office clerks and others for information. Often they will tell you things their superiors would just as soon you didn't know. Pursue the problem with zeal. Particularly with large bureaucracies, making a big issue out of the problem will move them to overcome their inertia and resolve your gripe.

One of the biggest problems is finding the right person to negotiate with. Don't start making your demands until you are sure you're dealing with the right person. Call the switchboard, talk to a secretary, contact the public-information office if there is one. Do whatever you must to find the right person in the right department.

Be aware that governmental agencies operate in the public eye and are extremely sensitive to media attention on their shortcomings. For that reason, your best allies may be those who can give your problem a public airing. Politicians, newspapers, action-line services of radio or TV stations, all can generate the sort of outcry you may need.

Negotiating with Doctors and Other Professionals (Dentists, Lawyers, Accountants, etc.)

"It simply isn't done." That's the attitude most people have about negotiating with professionals. Well, it is done—by me and lots of other people—and while negotiations with professionals have to be handled somewhat delicately because you want to establish a close working relationship, that's no reason to sidestep them altogether.

For starters, don't feel as though you're not at liberty to discuss price with professionals. It's perfectly legitimate—and well within your rights as a client—to do so, and if the professional tries to make you think otherwise, my feeling is that you should take your business elsewhere. Get a clear understanding in advance, before services are rendered, as to what the fee is. If the fee seems unrealistically high or more than you can afford, say so, and either reach an agreement or move on to someone else. It's especially important to do this before you've established a working relationship with the professional, since it's much harder to switch practitioners once you've invested time and energy and trust in someone.

This is not to say that money is the only issue. On the contrary, it may pale in comparison to factors such as the amount of time and effort—not to mention the quality of that effort—that the professional will devote to your problem. Equally important is the personal relationship you have with the professional. No matter how technically competent he is, if you find him gruff, arrogant, abrasive, inaccessible, if he refuses to explain to you what's going on and treats your questions as a major imposition and otherwise tries to intimidate you with professional mumbo-jumbo, you're dealing with the wrong person.

Whether it concerns fees or other matters, if you have a problem with a professional that you cannot resolve directly with him, your first line of defense is his professional association. County medical and dental societies, bar associations, and other groups are seriously concerned about the standards and reputation of their professions and will give your complaint a hearing. Many professionals are also regulated by state agencies, and you can appeal to those agencies as well if you're unable to resolve the issue elsewhere.

But again, don't get trapped into thinking that professionals are somehow above negotiation. Be aware that you can get equal quality of services at widely varying fees. It's entirely possible, by scouting around, that you can find, say, a top surgeon who will charge as much as fifty percent less than another surgeon. It's also perfectly permissible to negotiate the fee with a particular doctor. When he says surgery will cost $1,000, you say, "I'm sorry, I can't afford that. Can it possibly be done for less?" The response is often an immediate reduction of some sort, frequently a substantial one if you can offer evidence that you really would be hard-pressed to pay that amount. The same is true with other professionals in many instances.

Although it's certainly not the optimum time, sometimes you can even negotiate a fee reduction after the services have been rendered. A friend of mine needed surgery, and was subsequently billed $700 by the surgeon. She had neglected to discuss the fee with him beforehand, and she was extremely upset by what she felt was his exorbitant price. At my prodding, she went back and discussed the matter with him. I dare say he wasn't thrilled with her approaching him, but after she explained her financial and insurance situation to him, he agreed to accept $400 for his service.

EPILOGUE

Parting Thoughts

I'VE SAID IT before, but before we go our separate ways, it bears repeating: Trust your instincts when you negotiate. They are among the most powerful negotiating assets you have. Listen to your instincts first and me second. You may run into an opponent who screws up every conceivable aspect of a negotiation, who betrays his needs, his pressures, and how he had to have a settlement by yesterday. On the face of it, I would advise you to hold out, to push the opponent to the very bottom of his Settlement Range. But suppose your instincts tell you otherwise. Suppose you have some indefinable sense, for whatever reason, that his pressures notwithstanding, you can't get a better settlement out of him. Maybe he's snowing you, maybe not. In any event, heed your instincts. You're on the scene, you know what's going on, and you will be off base a lot less of the time by trusting yourself than you will be by blindly following any set of rules I or anyone else might give you.

I have no doubt that with everything you've learned in reading this book, you'll be getting much more of what you want out of the negotiations that punctuate your day-to-day life. But in addition to showing you how you can reap such benefits, I've tried hard in these pages to portray the life skill of negotiation as it truly is—an enjoyable, entertaining process. Sure, it's a skill you can employ to get more of what you want, and sure, it's a test—of wits, nerves, fast thinking, mental flexibility, creativity, and basic human psychology. But it's also enjoyable and entertaining.

So while you're on your way toward bigger and better settlements, I hope you learn to enjoy the process by which you get them. And remember, if you feel you need a refresher course in what to do and how to do it, by all means dip back into these pages. Negotiation isn't the sort of enterprise that can be fully digested and mastered in several sittings. It takes practice and, fortunately, practice isn't hard to come by, since there's always another negotiation around the corner.

Relax, go with the flow, trust your instincts and, above all, enjoy yourself as you negotiate your way toward a richer, more rewarding life.

Now, we can be on our way, if you'll just make me a reasonable offer on that typewriter. . . .